THE SOMME

Also by Martin Gilbert

THE CHURCHILL BIOGRAPHY

Volume III: The Challenge of War, 1914–1916
Document Volume III (in two parts)
Volume IV: World in Torment, 1917–1922
Document Volume IV (in three parts)
Volume V: The Coming of War, 1922–1939
Document Volume V: The Exchequer Years, 1922–1929
Document Volume V: The Wilderness Years, 1929–1935
Document Volume V: The Coming of War, 1936–1939
Volume VI: Finest Hour, 1939–1941
Churchill War Papers I: At the Admiralty, September 1939–May 1940
Churchill War Papers II: Never Surrender, May–December 1940
Churchill War Papers III: The Ever-Widening War, 1941
Volume VII: Road to Victory, 1941–1945
Volume VIII: Never Despair, 1945–1965
Churchill: A Photographic Portrait
Churchill: A Life

OTHER BOOKS

The Appeasers (with Richard Gott)
The European Powers, 1900–1945
The Roots of Appeasement
Children's Illustrated Bible Atlas
Atlas of British Charities
Atlas of American History
Atlas of the Arab–Israeli Conflict
Atlas of British History
Atlas of the First World War
Atlas of the Holocaust
The Holocaust: Maps and Photographs
Atlas of Jewish History
Atlas of Russian History

THE

SOMME

HEROISM AND HORROR IN
THE FIRST WORLD WAR

MARTIN GILBERT

HENRY HOLT AND COMPANY
NEW YORK

Henry Holt and Company, LLC
Publishers since 1866
175 Fifth Avenue
New York, New York 10010
www.henryholt.com

Published simultaneously in the United Kingdom
by John Murray Publishers.

Library of Congress Cataloging-in-Publication Data
Gilbert, Martin, 1936–
    The Somme : heroism and horror in the First World War /
Martin Gilbert.—1st ed.
        p.   cm.
    Includes bibliographical references and index.
    ISBN-13: 978-0-8050-8127-5
    ISBN-10: 0-8050-8127-5
    1. Somme, 1st Battle of the, France, 1916. I. Title.
D545.S7G627 2006
970.4'272—dc22   2006041169

First Edition 2006

Printed in the United States of America

1   3   5   7   9   10   8   6   4   2

To my teacher and friend
Alan Palmer

Contents

CONTENTS

Illustrations

Maps

Acknowledgements

WHILE A SCHOOLBOY in London more than half a century ago, thirty-five years after the Battle of the Somme, I was taught history at Highgate School by Arthur Preston White, who had served in the battle as a lieutenant and had written letters from the battlefield to his sister. 'Jumbo', as he was known, was in the habit in class of bursting into military song. From that time, as a fifteen-year-old, I had a curiosity about the battle. A decade later, in 1961, as a Junior Research Fellow at Merton College, Oxford, I heard about the Somme from another former lieutenant who had served there, J. R. R. Tolkien, a Fellow Emeritus of the college. Two years after that I had a number of conversations with A. P. Herbert, who had both fought on the Somme and written about his experiences.

I first visited the Somme in the 1970s, when I discussed the battle with several of those who were helping me with my work on the Churchill biography. Among them were three former Guards officers: Harold Macmillan, who had been seriously wounded on the Somme on 15 September 1916, and Field Marshal Earl Alexander of Tunis and Viscount Chandos, both of whom, as Captain Harold Alexander and Captain Oliver Lyttelton, were in the same fierce struggle that day. I also discussed the battle with Paul Maze, the French painter who served as a sergeant with the British forces on the Ancre in November 1916, and John Bentham, a veteran of the Royal Naval Division, who also fought in the November battle.

For help in the search for materials, I am particularly grateful to my friend Max Arthur; to Terry Charman, Historian, Imperial War Museum; to Richard Davies, Special Collections, Brotherton Library, Leeds University Library; to Gary Garrison; to Andrew Mackinlay, MP; to Professor Peter Neary; to Allen Packwood, Churchill Archives Centre, Churchill College, Cambridge; to George Palfrey; to the late

A. J. Peacock, Editor of *Gun Fire*; to Pawel Szymanski; to Vicky Wylde, Senior Collections Assistant, Imperial War Museum; and to Debbie Young, Somerset Military Museum. A special debt is due to Major and Mrs Holt (Tonie and Valmai Holt) for making the battlefield of the Somme accessible on the ground, wood by wood and cemetery by cemetery, to historians and visitors alike.

I am grateful to all those who gave me permission to quote from material that is their copyright. As it has not been possible to trace all the copyright holders, I apologize to those I have been unable to contact. Permission has been gratefully received for specific quotations and use of material from the National Archives, Kew; Churchill Archives Centre, Churchill College, Cambridge; the Imperial War Museum, London; Max Arthur; Eric Bogle; and Ron Venus.

My publishers have been supportive throughout: I would like to thank Jennifer Barth of Holt, New York; Doug Pepper and Chris Bucci at McLelland and Stewart, Toronto; and Roland Philipps and Caroline Westmore at John Murray, London; as well as Bob Davenport and Josine Meijer. For permission to reproduce the photographs I am grateful to the Imperial War Museum (Nos. 2, 4–21, 24, 27–40, 44, 46 and 47), the Liddle Collection, Leeds University Library (42); and Popperfoto (1, 3, 22, 23, 25–6, 41, 43 and 45). Numbers 48 and 49 are my own.

For help during my most recent visit to the Somme, I would like to thank the staff at the Newfoundland War Memorial Park; the staff of the Ulster Tower café and bookshop; Philippe Feret of the Beaucourt Station café; Avril Williams and her staff at Auchonvillers – 'Ocean Villas' to the soldiers of 1916 – and the almost always unseen yet in the most important sense ever-visible gardeners and keepers of the Commonwealth War Graves Commission, whose work and dedication have maintained so many places of repose on the Somme battlefield: my final maps show their locations.

As he has done for almost twenty years, Tim Aspden turned my rough drafts into maps of the highest quality. Kay Thomson was, as always, a font of indispensable help. My son David organized a journey to war memorials in the Leeds area. My wife, Esther, accompanied me on my most recent visit to the Somme, and has given good guidance.

To my teacher Alan Palmer, whose encouragement, beginning at school, has been consistent for more than fifty years, I dedicate this most recent assignment.

Preface

Even unto them will I give in mine house and within my walls
a place and a name better than of sons and of daughters: I will
give them an everlasting name, that shall not be cut off.

Isaiah 56:5

THE BATTLE OF the Somme was one of the most costly battles in the history of warfare. On the first day alone, 19,240 British soldiers were killed and more than 36,000 wounded. Between 1 July 1916, when it began at the height of summer, and 19 November 1916, when it ended in the snow and fog of winter, more than 300,000 British, Commonwealth, French and German soldiers had been killed, and twice that number wounded.

The area of the battlefield is small: fifteen miles in length and six miles at its greatest depth. Today it is an area of peaceful rolling hills, woods and cultivated fields, with its once obliterated villages rebuilt. It is also an area of scattered war cemeteries, and other memorials to the battle.

The largest of all the Western Front memorials is on the Somme: the Thiepval Memorial to the Missing. Inscribed on its massive columns are the names of 73,335 British and South African soldiers who were killed and whose bodies were never identified. The names of the other Commonwealth soldiers whose bodies were never identified, as well as the French and German, are on other memorials, further from where the battle was fought. French and German cemeteries are also a solemn feature of the Somme landscape: the German cemetery at Fricourt has 17,000 burials, of whom 12,000 lie in four mass graves.

What happened on the battlefield? Why was the battle fought in the first place? Why was it so prolonged, at such heavy cost? What was its impact on the wider war? These questions have haunted survivors of the battle, the relatives and friends of those killed, and those born long after it. Poets, historians, writers, novelists, journalists, film-makers, teachers and schoolchildren have been among those drawn to its story.

My most recent journey to the Somme was in November 2005, eighty-nine years after the last weeks of the battle. The battlefield, although much changed over ninety years, and much visited each year – even more in the twenty-first century than before – still has the power both to haunt and to inspire.

There are few battles in history that have generated so many pub-lications as the Battle of the Somme. Those I have consulted, and from which I have quoted, are listed in the bibliography. Among the most important and detailed books are the histories of the various corps, divisions, regiments and battalions that took part in the battle, and the official history of the whole campaign, published in two volumes in 1932 and 1938.

Research on what Marshal Joffre called 'the English battle' has been continuous. In each decade since 1916 substantial works of research and narrative have been published. The first decade of the twenty-first century is no exception. Among the important books published in the single year 2005 were Robin Prior and Trevor Wilson, *The Somme*; Gary Sheffield and John Bourne, *Douglas Haig: War Diaries and Letters*; and Jack Sheldon, *The German Army on the Somme, 1914–1916*.

Participants and historians have written about many aspects of the four-and-a-half-month conflict, including the central role of artillery, the recruiting and the preparations, the war in the air, the first appear-ance of the tank in warfare, shell shock, desertion, the casualties, the cemeteries, the poetry written on the battlefield and about it, and the life and fate of the PBI – the Poor Bloody Infantry – who in the last resort are the people who have to fight the battles face to face with the enemy. All these aspects have their place in this narrative.

As a historian of the human condition, I have always tried to give a place and a name to those on whose shoulders fell the burden of the decisions of others – their rulers and their commanders – and who did their duty without questioning, or seldom questioning, either the cause or the plan. Their stories deserve to be told in every generation, as an integral part of war, and as a testimony to human suffering and to the human spirit.

To avoid anonymity, I have given wherever possible the names of the individuals whose stories are told in these pages. To enable the reader who might visit the battlefield to pay his or her respects at the graveside, I have also given the names of the cemeteries in which many of the individuals lie, or the monument to the missing on which their names are listed. Were one to write a third of a page about every soldier killed on the Somme, it would require at least six hundred books as long as this one.

The war of 1914–1918 was known as the Great War. Those who fought it, and those who lived through it, believed it would be, as H. G. Wells called it, 'The War that will end all War'. That made the suffering seem more acceptable. At the same time, the details of that suffering were to a large extent withheld from the public in all lands. Every bloody encounter was portrayed as a victory, every terrified combatant as a hero, every battalion sent up the line as reinforcement as the last one needed for the final push. The Battle of the Somme was to be the Big Push, the battle to end all battles. That gave it an intensity few other battles had. In that purpose it failed, but the sustained and costly efforts to make it succeed were widely seen as both noble and imperative. Who are those who came afterwards to say that they were not?

Every book on the Somme contributes in its own way to perpetuating the memory of those who fought and those who fell. This book seeks to make its contribution to that act of remembrance.

Martin Gilbert
28 February 2006

Prelude: 'Chewing barbed wire'

IN AUGUST 1914 the empires of Europe embarked on a war that each of them believed would be swift and victorious.

Austria–Hungary was confident it could crush Serbia within a few weeks, avenging the assassination that summer of Archduke Franz-Ferdinand of Austria, killed in Sarajevo by a Serb nationalist.

Germany, with territorial desires on the industrial region of north-west France, was confident it could reach Paris within a few months and dictate peace terms, as it had done in 1871 – and was to do again in 1940. German reservists leaving Berlin by train for their mobilization depots in August 1914 painted on their carriages the slogan 'On to Paris!'

'I hope we shall get to England,' one German soldier wrote to his landlord on October 20, as he set off for the front; but Adolf Hitler was to be disappointed, both then and in 1940.

France, hoping to regain the eastern provinces of Alsace and Lorraine that Germany had annexed in 1871, was confident it could counter-attack and defeat Germany by the end of the year: French soldiers leaving Paris by train were cheered by enthusiastic crowds willing them 'to Berlin!'

Great Britain was certain that its small professional army, fighting alongside the French – with whom it had signed an Entente Cordiale in 1904 – could drive the Germans from the soil of northern France by Christmas. Britain was also confident it could drive the Germans out of Belgium, all but a tiny corner of which the German Army had overrun on its drive towards Paris. On August 4 Britain declared war on Germany in response to its invasion of Belgium, to whom Britain was bound by one of its oldest treaties of alliance, signed in 1839, and never before put to the test.

Russia – the Empire of the Tsars – whose territory stretched from the Baltic Sea to the Pacific Ocean, believed it could help its French ally by pressing in on the German Empire from the East. It also saw itself as the champion of fellow Slavs: Poles under German rule in the eastern regions of Germany, Serbs threatened by Austria–Hungary, and the many Slav minorities in Austria–Hungary itself, Poles, Czechs, Slovenes, Slovaks, Serbs and Ruthenes among them.

The Germans were confident that, with the help of Austria–Hungary, with whom they had an alliance dating back a quarter of a century, they could force Russia out of the war and gain control of Russian Poland, with its capital, Warsaw, and its industrial city, Lodz. Germany also wanted to establish control over the Russian province of Courland, including the Baltic port city of Riga, and the land bordering on German East Prussia, including the cities of Vilna and Brest-Litovsk – integral parts of the Russian Empire for more than a hundred years.

The hopes of each combatant for rapid territorial gains and swift victories were illusions. By Christmas 1914, within six months of the start of the war, Germany and Austria–Hungary had both lost territory to Russia on the Eastern Front. On the Western Front, the triumphant German march on Paris had been halted at the Battle of the Marne in mid-September, and pushed back a week later at the Battle of the Aisne.

Following the Battle of the Aisne, the Germans attempted to break through to the English Channel. They were stopped by the end of October, at the first Battle of Ypres, a Belgian town that was to remain within the Allied lines for the rest of the war. Throughout November and December, when winter made fighting almost impossible, the contending armies in the West dug trenches and gun emplacements in a continuous line stretching from the North Sea to the Swiss border. Then, protected by their trenches, they faced each other across the No-Man's Land that separated the trenches.

Briefly, at Christmas 1914, and again on New Year's Day, soldiers on both sides laid down their weapons, crossed into No-Man's Land, and fraternized. Some swapped beer or showed each other photographs of their families. Some played football. The higher commands on both sides ordered an end to this intimacy. A year later there were only minor truces.

Hardly had Britain declared war on Germany than the Secretary of State for War, Field Marshal Earl Kitchener of Khartoum – the victorious commander of the forces that had defeated the Mahdi of the Sudan sixteen years earlier – recognizing that war in Europe would require far more than the existing 160,000 men of the Regular Army, cast about for a means to raise volunteers on a substantial scale. His initial aim was an additional army of 100,000 men. Britain, which for the previous century had prided itself on the adequacy of its small, professional regular army, would have to accept that a nationwide effort was needed if the swift German military successes in Europe were to be checked and defeated.

At a meeting in the War Office on 19 August 1914, fifteen days after Britain had declared war on Germany, General Sir Henry Rawlinson – who was later to command the main British and Empire force on the Somme, the Fourth Army – suggested that men would be more willing to enlist if they knew they would serve with those whom they knew: friends, neighbours and workmates. Rawlinson asked a business acquaintance, Robert White, to raise a battalion of men who worked in the City of London. Within two hours of White opening a recruiting office, more than two hundred City workers enlisted. Six days later, the Stockbrokers' Battalion had 1,600 men.

When the Earl of Derby – the dominant political figure in Lancashire – heard of White's success he decided to form a battalion in Liverpool, opening a recruitment office there on August 28. By the end of the day 1,500 men had enlisted. It was Derby who first used the term a 'battalion of pals' to describe men who had been recruited locally.

On August 30, at St Swithun's Church, East Grinstead, the Reverend W. Youard gave a sermon calling on the young men of his parish to volunteer. Youard suggested that all local sports clubs close down so that men would not be tempted to stay behind. The creator of Sherlock Holmes, Sir Arthur Conan Doyle, who lived nearby, joined the campaign, telling the local men, 'If the cricketer had a straight eye, let him look along the barrel of a rifle. If a footballer had strength of limb, let him serve and march in the field of battle.' In response, Kitchener approved the creation of a Sportsman's Battalion. It included two England cricketers, Patsy Hendren and Andrew Sandham, and the Lightweight boxing champion of England, Jerry Delaney. The Sportsman's Battalion also included artists, authors, big-game hunters, clergymen and oarsmen.

A nationwide effort had begun. Kitchener encouraged towns and villages all over Britain to organize similar recruiting campaigns. Battalions were raised by local authorities, industrialists and committees of private citizens. A typical example was that of several army-age young men who had attended Winteringham Secondary School in Grimsby. They suggested to their former headmaster that he should form a battalion from his former pupils. By the end of October he had recruited more than a thousand former schoolboys into what they called the Grimsby Chums. Other schools, including five of Britain's leading public schools, quickly formed their own battalions. The four Pals battalions recruited in Hull were known as the Hull Commercials, the Hull Tradesmen, the Hull Sportsmen and the Hull T'Others.

In the two months following the outbreak of war, more than fifty cities and towns in Britain formed Pals battalions. Lancashire, Yorkshire, Northumberland and Durham were the counties that raised the most. Larger cities formed several battalions: Manchester had fifteen; Hull had four; Liverpool, Birmingham and Glasgow had three. Many towns were able to raise at least two battalions. In Glasgow, one battalion was drawn from the drivers, conductors, mechanics and labourers of the city Tramways Department.

On 10 September 1914 the British Prime Minister, H. H. Asquith, told the House of Commons, 'We have been recruiting during the past ten days substantially the same number of recruits as in past years have been recruited every year.' These men would be needed; at the very moment when the debate in Britain was whether the war would be over before Christmas, or might last as long as the festive season, Kitchener predicted a sustained and harsh conflict that would require, if Germany were to be defeated, the appearance on the battlefield of an overwhelming force of new, well-trained and well-led divisions, able to deliver a decisive blow. The men of the New Army – soon known as Kitchener's Army – were recruited from offices, football teams, cricket teams, coal mines and factories. Post Office employees, railway employees, tramway employees, coal miners, clerks: all clamoured to be allowed to serve. Whole streets of young men rushed to join up in a fever of patriotism that swept both Britain and its Empire.

Typical of the enlisting zeal, on 25 November 1914 eleven football players from the Heart of Midlothian team enlisted for a new battalion in Edinburgh. Two more members of the team joined up on the following day, with seven players from Raith Rovers – the team from Kirkaldy, in Fife – and six players from Falkirk. Then several players from another Edinburgh club, Hibernian, enlisted. It took only ten more days before 1,550 football players and fans had joined up, forming a complete battalion, the 16th Battalion, Royal Scots Fusiliers. It was soon known as the Sportsmen's Battalion, the Football Battalion, and, most widely, McCrae's Battalion, after Sir George McCrae, a former Member of Parliament for Edinburgh East, and Chairman of the Local Government Board for Scotland, who gathered its troops, prepared them for war, and was to command them on the Somme. 'If McCrae's are going out', it was said in Scotland, 'the Germans haven't got long to live.'

Because many volunteers were smaller than the Army's minimum height requirement of five foot five, the requirement was reduced to five foot one. Men between five foot one and five foot four were put into self-contained Bantam battalions. Four of these battalions were formed into a Bantam division, the 35th Infantry Division, of 4,000 men. Being smaller than their fellow New Army men, the Bantam soldiers had one advantage: they were less immediately visible to German snipers.

By the end of 1914, half a million New Army volunteers – five times Kitchener's initial target – were under training in England. Those who clung to the hopes that the small, professional army was enough to defeat the Germans called them, derisively, the Featherbed Soldiers, but Kitchener was confident that they could be trained to the highest fighting standards. Central to his plan was that they would enter the conflict as a single entity. To this end he resisted all attempts to transfer the New Army battalions to the battlefield as each one was trained. According to his calculations, they would be ready, as a well-trained, single, powerful entity, by the early months of 1916. He would not allow them to be thrown into the battle before then, either as a complete force or piecemeal.

On 3 October 1914, while the New Army battalions were being raised in Britain, the largest crowd ever assembled in St John's, Newfoundland, the capital of Britain's smallest Dominion, gathered to cheer the departure across the Atlantic of the first contingent of the Newfoundland Regiment: 535 volunteers who were determined to make their contribution to the defeat of Germany. 'You'll be back in six weeks,' called out some of the watching crowd. One onlooker called out in mock derision, 'There goes the picnic party!' A few months later he too volunteered; he was killed on the Somme, at Gueudecourt, in October 1916.

Known as the First Five Hundred, the first Newfoundland volunteers began their training in Britain in the rain, mud and icy winds of Salisbury Plain. A few miles away, men from their neighbouring, larger Dominion, soldiers of the Canadian Infantry Brigade, were also in training. They too would fight on the Somme.

Throughout 1915, the British and French armies attempted to break through the German lines, determined to drive the German troops from north-eastern France and from Belgium. It was a noble vision. The French city of Lille, only seven miles behind German lines, would be liberated. The most productive industrial region of France would be renewed. Brussels, the Belgian capital, would see an end to German military rule, and be restored to its King. None of this happened: the Anglo-French offensives of 1915 were halted by an enemy that had dug deep trenches from which its troops could fight, built fortified strongpoints from which machine-gun fire could be directed against the attacker, and erected barbed-wire defences that could be breached only after facing intense rifle and machine-gun fire.

Along the narrow but unbroken line of the trenches, stretching from the North Sea to the Swiss border, the soil, farms and woods of France and Flanders were scarred and ravaged by a year of fighting. Artillery on both sides fired their explosive shells against the facing defenders. Tens of thousands of soldiers were killed in each of the contending armies. At the end of 1915 the line of trenches on the Western Front, with its ever-thickening barbed-wire entanglements on both sides, its ever-stronger machine-gun defences on the German side, and its well-defended artillery positions, was virtually the same line as at the start of the year.

A series of British attempts to break the line, most notably at Neuve-Chapelle in March and at Loos in September, had failed to do so, at heavy cost in dead and wounded. At Neuve-Chapelle, 11,000 British soldiers were killed or wounded. At Loos the number of casualties was 61,000, of whom 7,760 were killed. As the cost in human life mounted, for almost no military gain, British policymakers began to wonder if the stalemate and slaughter of trench warfare was the way to victory. Winston Churchill, whose twenty-eight-year-old cousin Norman Leslie, a captain in the Rifle Brigade, was killed in action in October 1914, was among those in the British government who felt there must be some alternative, as he expressed it, to 'chewing barbed wire in Flanders'.

One such alternative had been found in early 1915: an attack on the Turkish Ottoman Empire. After Germany had won Turkey to its side in October 1914, most politicians and military commanders in Britain and France were confident they could bring the so-called 'Sick Man of Europe' to its knees. Two areas seemed possible points of attack. The first was Turkey-in-Europe, centred on Constantinople. The second was Turkey's vast Near Eastern regions, including Syria, Palestine, the Sinai desert bordering on Egypt, and Mesopotamia (now Iraq), where British troops had landed in October 1914, advancing to Basra, and with their sights on Baghdad.

In April 1915, Italy joined Britain, France, Russia and Serbia – the Entente Powers, soon to be known as the Allied Powers. The Italian government was confident that it would secure large swathes of Austro-Hungarian and Turkish territory the moment these two empires had been defeated. But a two-phased Anglo-French effort to reach Constantinople in early 1915 ended in failure. That March, a naval attack, for which Churchill, then First Lord of the Admiralty, was responsible, tried to push through the Dardanelles by ships alone, but was foiled by an undetected Turkish minefield. Sixty-seven British and 600 French sailors were killed in the attempt, which, to Churchill's chagrin, was not renewed, even with increased minesweeping vigilance.

In April 1915 a military landing, for which Lord Kitchener, as Secretary of State for War, was responsible, was made on the Gallipoli Peninsula, which overlooked the Dardanelles. It met with strong opposition from Turkish forces commanded and led by German officers. In the assault on the Gallipoli Peninsula, 34,000 British and Empire troops were killed, including Australian and New Zealand (Anzac) forces who had come by sea halfway round the world, and some of the First Five Hundred from Newfoundland. Also killed were 10,000 French troops and 80,000 Turkish soldiers. But the peninsula could not be taken, and after nine months of intense fighting the Gallipoli enterprise was abandoned.

Churchill, the architect of the naval assault at the Dardanelles, while remaining a Member of Parliament, left the government and went to the Western Front as a lieutenant colonel, commanding a Scottish battalion in the trenches just south of Ploegsteert Wood. Kitchener, the architect of the military landings at Gallipoli, remained in London as Secretary of State for War, preparing for the campaigns of 1916, and for the first appearance of his New Army on the battlefields of Europe.

An Allied army of 133,000 men was evacuated from Gallipoli in three stages, the first two on 20 December 1915, from Suvla and Anzac, the third on 9 January 1916 from Helles. Those evacuated included British, French, Australian, New Zealand, Newfoundland and Indian troops. Among them was a future British Prime Minister, Clement Attlee. The evacuation took place without casualties. The troops were available to fight elsewhere, including on the Western Front.

In the summer of 1915 the Austro-Hungarian Army struck at Serbia, which had repelled its first attacks in August and September 1914. To come to the aid of Serbia, British and French troops landed at the Greek port city of Salonika, with its direct road and rail access northward to Serbia. But it was too late. Austro-Hungarian troops, having defeated the outnumbered Serbian Army and overrun Serbia, hurried southward and established an impenetrable line of trenches twenty miles north of Salonika. In a hilly, precipitous landscape, they pinned down the Anglo-French forces into a small perimeter, with their backs to the Aegean Sea.

There was going to be no swift victory – possibly no victory at all – either against the Turks, who were tenaciously defending their positions in Mesopotamia, or against the Austrians north of Salonika: the two fronts so much favoured by those British and French leaders and strategists who were known as the Easterners. The focus of potential victory turned once more to the trench lines on the Western Front.

To prepare for the coming battles, the British Army established, on 14 October 1915, the Machine Gun Corps, to provide trained machine-gunners for every battalion. The Lewis gun, designed by an American Army colonel, Isaac Newton Lewis, was superior to the existing Vickers gun, and would be available in the new year. It could fire up to seven hundred bullets a minute, in short, lethal bursts. It needed only one man to carry and fire it, and a second man to carry the ammunition, as against four men to do the same tasks for the Vickers gun.

Because the Machine Gun Corps did such destructive work, it quickly became the target of every weapon on the battlefield. For this reason its members were known as the Suicide Club. But it was they, and their German opposite numbers, who dealt out the deadly fire, as the infantrymen on both sides were to discover. On the Machine Gun Corps Memorial at Hyde Park in London is inscribed a verse from the Book of Samuel: 'Saul has slain his thousands, and David his ten thousands.'

I

The prospect: 'To break through and win victory'

THE INFLUENCE OF those in British policymaking circles who wanted to find an area of potential victory other than the Western Front had been much weakened by the Gallipoli evacuation, and by the lack of progress on the Salonika and Mesopotamia fronts. As a result of these setbacks, the Allied leaders looked to the Western and Russian fronts for victory. On 6 December 1915, only two days after the decision was made in London to evacuate the Gallipoli Peninsula, a meeting was held at French military headquarters at Chantilly, intended to produce a grand design for the defeat of Germany and Austria–Hungary in 1916.

The meeting at Chantilly was presided over by the Supreme Commander of the French forces, General Joffre. The senior British representative was the Commander-in-Chief of the British Expeditionary Force, Field Marshal Sir John French. Senior Russian and Italian generals were also present. A bold plan was devised. Large-scale offensives would be carried out as simultaneously as possible by Britain, France, Italy and Russia on different fronts, preventing the resources of Germany and Austria–Hungary being concentrated in any single war zone.

Russian forces, after an initial advance deep into East Prussia, had been driven out by the Germans in 1915. By the beginning of 1916 Russia had lost large swathes of its own western provinces to Germany. Under the plan agreed at Chantilly, the Russian Army would carry out a double-pronged attack, combining a northern offensive against the Germans and a southern offensive against the Austro-Hungarians.

Italy, having earlier been unsuccessful on its Austrian front in the second half of 1915, would strike again across the Isonzo River with a view to penetrating deep into Austria (it was only thirty miles from the Isonzo to the Austrian city of Villach).

Britain and France would carry out a joint offensive on the Western Front, in Picardy, on either side of the River Somme. Because the Russian Army needed time to recover its equilibrium after the setbacks of 1915, the date set at the Chantilly Conference for the combined British, French and Russian offensives was spring 1916, six months ahead.

On 19 December 1915 Sir Douglas Haig, commander of the British First Army, succeeded Sir John French as Commander-in-Chief of the British Expeditionary Force. He was fifty-four years old, a veteran of the fighting in the Sudan in 1898, in South Africa in 1900, and of the previous year's fighting on the Western Front – a front on which he believed that victory over Germany could be secured. It was not at Montreuil, Haig's headquarters in France, however, but in London that the decisions were to be made as to how the British Expeditionary Force should be used.

On December 28, nine days after Haig's appointment, the War Committee in London – the Cabinet's inner war policymaking group, presided over by the Prime Minister, H. H. Asquith – discussed and endorsed the decisions of the Chantilly Conference. The official minutes of the committee recorded its conclusion that France and Flanders were to be 'the main theatres of operations', that every effort should be made to carry out the offensive 'next spring', and that it should be done in close co-operation with the other Allied Powers.

A day after the committee meeting, one of its members, A. J. Balfour – a former Prime Minister who had been First Lord of the Admiralty since May 1915 – put the case forward for the Easterners, who still felt victory could be secured by attacks on the perimeter. He was convinced that the major Western Front offensive – as agreed to both by the generals at Chantilly and by his own political colleagues in London – would almost certainly fail. The Germans, he pointed out, 'are straining every nerve to make their line impregnable'. The British forces 'have found no sufficient reply to the obstacles provided by successive lines of trenches, the unlimited use of barbed wire, and the machine guns'.

Balfour went on to ask his colleagues whether the Entente Powers – Britain, France, Italy, Russia and Serbia – could afford to fight in conditions 'which may involve a far heavier loss of men for them than for their opponents'. He was worried that, at the end of the planned offensive, the strategic position would be unchanged, 'while the attackers have lost far more men than the attacked', creating a condition of 'extreme peril for the Entente'.

Balfour was rebuked by Lord Kitchener, who, in his written reply, set out the reasons for continuing with the offensive. Germany's 'primary objective', Kitchener wrote, was 'to establish a predominant position in Europe, first by crushing France completely, and then by compelling her other adversaries to accept the terms she chooses to dictate'.

The strength of the Germans' position was clear to Kitchener. 'They are in occupation of the whole of Belgium and all the north-eastern provinces of France comprising the most valuable mining and manufacturing districts in that country. They may well conclude that, providing they can continue to hold their gains, they will be in a favourable position to impose their own peace terms, and that the Allies will tire of the struggle before they themselves do so.' Kitchener was also worried that, unless there was a major offensive in the spring of 1916, it would be very difficult for Britain 'to sustain the strain imposed on us by keeping our forces in the field during the winter for a spring campaign of 1917, and that France will be also in a similar condition'. If, as Balfour advocated, the next Allied offensive were delayed, Kitchener insisted that Britain would 'be running a great risk of losing the war through the exhaustion of our resources'.

In France, on 8 January 1916, Sir Douglas Haig travelled from his headquarters at Montreuil to Hinges, for a conference with his three army commanders. He asked them to 'work out schemes' for preliminary operations 'to wear out the Enemy and exhaust his reserves', and for 'a decisive attack made with the object of piercing the enemy lines'. Ten days later, during a full day's discussion with his Chief of Staff, General Kiggell, and Kiggell's deputy, General Butler, Haig, who was growing in confidence, elaborated on his concept of a 'decisive attack'. Once the Germans had been worn down and used up their reserves – but not until then – a 'mass of troops' would be thrown in 'at some points where the Enemy has shown himself to be weak', with the definite objective 'to break through and win victory'.

In London, Kitchener had been emphatic at the end of December that the British forces in France needed to renew their offensive. When a Conservative member of the War Committee, Austen Chamberlain, asked on January 13 if a German offensive on the Russian front might call for the British to 'settle down to the defensive' in France, Kitchener again argued the case for action, telling his colleagues that 'the only chance of finishing the war this year was by a great offensive in the West.'

Kitchener looked to victory on the Western Front in 1916. Many of his colleagues, including the Chancellor of the Exchequer, Reginald McKenna, feared 'the exhaustion of our resources', warning ominously that 'if we were exhausted, we were done.' If this were so, commented the Minister of Munitions, David Lloyd George, 'we should have nothing to bargain with.' The possibility of having to negotiate a compromise peace was never far from the surface.

As the debate continued, Lloyd George pointed out that Britain had already participated in two offensives on the Western Front in 1915, 'both of which had come to nothing'. His was the voice of caution: 'We could not have another of the same sort. That would amount to a defeat. Therefore we ought to delay until we were really strong enough.'

Lloyd George's dislike of a renewed offensive on the Western Front was strong. 'In the main,' he told the War Committee, 'it was our business to sit tight on the Western frontier,' and take the offensive against the Turks 'in Egypt, Mesopotamia, or Salonika'. Or, he argued, Britain and France could remain on the defensive on the Western Front, while sending heavy guns and equipment to the Eastern Front, to support the forthcoming Russian offensive against Germany. 'Russia had a long front,' Lloyd George noted, 'and it might be easier to break through on it.'

As the debate for and against another offensive on the Western Front gathered momentum, Kitchener's viewpoint was crucial. His colleagues in the War Committee – Liberal politicians who had brought him into their midst to ward off Conservative criticism that they were not truly war-minded – spoke with an authority, based on his rank and high place in public esteem, that could not easily be challenged. On January 14 he wrote privately to Haig, 'There is no doubt a strong feeling against another offensive in France, owing to failures hitherto. But, unless we can impose a peace by force of arms this year, we will run a terrible risk of an unsatisfactory stalemate peace which will certainly necessitate hostilities again in about five years.'

Kitchener added that the Chief of the Imperial General Staff, General Sir William Robertson, the most senior military official in London, was 'fighting splendidly' for a Western Front offensive in 1916, 'but has his work cut out for him by the politicians'.

When the War Committee met on February 22 it had in front of it a letter from Haig, stating that May or June would be the earliest possible date for a British offensive on the Somme, along a fourteen-mile front. Once more the committee endorsed the Western Front offensive, for the dates Haig had given.

The Department of the Somme was created in 1790 as an administrative entity consisting of almost all the ancient French province of Picardy. Its rolling hills had seen many battles. Julius Caesar and his Roman legions fought their way through this rural countryside fifty-seven years before the birth of Christ. One legacy of Rome was the road that, straight as a die, still links Albert and Bapaume, striding across the 1916 battlefield.

The Romans were not the last invaders before the armies of the German Kaiser in 1914. In the ninth and tenth centuries it was the Nordic Vikings who ravaged the land. In 1330, as part of the destructive Hundred Years War, English soldiers tramped the lanes of Picardy, led by their warrior king Edward III. The English defeated the French then, and did so again in 1415, led by King Henry V. On his way to victory at Agincourt, Henry and his army went through Beaumont-Hamel, where the descendants of his soldiers were to fight and fall in July and November 1916.

In the early seventeenth century, Saxon troops of the Holy Roman Emperor marched through the Somme, reaching Corbie, which they besieged for four years, before Louis XIII drove them away. During the fighting between 1636 and 1640, the chateau at Querrieu was burned down. The rebuilt chateau was to be General Rawlinson's Fourth Army headquarters in 1916.

Germans and Frenchmen fought on the Somme again in 1870, during the Franco-Prussian War. A memorial at Pont-Noyelles, less than a mile from Querrieu, commemorates the victory on 23 December 1870 of General Faidherbe, commander of the French Army of the North, against the invading Prussian Army. Another Franco-Prussian War memorial stands today at Le Transloy, towards which Rawlinson's Fourth Army struggled in vain in October 1916.

The French again fought the Germans on the Somme during the opening months of the First World War. On 28 August 1914, at Sailly-Saillisel, Rocquigny and Morval, French reservists had been outnumbered and outgunned as the German Army swept past on the way to Paris. In the local cemetery at Le Transloy is a memorial column in memory of the French soldiers killed during the fighting that day, hampered in their defensive action by the dense fog that can be a feature of the Somme. Many were killed by the Germans as they lay wounded.

What was to become the Somme battlefield in July 1916 has many resonances from this earlier struggle. Visible from Caterpillar Valley Cemetery today is a memorial cross to Captain Henri de Monclin and those of his soldiers killed in the fighting there on 28 September 1914. The town of Albert, which was to become a pivot of the British offensive in 1916, was first shelled by the Germans on 29 September 1914, as they fell back from their thrust to Paris.

By the winter of 1914/15 the opposing armies were separated by a line of trenches from the North Sea to the Swiss border. That line ran through the Somme, and was defended by Breton soldiers, far from their homes in Brittany. A memorial in the village of Ovillers – later one of the objectives of the 1 July 1916 attacks – recalls the death of those Bretons who fell there in action on 7 December 1914.

Calm fell on Picardy and the Somme in January 1915, but it was deceptive. With methodical determination, from the first months of 1915 the Germans began to fortify their line of trenches with deep dugouts and concrete strongpoints. Those just east of the River Ancre were put in place by General von Wundt, commanding the 51st Reserve Infantry. Two strongpoints that were to prove severe obstacles to the attackers on 1 July 1916 were the Schwaben Redoubt and the Leipzig Redoubt.

British troops took over a fourteen-mile sector of French-held trenches in the chalky, rolling countryside north of the River Somme during a routine adjustment of the Allied front line at the end of 1915. They were not pleased with what they found. According to their standards – which were still not as high as those of the Germans – the

French trenches had not been properly maintained. Because the Somme had been a quiet part of the Western Front for most of 1915, the French had allocated relatively few troops to defend it. In many places the raised parapets were no protection from an enemy sniper. In many sections one front-line trench did not connect with the next. The parados – the parapet behind the trench, giving protection from the rear – was frequently overgrown with brambles. Barbed wire had not been put in place at the edge of No-Man's Land. An air of neglect permeated the line.

Some of the German divisions facing the French in the line of trenches north of the Somme had been there since the end of 1914. The German soldiers had been diligent in preparing deep trenches and strong dugouts; nor had there ever been a day without some clash, some artillery bombardment, some trench mortar attacks, some burst of machine-gun fire, which led to death and injury.

A British second lieutenant, Hugh Freston, of the 3rd Battalion, Royal Berkshire Regiment, joined his battalion near Albert six days before Christmas 1915. In the trenches facing La Boisselle on 24 January 1916 he was inspecting a dugout that had been heavily shelled, and was talking to some stretcher-bearers, when more shells fell and he was killed. He was twenty-four years old. In one of his poems he had written:

> After I am dead,
> And have become part of the soil of France,
> This much remember of me:
> I was a great sinner, a great lover, and life puzzled me very much.
> Ah love! I would have died for love!
> Love can do so much, both rightly and wrongly.
> It remembers mothers, and little children,
> And lots of other things.
> O men unborn, I go now, my work unfinished!
> I pass on the problem to you: the world will hate you: be brave!

Second Lieutenant Freston is buried in Bécourt Military Cemetery on the outskirts of Albert.

In response to the decisions of the Chantilly Conference to embark upon attacks on the Somme in the spring of 1916, a vast British army was on its way to billets in France in readiness for the Somme offensive.

Two hundred thousand fighting men were available for the Big Push. These included regular soldiers of the British Army who had been in action since the first weeks of the war; Territorial soldiers, part of more than seventy battalions raised in Britain between 1907 and 1914 under a pre-war volunteer recruiting scheme for home defence; men of the 29th Division, veterans of the fighting at Gallipoli, including Australians, New Zealanders and Newfoundlanders; and, numerically the largest group, the men of Kitchener's New Army.

One of the New Army soldiers, the footballer Pat Crossan – a member of McCrae's Battalion, and an exceptionally fast right back – wrote to his pre-war manager on February 10, 'I think that instead of fighting we should take the Fritzes on at football. I am certain we would do it on them.'

Many of the Pals battalions, like the Accrington Pals, the Bradford Pals, the Halifax Pals, the Leeds Pals, the Liverpool Pals and the Salford Pals, were from the north of England, but Pals battalions came from all over Britain. The Swansea Pals were to be among the pride of Wales. These battalions, each of a thousand men and more, representing the close-knit, territorial nature of pre-1914 British life, were to fight – and die – on the Somme amid a fierce comradeship.

In France, preparations for battle were continuous. On March 1, General Sir Henry Rawlinson took over command of the Fourth Army, which would bear the brunt of the fighting. Two days later, Lieutenant Bernard White, of the 20th (1st Tyneside Scottish) Battalion, Northumberland Fusiliers, a twenty-nine-year-old publisher and writer, wrote to a friend, 'We are here for a short rest before going into the trenches again. "Rest" is a military term meaning "out of danger from anything but long-range fire and aerial bombs"; but it does not necessarily mean ease. There are kit inspections, anti-gas helmet inspections, ration inspections, rifle inspections, foot inspections to be arranged. Also route marches, bathing parades, laundry parades, working parties (arranged for the sublime and impudent slackers that accompany us).'

'Trench warfare is monotonous', Lieutenant White explained, 'but fairly safe. Snipers do the most damage, although shellfire is worse when it is unexpected. Given a little warning, one can get under cover from these veritable machines of iniquity; but if one comes plump into a billet, then it is sure to take its toll of life, for its ravages are widespread.'

Lieutenant White was killed on the first day of the Battle of the Somme. His body was never identified. His name is inscribed on the Thiepval Memorial to the Missing.

On March 6, at his headquarters chateau at Querrieu, General Rawlinson held his first conference with his corps commanders, Generals Congreve, Morland and Hunter-Weston. After outlining the overall plan, he asked them to make their preliminary preparations, selecting sites for artillery batteries, building observation posts for the artillery, and laying telephone cables. This last was the task of the Royal Engineers, who, on April 1, began to lay cable lines forward of divisional headquarters, digging them six feet deep to protect them from shelling by German 5.9-inch shells. More than 7,000 miles of deep-dug wire were laid during the coming three months, in addition to 43,000 miles of above-ground cable. Plans were also begun for different means of communication, principally wireless, soldier runners, dogs and pigeons.

Britain's Carrier Pigeon Service consisted of four hundred men, employing 22,000 pigeons and 150 mobile lofts on the Western Front, at the time of the Armistice in November 1918. More than 100,000 pigeons were used by British forces during the First World War. During the fighting on the Somme, the French Army used 5,000 carrier pigeons. Only two per cent of the birds released failed to return.

To ensure that the advancing troops would be able to communicate their whereabouts as they moved forward – a crucial element in artillery co-operation – lamps, flags, discs, shutters and fans were assembled, to be used in signalling to the Royal Artillery observers watching from vantage points on hills and in trees, and to the Royal Flying Corps observers who would be flying over the battlefield. Klaxon horns were distributed to the aviators. A long blast on the horn would mean 'Where are you?', to which the reply would be given by coloured flares.

Even in the build-up before the battle, death was a daily occurrence. On April 22, twenty-one-year-old Private William McBride, Royal Inniskilling Fusiliers, was killed just south of the River Ancre. His grave is in the Lonsdale war cemetery at Authuille, south of Thiepval Wood. Two days later nineteen-year-old Private George

Curnew, 1st Battalion, Newfoundland Regiment, was killed by a German sniper less than two miles to the north, while working on the parapet of the trenches to which the Newfoundlanders had been sent, opposite the German-held village of Beaumont-Hamel. He is buried in Mesnil Ridge Cemetery.

It was a slow, steady process of attrition, soon to be accelerated and multiplied many-thousandfold.

As British plans for a Somme offensive went ahead, the German High Command launched a military offensive 150 miles to the south-east, against the French fortress of Verdun. Even if the German soldiers could not capture the city itself, the German Commander-in-Chief, General Erich von Falkenhayn, believed that an unrelenting German assault could bleed the French armies defending it.

With the launching of the German attack on Verdun, the French faced a fearsome struggle. While the outcome of that struggle was still unclear, Haig was making his plans for a British offensive that would lead to an end to the stalemate of trench warfare. On March 24 he drafted instructions for the training of the cavalry divisions at his disposal. When a break in the German lines had been made, 'cavalry and mobile troops must be at hand to advance at once to make a bridgehead (until relieved by infantry) beyond the gap with the object of checking hostile reserves which the Enemy might rush up, and to give time for our own divisions to deploy.' At the same time, mounted troops would co-operate with the main attacking force 'in widening the gap', both by operating in the rear of any German defences that were holding out and by extending the flank of the 'bridgehead' as a protection to the outer flanks of the attacking forces.

In addition to the men of Kitchener's New Army, and the Territorials, an important influx of troops in preparation for the Battle of the Somme came with the men of the 29th Division, who had been evacuated from Gallipoli three months earlier. Among the first to arrive in France were the men of the Newfoundland Regiment. On March 25, having travelled by ship from Suez to Marseille, and then by train from Marseille to Pont-Remy, eight miles south-east of Abbeville, they reached Pont-Remy Station at two in the morning. From the station they crossed a river on the bridge – the *pont* – that gave the town its name. That river was the

Somme. From there they marched three miles in the darkness, in cold and rain, to their billets at Buigny-l'Abbé.

The urgency for a plan of attack on the Somme intensified as the German assault on Verdun claimed increasingly heavy losses. Within a month of the German assault, the French had suffered enormous casualties: 90,000 men had been killed and even more tens of thousands injured. The ring of fortresses held, but at an Anglo-French conference in Paris on March 28 the French political and military leaders spoke openly of their heavy losses at Verdun, and impressed upon the two senior British representatives, Lord Kitchener and General Sir William Robertson, that it was 'time for the British to play their part'.

Kitchener reported this call to Haig, whom he visited at Montreuil on March 29, on his way back to London. Haig told him that 'I never had any intention of attacking with all available troops except in an emergency to save the French, and Paris perhaps from capture.' Haig added, ominously, 'I have not got an army in France really, but a collection of divisions untrained for the field.' The actual fighting army would 'evolve' from these divisions.

An essential element in the early planning stages of the offensive, whatever the precise date might be, was to establish a site to which the seriously wounded men could be brought from the battlefield for emergency treatment, before being sent by train to the main base hospitals near the coast – the largest in Etaples, others in Rouen and Boulogne. On April 1 a casualty clearing station was set up near the village of Heilly, less than eight miles from the front-line trenches facing La Boisselle. Within two months, ten more casualty clearing stations had been set up.

The numbers that would be involved in the Big Push were enormous. Facilities had to be found, in the first instance, for at least seven weeks' lodging for more than 400,000 men and 100,000 horses. The road and rail communications in the area immediately behind the front were poor, with only one road of sufficient quality to be used night and day to take troops and supplies up to the front. This was the road linking Contay, Hédauville, Englebelmer, Martinsart and Aveluy. Because the local chalk was too soft for roadbuilding, heavier chalk that could take the mass of transport that would use the roads was brought from Cornwall and the Channel Islands.

To ensure sufficient water for the troops, for drinking, washing and laundry, as well as for the supply, artillery and cavalry horses, pumping sets were brought from Britain, including two powerful steam fire engines from the London County Council. More than 300 lorries, some with 550-gallon tanks, brought water to the billets. Pipes were laid down to take water forward as far as possible, to water points at the front. Initially these water points consisted of waterproof canvas tanks holding 2,000 gallons each. Steel 'bandages' were prepared for the swift repair of water pipes damaged by German gunfire.

On 1 April 1916 it was decided that a new standard-gauge railway line would be needed, running seventeen miles between Candas and Acheux. This would provide four supply railheads, and could carry fifteen trains a day. A second new line, giving three railheads, was built on the ten-mile stretch from Daours to Contay, and the existing spur line from Dernancourt was extended to supply the artillery positions near Méaulte. This spur was eventually extended further, forming what became known as The Loop, east of the Fricourt–Bray road. A major railway supply siding was laid out at Buire – known to the British as Edge Hill – to which a mass of materiel – the equipment, apparatus and supplies of a twentieth-century military force – would be brought, and then moved forward by road. New sidings, depots and platforms were also built at Vignacourt and Flesselles. In all, fifty-five miles of new railway track were laid.

A total of seventeen railheads were established. Two of them, at Doullens and Vecquemont, were designated specifically for ambulances. Forward bases for ambulances were established at Louvencourt, on the Doullens–Albert road, and at Warloy-Baillon, six and a half miles from the front line, where a cemetery extension was begun in readiness for those battle casualties who could not be saved. At Acheux, five miles from the front facing Beaumont-Hamel, VIII Corps established its collection station for the wounded: the war cemetery at Acheux was to see 180 burials. Seven miles south-west of the front line facing Mametz, an area was chosen for a concentration of field ambulances, and for the main dressing station of XIV Corps. There too a cemetery was to be built, in a nearby wood. It became known as Dive Copse Cemetery, after the officer commanding the dressing station.

The town of Corbie, near the conflux of the Somme and the Ancre, also saw intense preparation for the arrival of the wounded, the town centre becoming a medical centre, with Casualty Clearing Stations Nos. 5 and 21 being established in the suburb of La Neuville. In the four British war cemeteries in Corbie are 2,224 burials, most from the battle that was soon to begin.

Sixteen miles behind the front line, the cathedral city of Amiens, the location since August 1914 of the 7th General Hospital, saw considerable preparations from April 1916 to receive the wounded of the Big Push. That April the 56th (South Midland) Casualty Clearing Station was established there, followed in July by the New Zealand Stationary Hospital. For those who were to die of their wounds while still being tended, a cemetery was established at Saint-Pierre, on the northeastern outskirts of Amiens, on the northern side of the main road to Albert. Today it contains 676 First World War Commonwealth burials.

It was not only the men who died after being brought back to casualty clearing stations who were to be buried in the cemeteries. The cemetery at Bouzincourt, four miles behind the front line, was to be used not only for burials from the field ambulances but also for the interment of many soldiers killed in action and brought back there by the burial parties.

For the new offensive, Haig hoped to make use of a new weapon of war: the tank. On April 14, when he was in London, he was told by the officer in charge of tank development, Colonel Ernest Swinton, that he could have 150 tanks by July 31. Haig said that 'was too late'. He wanted fifty by June 1 as a matter of urgency. He then showed Swinton a trench map 'and impressed on him the necessity for thinking over the system of leadership and control of a group of "Tanks" with a view to manoeuvring'.

In the event, no tanks were to be made available until mid-September, two and a half months after the start of the battle.

The German bombardment of the forts protecting Verdun was massive and continuous. But in France there were those who hesitated to advocate a large-scale Anglo-French counter-offensive. On May 4, the chairman of the Senate Military Committee, Georges Clemenceau, went to see Haig at Montreuil and asked him to exercise a 'restraining hand' on the Supreme Commander of the French forces, General Joffre, and to prevent 'any offensive on a large scale from being made until all is ready, and we are at our maximum strength'. Clemenceau warned Haig that, if Britain and France were to attack and fail, there would be 'a number of people' in France who would say that the time had come to make peace with Germany. Haig replied cautiously that the British divisions 'want much careful training before we could attack with hope of success'.

On the day after Clemenceau's visit, Haig inspected the Australian and New Zealand Divisions. 'They are undoubtedly a fine body of men,' he wrote in his diary, 'but their officers and leaders as a whole have a good deal to learn.' A portion of their front had been shelled on May 4, 'and a small party of Germans entered their trenches. I understand that the severity and accuracy of the enemy's artillery fire was a revelation to them!' It was Haig who used the exclamation mark.

Haig also visited the Canadian forces, whom he found 'in the best of spirits, determined to give the Enemy more than they had received in hard knocks from him'. As to the South African Brigade, it was, Haig noted in his diary, 'as fine a unit as there is in the Army'.

A difference of opinion had emerged among Haig's commanders. General Rawlinson, commanding the Fourth Army, which would undertake the main assault, saw success as the overrunning and capture of the German trench lines facing his troops, not in the type of break-through that Haig envisaged. On May 10, Haig saw the commander of VIII Corps, General Hunter-Weston, who had fought at Gallipoli, and who shared Rawlinson's view. 'I impressed on him', Haig wrote in his diary, 'that there must be no halting attacks at each trench in succession for rear lines to pass through! The objective must be as far as our guns can prepare the Enemy's position for attack – and when the attack starts it must be pushed through to the final objective with as little delay as possible.'

Haig added that Hunter-Weston's experiences at Gallipoli 'were under very different conditions: then he landed from ships, a slow pro-ceeding: now his troops can be forward in succession of lines in great depth, and all can start at the same moment!'

The situation at Verdun as revealed by the French was causing alarm among those few British policymakers who were aware of its severity. On May 10, the day on which Haig warned Hunter-Weston of the dangers of hesitation on the battlefield, Sir William Robertson told the War Committee in London that, while the French estimated their casualties at Verdun – of dead and wounded – at 115,000, he believed that they were 'somewhat heavier', and that the German casualties there were not as great as claimed by the French. A week later Lord Kitchener warned the committee that the German aim of wearing out the French forces at Verdun was succeeding, and that the Germans would 'wear through and go on to Paris'.

The effect of this danger on the British forces, and on the whole prospect of the war, was self-evident. On May 19 the Director of Military Operations at the War Office, General Sir Frederick Maurice, explained that, before Verdun, General Joffre had intended to employ forty French divisions as France's contribution to the Somme offensive, but that as a result of the fighting at Verdun he could contemplate only twenty-five, and even then could not guarantee that number in a month's time.

Joffre also conferred with Haig, pressing the British Commander-in-Chief to relieve the strain on the hard-pressed French divisions at Verdun by carrying out a large-scale British attack on the German trenches. Joffre wanted the attack to take place on July 1. He did not mind where it took place, as long as it forced the Germans to take troops and artillery away from Verdun.

Haig agreed to come to the aid of France. No breach in the German trench defences had been made between August 1914 and December 1915 while his predecessor Field Marshal Sir John French had been in command of the British forces. Haig was determined to change this. He had been on the Western Front since the start of the war, commanding the largest of the British armies. He had confidence in his powers of command, in the strategy that he had devised, and in the abilities of his troops.

Haig was pleased that the battle would take place on the Somme, the area agreed upon at Chantilly the previous December. It was ideally suited for close liaison with the French as far as creating a wider front was concerned. British and British Empire forces north of the river, and French forces south of the river, would attack simultaneously. But the British would have a far longer front line, would provide by far the larger number of troops, and would face a far larger number of German divisions.

Despite his keenness for the plan, and his confident hopes for a break-through, Haig, having continued to watch the troops in training, was uneasy about the French call for an attack that July. He no longer felt, as he had done earlier, that his troops, especially those from the New Armies – more than half of his force – and the troops of the Territorial Army, would be ready in June. His preferred date was August 15. Haig was being realistic, but he was not to be the arbiter of the date.

Meanwhile, every preparation for battle was under way. On May 24, General Rawlinson wrote to the War Office in London, 'I hope you are sending us out plenty of big cylinders with chlorine gas in them for when the west wind commences, we shall want them badly.'

On May 25, when Sir William Robertson visited Haig at Montreuil, Haig pointed out that if the attack was held off from July, the date Joffre had requested, to August 15 'we would be much stronger.' But Haig also explained to Robertson 'what might be the results if we did not support the French', and that he had therefore come to the con-clusion 'that we *must* march to the support of French'. Haig under-lined the word 'must'.

Haig's next visitor, on May 26, was Joffre, who stressed that the French 'had supported for three months alone the whole weight of the German attacks at Verdun'. If this went on, Joffre warned, 'the French Army would be ruined'. He was therefore of the opinion that July 1 was 'the latest date for the combined offensive of the British and the French'. Haig tried to talk him through the various dates on which British preparedness would be increased, speaking successively of July 1, July 15, August 1 and August 15. When Haig mentioned August 15, 'Joffre at once got very excited and shouted that "the French Army would cease to exist, if we did nothing till then"!'

Haig then pointed out that 'in spite of the 15th August being the most favourable date for the British Army to take action, yet, in view of what he had said regarding the unfortunate condition of the French Army, I was prepared to commence operations on the 1st July or thereabouts. This calmed the old man, but I saw that he had come to the meeting prepared to combat a refusal on my part, and was pre-pared to be very nasty.'

Haig's reluctance to start the offensive before August 15 was essen-tially overruled by the French Supreme Commander. The British government was pledged and determined to help France escape the danger of defeat at Verdun, and beyond. France's defeat would be Britain's danger. Haig had no alternative but to defer to French demands. The Big Push was planned to begin on June 29.

The troops, who were privy neither to the plan nor to the dispute about the date on which it would be launched, knew that something massive was in prospect, as a continual stream of men, guns and ammunition was assembled behind the front line. The Big Push would be the first British offensive action on any scale for almost a year. The tactical plan was clear. They would gather in their trenches and then, at the blow of a whistle, emerge from them – go 'over the top' – and move forward, some walking, some running, depending on the circumstances, crossing the tract of No-Man's Land in front of the German defenders, breaking into successive German lines of trenches, reaching the villages that lay beyond the trenches, and advancing steadily eastward, liberating the villages and towns of France from German occupation under which they had suffered for more than a year and a half.

From the outset of his command, Haig's plan had been ambitious. He was convinced that if his troops could make a breach through the German trench lines and defences, then the cavalry could ride through the gap and push deep into German-occupied France. His belief in the role of cavalry had been hardened in mid-May, after a dispute with the War Committee about whether horses needed to be maintained in such large numbers on the Western Front. Asquith had been particularly opposed to Haig's cavalry concept, telling the War Committee, as its minutes recorded, that 'the horses out in France were of no use now. They were only there for prospective use when we had broken through. We were maintaining in France an enormous number of horses which were temporarily useless.'

For Haig, this politician's view showed abysmal ignorance of what was possible, and hopefully imminent, on the Western Front. As he explained to the British General Staff a month after the War Committee meeting, 'the advance was to be pressed eastward far enough to enable our cavalry to push through into the open country beyond the enemy's prepared lines of defence.'

Since the retreat from Mons to the Marne in August 1914, cavalry had been the unused arm of war. Throughout 1915 and the first six months of 1916, the soldiers and their horses had waited for a chance to gallop forward through a gap in the German lines, but no gap had been created. The German trench fortifications were too strong and too deep for infantry to effect a breach. At Neuve-Chapelle in March 1915 and at Loos six months later, the German front line had held firm against ferocious infantry assault. In these two battles, terrible casualties had been incurred for gains of less than a thousand yards.

If Haig's plan were to succeed, as he was confident it would, all this would change. The infantry would break through, the German front line would part, and the cavalry would follow. The hunt would be on. Germany, which for almost two years had held a defensive line of the trenches stretching from the North Sea to the Swiss border, would be defeated. The losses of earlier battles would be avenged.

Victory would see the humbling of the German Empire, the humiliation of the German Kaiser, the liberation of Belgium and north-eastern France, and a moment of glory for Britain and its Empire. That Empire had sent troops to fight from Canada, Newfoundland, Australia, South Africa and New Zealand. But Winston Churchill, who had served as a battalion commander on the Western Front from January to May 1916, was uneasy at what was in prospect. In May 1916, after his battalion was amalgamated with another, he returned to his parliamentary duties. In a speech on May 23 he asked the House of Commons to realize the harshness of front-line service: 'I say to myself every day, what is going on while we sit here, while we go away to dinner or home to bed? Nearly a thousand men – Englishmen, Britishers, men of our race – are knocked into bundles of bloody rags every twenty-four hours, and carried away to hasty graves or to field ambulances.' It was six weeks before the start of the Somme offensive. Churchill spoke in Parliament against the 'futile offensives', but his voice was drowned in the general patriotic call for a renewed attack.

In the South Atlantic Ocean, the explorer Ernest Shackleton, having spent two years in the remote Antarctic, reached the small island of South Georgia on May 20. The first question he asked Mr Sorlie, the manager of the tiny British whaling station, was 'Tell me, when was the war over?' To which Mr Sorlie replied, 'The war is not over. Millions are being killed. Europe is mad. The world is mad.'

*

On the last day of May 1916, as a vast British army was assembling for the new offensive, the British Grand Fleet and the German High Seas Fleets clashed for the first time since the outbreak of war. At this battle off the Danish Jutland coast, the Royal Navy, on which Britain based its imperial power and war-making confidence, failed to destroy its German naval adversary, despite earlier hopes of the British admirals that it would. For their part, the Germans failed, despite their fervent hopes, to destroy the British Fleet.

The German High Seas Fleet returned to its ports, and remained there, no longer a decisive factor in the conflict, for the rest of the war. Its failure to defeat the British at sea left the Royal Navy masters of the English Channel, enabling troops and their munitions to continue to be transferred from Britain to France without interruption or loss.

As May came to an end, many of those troops were undertaking front-line trench duty. The Newfoundlanders, marching forward from their new billets in Louvencourt, began their second tour of front-line duty on May 18. Their official historian notes that this was also their second encounter with the 'Somme rat' – 'a breed unsurpassed in size and daring anywhere along the Front'. To leave the unfinished portion of the day's ration in one's haversack without protection of the mess tin 'was to invite both the destruction of the haversack and the loss of the rations'. These rats, the official historian adds, 'as heavy as cats, would roam about trenches and dugouts all night, disturbing much needed sleep and offering themselves as revolver targets for officers, and Lewis gunners' – the No. 1 Man on the Lewis gun being equipped, like the officers, with a revolver.

Selected troops, many of whom had never been in action before, were sent to training camps – the largest being at Etaples on the coast – to practise digging trenches and vaulting over them. They also learned how to use their bayonets effectively, practising the disembowelling of straw sacks.

Among those sent back from the front for a refresher course at Etaples was Second Lieutenant Siegfried Sassoon, 1st Battalion, Royal Welch Fusiliers, whose brother Hamo had been killed at Gallipoli the previous November. Siegfried Sassoon had earlier won the Military Cross in a raid on the German trenches in front of Fricourt. The Military Cross had been instituted on 28 December 1914 for junior officers – captains, lieutenants and second lieutenants – for 'gallantry in the field'. The refresher course made a powerful impact on Sassoon. As he later wrote in his *Memoirs of an Infantry Officer*, 'Man, it seemed, had been created to jab the life out of Germans. To hear the Major talk, one might have thought he did it himself every day before breakfast. His final words were: "Remember that every Boche you fellows kill is a point scored to our side; every Boche you kill brings victory one minute nearer and shortens the war by one minute. Kill them! Kill them! There's only one good Boche, and that's a dead one!"'

After bayonet practice, Sassoon recalled, 'I went up the hill to my favourite sanctuary, a wood of hazels and beeches. The evening air smelt of wet mould and wet leaves; the trees were misty-green; the church bell was tolling in the town, and smoke rose from the roofs. Peace was there in the twilight of that prophetic foreign spring. But the lecturer's voice still battered on my brain. "The bullet and the bayonet are brother and sister." "If you don't kill him, he'll kill you." "Stick him between the eyes, in the throat, in the chest." "Don't waste good steel. Six inches are enough. What's the use of a foot of steel sticking out at the back of a man's neck? Three inches will do for him; when he coughs, go and look for another."'

Sassoon had already seen action. For most of those in training, the Somme was to be their first encounter with war: both bullet and steel. The steel was to be not only that of the bayonet, but also that of the artillery shell, the single most destructive weapon of battle.

2

June 1916: 'There is much in the wind'

O N WHAT WAS soon to be the Somme battlefield, men and supplies were being assembled in considerable numbers. Each corps
constructed a large 'cage': a barbed-wire enclosure in which German
prisoners of war would be held. The Fourth Army consisted of
519,324 men, prompting General Rawlinson to write in his diary,
with some pride, 'It is not the lot of many to command over half a
million men.' This was three times the number of men who had
assembled for the Battle of Loos, the largest previous effort of the
British Expeditionary Force.

The area chosen for the attack was one of existing trench lines,
stretching across a rolling landscape, weaving in and out of woods and
villages. The German trenches were particularly well fortified, as
befitted an army committed to the defensive. In the cellars of the
village houses, strongpoints and deep dugouts were built.

As preparations for the British assault gathered momentum, daily
clashes between the two opposing forces took place at some point
along the facing front lines, which were sometimes several hundred
yards apart, sometimes only fifty yards distant. Sniping was continuous. The artillery of both sides, situated well behind the front, kept
up a spasmodic but deadly barrage.

Beneath the front-line trenches, British 'moles' were at work, tunnelling below No-Man's Land and reaching beneath the German
front-line trenches, where they laid massive explosive charges. 'The
ground being hard chalk,' wrote the official British war historian,
Brigadier General Sir James Edmonds, 'the tunnellers were forced to
work with push-picks to avoid being heard; when close to the
enemy progress was continued by boring holes in the face with car-
penters' augers. Vinegar was poured into the holes and, thus sof-
tened, the chalk surrounding each hole was then scraped out. One

auger actually penetrated into a German officers' dugout unnoticed by the enemy.'

Because of the tunnellers' closeness to the German positions, General Edmonds pointed out, the tunnelling had to be carried out in silence. The bayonets were fitted with a special spliced handle, the men were barefoot, and the floor of the gallery was carpeted with sandbags. The sapper inserted the point of the bayonet in a crack in the 'face' or alongside a flint, gave it a twist, and dislodged a piece of chalk, which he caught with his other hand and laid on the floor. If he needed both hands on the bayonet, a second sapper caught the stone as it fell.

The tunnels were extremely narrow: about four and a half feet by two and a half feet. An advance of eighteen inches in twenty-four hours was considered satisfactory. The spoil was packed in sandbags, passed out along a line of men seated on the floor, and stacked against the side of the tunnel, ready for use later to 'tamp' the charge. The tunnel at Y Sap, which penetrated below the German trenches at La Boisselle, was 1,030 feet long, the longest ever driven in chalk during the First World War. The explosive used in the charge was ammonal – 65 per cent ammonium nitrate, 17 per cent coarse aluminum, 15 per cent TNT and 3 per cent charcoal, a mixture that detonates with a velocity of 4,400 metres a second. It remains in use today as an industrial explosive.

Eight large and eleven small mines were laid: two large and nine small at Casino Point, three large ones at the 'Tambour' opposite Fricourt, two large and two small ones near La Boisselle, and one large one at Beaumont-Hamel. General Edmonds noted, 'Lack of manpower prevented more being undertaken.' It was a formidable mining enterprise.

For the troops being assembled for the Big Push, entertainment was provided in many towns and villages behind the lines. Amiens, with the largest cathedral in France – where Edward III had attended Mass on his way to the Battle of Crécy in 1346 – was a favourite place for rest and recreation. Dennis Wheatley, Royal Field Artillery, later a successful crime writer, enthusiastically recommended Madame Prudhomme's brothel. The writer Jean Cocteau stayed in Amiens in June while waiting to be posted to the French Evacuation Hospital

No. 13 at Marcelcave, to work with the ambulance service. Its fine hotels and restaurants were patronized by officers, journalists and visiting dignitaries. Raymond Asquith – the Prime Minister's son, and a Guards officer – wrote of a visit to Amiens where he 'ate and drank a great deal of the best, slept in downy beds, bathed in hot perfumed water, and had a certain amount of restrained fun with the very much once-occupied ladies of the town'.

Five miles from Amiens, in one of the large barns at Querrieu, a few hundred yards from Rawlinson's magnificent chateau, there were film shows and concerts. In his novel *The Golden Virgin*, based on his personal experiences, Henry Williamson recalled some of the actors at a concert 'dressed up as girls with varied types of wigs' and garish make-up, and how each herded man in the audience was 'fascinated, filled with longing'.

One popular entertainer was Captain Basil Hallam Radford. A leading singer and comedian on the pre-war London stage, where he was known as Basil Hallam, at the outbreak of war Radford was rejected by the infantry because of a steel plate in his leg from a former accident. He persevered, played one more season in London at the Palace Theatre, and in the summer of 1915 was accepted by the Royal Flying Corps; in 1916 he was posted to France, to No. 3 Army Kite Balloon Section. At Querrieu, as in London, his pre-war character Gilbert the Filbert was an immediate favourite:

> I'm Gilbert the Filbert, the Knut with a 'K'
> The pride of Piccadilly, the blasé roué
> Oh, Hades, the ladies, who leave their wooden huts
> For Gilbert the Filbert, the colonel of the Knuts.

At the beginning of June 1916, the 10th Battalion, Loyal North Lancashire Regiment, was sent to Bienvillers, south-west of Arras, with the usual routine of five days in the front-line trenches followed by five days in reserve billets. The nature of this existence was described by Captain Richard Dennys, a pianist, painter, actor and writer, in a letter to a friend. 'Billets again and a bit of rest,' he wrote, 'but we've been having a fairly lively time in the trenches – two raids on the Boche by people close on our left with resulting bombardments on their part. Unpleasantly warm! My headquarters dugout was smashed to pieces the day before we took over, and during the 2nd bombardment the other to which I had repaired was buried in debris. A shell burst just near the door and you never saw such a mess! Bed a foot deep in earth, door blown in and utter confusion of all papers and things. Two shells through the mess kitchen and others in profusion all round. They have got Company HQ marked all right! Yes, we are full of activities. There is much in the wind. You should have news of this part of the world at no distant date.'

That some major Western Front offensive was in the offing was clear. On June 2 it was announced that for all munitions workers in Britain the June 11 Whitsuntide holiday would be postponed until the end of July. Also clear was the French need for help to take pressure off troops pinned down and suffering daily losses at Verdun. The War Committee in London had still not made up its mind, however, to endorse the Somme offensive. On June 5, before its next scheduled meeting, Lord Kitchener, on his way to North Russia on board the cruiser HMS *Hampshire*, perished when the ship hit a mine west of the Orkney Islands, during a Force 9 gale. Kitchener, his Staff, and 643 of the crew of 655 were drowned or died of exposure. Kitchener's body was never found. On the day of his death the last division of his New Army crossed the English Channel to take up its positions on the Somme.

A nation's war hero was dead. The War Committee had lost its military expert, the only Secretary of State for War since the outbreak of hostilities almost two years earlier. At its meeting on June 6 – the day after Kitchener's death and a mere twenty-three days before the battle was meant to begin – the Minister of Munitions, David Lloyd George, reported on his recent talks with his French opposite number, the French Minister of Munitions, Albert Thomas. The French, reported Lloyd George, were becoming 'rattled'. They had borne the brunt of the fighting for two years, and were growing exhausted. The British must come to their aid, or their army would be knocked out.

Lloyd George also warned his colleagues that the French were beginning to believe that Britain was accumulating military resources for some future project entirely to its own benefit, and was disregarding France's immediate needs.

The dangers to France were not belittled in London. General Philippe Pétain, the commander in the Verdun region, had reported that his sector could not hold out beyond June 20. While Joffre disputed this, saying that Verdun could hold out until early July, it was clear that the moment of grave danger was drawing near.

The Chief of the Imperial General Staff, General Sir William Robertson, pointed out to the War Committee at the same meeting on June 6 that the British had never refused to give assistance to the French High Command, whenever they had requested it. Lloyd George was also worried about what was happening at Verdun, telling the committee that the French were 'not quite holding their own' there.

The War Committee, presided over by Asquith, who had temporarily taken over Kitchener's portfolio as Secretary of State for War, met again on June 7. Haig – who, in anticipation of the Battle of the Somme, had established his headquarters at Beauquesnes, almost ten miles behind the front line, in the Château Val Vion – had been asked to cross over from France to attend. He reported widespread feeling in France at the highest level – including, he said, President Poincaré – that the Germans would take Verdun. The French, Haig added, felt that, having started the war as the strongest of the Allied Powers, 'they were now going down and down.' Haig had told Joffre he would launch the British attack on June 29, but preferred August 15. Joffre had said that July 1 would be 'soon enough'.

In the assembly areas, June 8 saw the first of seven daily ammunition trains arrive at the railheads. The ammunition was then taken up, often by horse teams, to the artillery batteries, almost all of which were in place. Also behind the lines, practice attacks were taking place across fields of ripening corn, the imagined German trench lines being indicated by flags and specially ploughed furrows.

The Newfoundlanders, noted for their thrift in a harsh climate, were particularly shocked at having to trample across acres of knee-high crops belonging to the villagers of Louvencourt, where they were billeted. This made them feel particularly ashamed as the villagers had welcomed them so warmly from their distant land. But practice was an essential part of the plan. 'We go over the ground exactly as we shall on the Great Day,' wrote one Newfoundlander, Lieutenant Owen Steele, on June 12. Eight days after that 'Great Day' he was killed by German shellfire while in reserve billets. Today he lies in the Mailly-Maillet Communal Cemetery Extension.

★

The final decision was yet to be taken by the War Committee in London for what was intended to be the June 29 opening of the Battle of the Somme. Much depended on whether Lloyd George could satisfy the War Committee that Britain had the necessary munitions of war to carry out a major offensive. It was only a year since the scandal of the shortage of shells at the Battle of Loos had forced Asquith's Liberal government – in power for a decade – to bring in the Conservative opposition as equal partners.

On June 21 the War Committee met to hear what Lloyd George had to report. He astonished them all, and in particular Asquith, with his statistical presentation of increased munitions production in Britain. While France was manufacturing 20 to 30 heavy guns each month, he told them, Britain was manufacturing 140 to 150. As for the all-important shell situation, it was such, Lloyd George revealed, that Haig would be able to order sufficient shells to fire almost 300,000 each week.

In the British sector, Rawlinson's Fourth Army would face thirty-two German battalions. One ominous fact, revealed by Military Intelligence, was that, because of the number of German troops known to be in reserve – sixty-five battalions – Rawlinson's numerical superiority on the battlefield would entirely vanish after just five days. This, comment the military historians Robin Prior and Trevor Wilson, was 'hardly the scenario for a decisive advance or any sort of breakthrough'. They add, 'It foreshadowed, at the very most, a gradual and costly pushing forward of no great significance.'

At a meeting of the War Cabinet on June 22, General Robertson, without mentioning the Intelligence report about German strength in reserve, told the War Committee that the British forces on the Somme had a 'superiority in men', although, he added, 'he thought the Germans were superior in guns.' An astonished A. J. Balfour pointed out to his colleagues, 'On the whole our superiority was great except in the one thing that really mattered.'

Another factor weighed more heavily with the War Committee than any relative British weakness in artillery. At their meeting on June 23 the committee members were, in the words of the minutes, 'impressed with the great progress that had been made in munitions production', and with 'the highly satisfactory position which had been reached'.

Throughout the morning of June 23 a mass of troops was moving forward from its reserve billets, along the dusty roads. Some officers feared that the dust clouds would alert the eagle-eyed German observers to the fact that a substantial attack must be in the offing. But in the early afternoon, as violent thunderstorms broke out, the area was deluged by rain, and it became impossible for the troops to make use of the recently dug communications trenches to move forward to the front line. Waist deep in mud and water, they had to wait until dusk to go over the open fields.

The preliminary artillery barrage was opened on June 24, along the whole fourteen-mile front facing the British forces. Its aim was to destroy the German front line entirely during five intense days of bombardment: the barbed-wire defences, and the trench fortifications, and the dugouts in which the German soldiers would be taking shelter from the barrage. During the course of a week, more than 1,500 guns and howitzers fired an astonishing 1,732,873 shells. On exploding, however, many of these shells merely churned up the already pockmarked and battered surface of the ground. They also caused less damage than hoped to the dugouts of the German defenders – dugouts that were sometimes two storeys deep, and strongly reinforced, often with concrete.

It also soon became clear that many of the British shells were duds, which failed to explode at all. But the impact of the noise and ferocity of the bombardment on the mood and morale of the British troops as the shells flew above them towards the German lines was considerable. The Germans were also impressed. 'The drumfire never ceased,' a German medical officer, Lieutenant Stefan Westmann, later recalled. 'No food or water reached us... men became hysterical and their comrades had to knock them out, so as to prevent them from running away and exposing themselves to the deadly shell splinters. Even the rats panicked and sought refuge in our flimsy shelters; they ran up the walls and we had to kill them with our spades.'

Reserve Lieutenant Wilhelm Geiger, of the 111th Reserve Infantry Regiment, also recalled the preliminary bombardment. 'I was fit to drop with tiredness and wanted to snatch some sleep before the deadly dance started up again outside,' he later wrote. 'Good old Jansen, the communication trench officer, took my place at the telephone. I took a cover down to the end of the passageway and lay down by the telephonists. A sandbag was my pillow and my coat the blanket for this brief rest on the ground. I had not even fallen asleep when there was a terrible crash. All the lights went out. There were shouts in the dark and a choking cloud of explosive gases. The doctors and I raced to the other end of the dugout.' There, the captain, the senior doctor and the captain's batman – the soldier servant attached to every officer – 'lay wounded under splintered beams and there sat Jansen on my chair, bent forward, dead with a splinter in his head. His hand still held the pencil that he was using to write a letter to his wife. It was, I believe, their sixth wedding anniversary! Hardly a moment earlier it had been me sitting in that same chair. It got him, not me. Luck?'

On June 25 the shrapnel shells the British artillery had been firing were changed to high explosive. It was felt that, once the German trenches had surely ceased to exist as recognizable entities as a result of the intense day-long shrapnel-shell bombardment, the surface nature of shrapnel would be wasted. From June 25, high-explosive shells mixed with gas shells streamed down in great arcs from the muzzles of the British howitzers. In the deep, concrete German dugouts the walls shook and the ground heaved with each concussion. Some Germans were killed as the trenches above them collapsed, but at thirty to forty feet most dugouts were deep enough and strong enough to survive; indeed, their deep reinforced-concrete shelters had been built to withstand a direct hit. Most had two exits in different parts of the trench system. The seven-day drumfire – the continuous artillery bombardment with the noise of uninterrupted drums – strained the Germans almost to breaking point. Weak from lack of food and water – for nothing could reach them in their deep hiding places – they awaited the inevitable attack.

On the evening of June 25, at the end of the first day of the intensified bombardment, General Rawlinson drove into Amiens for the Old Etonian Dinner; 167 officers, all former Eton schoolboys, were gathered there that night. In all, 1,157 Old Etonians were killed in the First World War, 148 of them on the Somme. They included several who appear in this narrative, including Lieutenant Colonel Guy Baring, Major Congreve VC, Major C. C. Dickens, Lieutenant Colonel the Earl of Feversham, and Lieutenant Neil Shaw-Stewart.

How many of the 1,157 were at the feast in Amiens is not recorded; but more than thirty Old Etonians were killed on the first day of the battle.

During brief pauses in the British artillery bombardment, small raids were made across No-Man's Land to report back on the situation in the forward German trenches and to bring back German prisoners for interrogation. A British intelligence summary for June 25 and June 26 noted, ominously in retrospect, that many raids attempted that night 'were unsuccessful in some sectors owing to intense machine-gun and rifle fire'. In the eight raids carried out by the 29th Division – the veterans of Gallipoli – not one German soldier was brought back.

The Big Push was due to begin on June 29. But front-line deaths were continuous. On June 25, following the death of thirteen men of the 2nd Battalion, Seaforth Highlanders, a war cemetery was begun at Mailly Wood, a mile and a half behind the front.

Systematic British shelling had begun against German ammunition dumps behind the lines. On June 25, Royal Flying Corps observers, flying in their two-seater Morane biplanes from their base at Vert-Galant, reported particularly large explosions of German ammunition at Longueval, Montauban, Mametz Wood and Pozières.

Photographic reconnaissance was also continuous. Cecil Lewis, who had joined the Royal Flying Corps a year and a half earlier, at the age of sixteen and a half, later wrote of how the whole section of the front from Thiepval, through La Boisselle, around the Fricourt Salient – a bulge in the German line that pushed into the British line – and on to Montauban 'was to be photographed every day, in order that Headquarters might have accurate information of the effects of the bombardment. This aimed at destroying all the enemy first- and second-line trenches, and so making the attack easy for the infantry. At leisure we had photographed the line before the bombardment started. But during this last week the weather was poor. On two days, low clouds and rain prevented us getting any photos at all. The 3rd and 15th Corps, for whom we were working, got in a panic. It was essential to know the effects of the shelling. Photos were to be got at all costs.'

There was, therefore, to be no delay. 'We went out in the afternoon. The clouds forced us down to two thousand feet. A terrific bombardment was in progress. The enemy lines, as far as we could see, were under a white drifting cloud of bursting high explosive. The shellbursts were continuous, not only on the lines themselves, but on the support trenches and communications behind. At two thousand feet we were in the path of the gun trajectories, and as the shells passed, above or below us, the wind eddies made by their motion flung the machine up and down, as if in a gale. Each bump meant that a passing shell had missed the machine by four or five feet. The gunners had orders not to fire when a machine was passing their sights, but in the fury of the bombardment much was forgotten – or perhaps the fact that we were not hit proves the orders were carried out. If so, they ran it pretty fine.'

On June 26, two days after the artillery bombardment had begun, and with another two full days of bombardment planned, heavy rain brought a setback to the British plan, making aerial reconnaissance impossible. But there was no shortage of warlike activity: that night, fifty-seven men of the Newfoundland Regiment, who had been specially trained near the village of Englebelmer in the use of bayonet, bomb and bullet, and been instilled with what their official historian calls 'an extra supply of hatred for the Hun', crossed No-Man's Land with the aim of entering the German front-line trench opposite theirs and bringing back prisoners for interrogation as to German strength and morale.

The Newfoundlanders carried with them two Bangalore Torpedoes to cut the German wire. These simple but potentially effective weapons consisted of a two-inch-diameter, twenty-foot-long steel pipe filled with explosives, with special igniters which went off when the torpedo was given a slight twist. It could then blow a six-foot gap in the German wire. On this raid, the first torpedo did its work well, blowing a gap in the German wire sufficient to let the raiders through, but it was discovered that there was a second belt of wire immediately behind the first. For this the second torpedo was brought up, but failed to go off. By the time the raiders began to use their wirecutters, the Germans were alerted. The raiding party beat a swift retreat.

On June 27, during a break in the weather, the artillery bombardment continued. That morning Haig drove the ten miles from his headquarters at Château Val Vion to Rawlinson's headquarters chateau at Querrieu, where the two men went up to 'The Grandstand' – the heights above Querrieu – from where they watched the barrage. It was twelve miles from their vantage point to the front lines.

Working at Val Vion, and travelling to the headquarters of his army commanders, Haig challenged what he regarded as their overcautious plans. On June 27 the commander of the Reserve Army, General Gough, whose headquarters were at Toutencourt, five miles from Val Vion, explained to Haig what he had in mind. Haig wrote in his diary, 'I thought he was too inclined to aim at fighting a battle at Bapaume, forgetting that it was at the same time possible for the Enemy to attack him from the north and cut him off from the breach in the line! I therefore insisted on the offensive move northwards as soon as Bapaume has been occupied.'

Haig then visited Rawlinson at Querrieu, writing in his diary almost contemptuously of the Fourth Army commander: 'He had ordered his troops to halt for an hour and consolidate on the Enemy's last line! Covered by an artillery barrage! I said this must depend on whether Enemy had reserves available and on the spot for counter-attack. I directed him to prepare for a rapid advance: and, as soon as the last line had been gained, to push on advanced guards of all arms as "a system of security" to cover his front. I told him to impress on his Corps Commanders the use of their Corps Cavalry and mounted troops, and if necessary supplement them with regular cavalry units.'

Haig added, 'In my opinion it is better to prepare to advance beyond the Enemy's last line of trenches, because we are then in a position to take advantage of any breakdown in the Enemy's defence. Whereas if there is a stubborn resistance put up, the matter settles itself! On the other hand if no preparations for an advance are made till next morning, we might lose a golden opportunity.'

That night, Haig sent his Chief of Staff, General Kiggell, to Toutencourt to learn more of Gough's plans. Returning to Val Vion after midnight, Kiggell reported that Gough would set up his headquarters in the town of Albert 'as soon as the Pozières heights were taken; he is then to be given certain divisions from Rawlinson's reserves. With these he will move on Bapaume in co-operation with the cavalry (3 divisions) which is now under him. I agree to this arrangement.'

Another brick in the command structure was put in place on June 27, when Major General Trenchard, commanding the Royal Flying

Corps, set up his headquarters at Fienvillers, five miles from the main airfield at Vert-Galant, which was halfway from his headquarters to Haig's at Val Vion. Trenchard had 185 aircraft under his command on the Somme, as against 129 on the German side. His aviators were able to ensure that not a single German aeroplane flew over the Fourth Army zone, either to bomb the men in their billets or to observe and photograph the preparations.

For the German soldiers in their front-line trenches, the British artillery bombardment had assumed hellish proportions. 'The enemy began to hammer at our trenches and links to the rear with an iron hail of fire of all calibres,' recalled Corporal Friedrich Hinkel, 7th Company, 99th Reserve Infantry Regiment; and he added, 'Artillery fire! Seven long days there was ceaseless artillery fire, which rose ever more frequently to the intensity of drumfire. Then on the 27th and the 28th there were gas attacks on our trenches. The torture and the fatigue, not to mention the strain on the nerves were indescribable!'

Corporal Hinkel continued, 'There was just one single heart-felt prayer on our lips: "Oh God, free us from this ordeal; give us release through battle, grant us victory; Lord God! Just let them come!" and this determination increased with the fall of each shell. You made a good job of it, you British! Seven days and nights you rapped and hammered on our door! Now your reception was going to match your turbulent longing to enter!'

With the United States neutral, Alan Seeger, a young American poet, had volunteered to fight with the Allies, and was serving with the French Foreign Legion. On June 28 he wrote home, 'We go up to the attack tomorrow. This will probably be the biggest thing yet. We are to have the honor of marching in the first wave.' Seeger added, 'I will write you soon if I get through all right. If not, my only earthly care is for my poems. I am glad to be going in the first wave. If you are in this thing at all it is best to be in to the limit. And this is the supreme experience.'

On the night of June 27/28 a second Newfoundland raiding party tried to penetrate the German trenches, to bring back prisoners for interrogation. They were more successful than their predecessors in entering the German front line, although heavy rain meant that as they crawled forward they became soaked to the skin and covered in mud. No Bangalore Torpedoes had to be used – the German wire had been cut by heavy British artillery fire – but as the Newfoundlanders advanced a German flare illuminated them as if it were daylight, and a fierce firefight began. Two Newfoundlanders managed to enter the German trench, but were taken prisoner. Four were killed.

For his efforts to bring back the wounded, Private George Phillips was awarded the Military Medal, and Private John Cahill was mentioned in dispatches. Phillips was killed in action at Gueudecourt four months later. His body was never found; his name is on the Newfoundland Memorial to the Missing. Cahill, who was thirty-six years old, died of wounds on July 5, while in German captivity. He is buried in the Achiet-le-Grand Communal Cemetery Extension, half a mile behind the German third line of trenches.

Haig was not pleased at the failure of the raids, commenting in his diary that the Staff of VIII Corps – under whom the Newfoundlanders were serving – 'has had no experience of the fighting in France and has not carried out one successful raid'. On his drives behind the lines, however, he was impressed by the mood of the troops, who knew that an offensive was imminent. Writing to King George V on June 28, Haig reported, 'Everywhere I found the troops in great spirits, and full of confidence of their ability to smash the Enemy when the moment for action arrives. Several officers have said to me that they have never known troops in such enthusiastic spirits. We must, I think, in fairness, give a good deal of credit for this to the Parsons.'

Haig also reported to the King that the French were 'still anxious' about the German attack on Verdun, and that Joffre was of the opinion 'that the Enemy will not desist until he is attacked in force elsewhere. This, as I think Your Majesty knows, we are in a position to do.'

Although the offensive was due to begin on June 29, the continuing heavy rain on June 28, and a realization that the artillery bombardment had not been as effective as intended, led Rawlinson to postpone the attack for forty-eight hours. This lessened the impact of the British artillery to stun and to surprise.

After the preliminary artillery bombardment had continued through the night of June 28/29, twenty-two-year-old Lieutenant

Robert Gilson of the Suffolk Regiment wrote home, 'Guns firing at night are beautiful – if they were not so terrible. They have the grandeur of thunderstorms. But how one clutches at the glimpses of peaceful scenes. It would be wonderful to be a hundred miles from the firing line once again.' Gilson was killed in action on the first day of the battle. He is buried in the Bécourt Military Cemetery on the outskirts of Albert.

The scale of the preliminary bombardment boosted the confidence of the waiting British and Newfoundland troops. 'Very hot stuff here,' Second Lieutenant George Norrie wrote to his mother on June 29, 'and I am enjoying myself. Talk about "shell-out" this show beats it – I think I was made for it.'

During June 29 the commanders reviewed their troops and spoke to them about the coming battle. A photograph survives of General de Lisle addressing the 1st Battalion, Lancashire Fusiliers, at Mailly-Maillet.

Lunching at Val Vion on June 29, General Hunter-Weston seemed to Haig 'quite satisfied and confident'. Haig told him that he knew of the difficulties his divisional commanders had faced in training their divisions and in preparing their trenches for attack, 'also that I have full confidence in their abilities to reap success in the coming fighting etc.' After lunch Haig drove to the headquarters of X Corps at Senlis-le-Sec, where he found General Morland 'quietly confident of success'.

Driving on to III Corps headquarters at Montigny, Haig saw General Pulteney, who 'also is quite satisfied with the artillery bombardment and wire cutting'. But after returning to Val Vion for dinner he was given a report by his Royal Artillery commander, General Birch, of Birch's visit that day to VIII Corps. 'The conclusion I come to', Haig confided in his diary, 'is that the majority are amateurs, and some thought that they knew more than they did of this kind of warfare because they had been at Gallipoli.'

On the evening of June 29, men of the Newfoundland Regiment again raided the German trenches opposite theirs, finding them 'full of Huns'. According to their official historian, 'They slew a lot but lost heavily themselves.' In another trench raid that night, Scottish infantrymen brought back forty-six German prisoners, who were interrogated as to the strength and morale of the German front line, both of which seemed to be excellent: a bad omen for the attackers.

Among the raids carried out on German front-line trenches on the night of June 29/30 was one made by the 18th Battalion, West Yorkshire Regiment: the 2nd Bradford Pals. Forty-two men volunteered for the raid. Despite the previous days' artillery barrages, the German defenders were ready. Thirteen of the attackers were killed, and one of them, Lance Corporal Gradwell, was taken prisoner by the Germans. Twelve men were wounded. Two of those killed, Private Arthur Firth and Private Kenneth Macaulay, were seventeen years old; they could not have been older than sixteen when they enlisted. Their bodies were never found; their names are on the Thiepval Memorial.

For his part in the raid, and for helping to bring in the twelve wounded men from No-Man's Land, Second Lieutenant Leslie Dalley was awarded the Military Cross.

During his drives on June 30, Haig regained his confidence with regard to the 'amateurs' in command. After visiting the headquarters of XV Corps at Heilly, he noted, 'Preparations were never so thorough, nor troops better trained. Wire very well cut, and ammunition adequate' – this, Haig commented, even though the corps had already expended twice as much artillery ammunition 'as was allowed!' Haig concluded, 'With God's help, I feel hopeful for tomorrow. The men are in splendid spirits: several have said that they have never before been so instructed and informed of the nature of the operation before them. The wire has never been so well cut, nor the artillery preparation so thorough. I have seen personally all the Corps Commanders and one and all are full of confidence.'

While Haig was visiting his corps commanders, the War Committee in London was given an account of the war beyond the Western Front. This, like the news from Verdun, put the onus on Britain to strike the Germans a serious blow. On the Eastern Front, in the northern sector that had earlier seemed so hopeful for a Russian advance, the Germans were in the ascendancy, while at the same time Russia's munitions situation had become perilous in the extreme. While Britain was producing 120,000 shells a week, the Russians could produce only 40,000. Yet the front along which the Germans were mounting their new offensive against Russia was 172 miles long. The British and French sectors on the Somme, combined, would be twenty-two miles.

The War Committee of June 30 listened to a report by Sir William Robertson of what would be attempted on the Somme. The objectives of the first day were one and a half miles deep. Twenty-six British divisions and fourteen French divisions were ready to attack. The Germans had only six divisions facing the British. Many miles of railway lines and water pipes had been laid. In conclusion, Robertson stated, 'we could get on alright'. The War Committee was content. The Big Push would go ahead.

The prospect of another offensive did not necessarily displease those who would have to lead it. A British officer, Major Robert Money, wrote in his diary in late June, 'It appears that in about a week's time we shall be required to prance into the Hun trenches – well cheerio and I hope the Huns will like it.' Major Money was impressed by the fact that, as he noted, 'nothing seems to have been spared to make this show a success – nothing seems to have been overlooked.'

In addition to Casualty Clearing Station No. 36 at Heilly, other casualty clearing stations were also being established behind the lines to take in the wounded, including a second casualty clearing station – No. 38 – at Heilly. Two more, No. 3 and No. 44, were set up at Puchevillers, just off the road that linked Haig's château at Val Vion with Rawlinson's at Querrieu. On Rawlinson's orders, eighteen ambulance trains were waiting in railway sidings to evacuate the wounded to the military hospitals at Etaples and Rouen. Each train had a staff of doctors and nurses, and could take four hundred men.

Among the tens of thousands of men gathering for the battle on the Somme was Lieutenant William Noel Hodgson, a Cambridge University graduate. Hodgson, an officer with the 9th Battalion, Devonshire Regiment, had won the Military Cross at the Battle of Loos in September 1915. In April 1916 his battalion was sent to the front-line trenches facing Mametz, with its billets three miles back, in Bray-sur-Somme. In May it was in training in Méaulte, and in June it was in bivouacs in the Bois-des-Tailles, a wood three miles behind the lines.

Hodgson was twenty-three years old. Known affectionately by his fellow soldiers as 'Smiler', as he waited at the Bois-des-Tailles on June 29 before moving up to the assembly trenches he wrote a poem to which he gave the title 'Before Action':

I, that on my familiar hill
  Saw with uncomprehending eyes
A hundred of Thy sunsets spill
  Their fresh and sanguine sacrifice,
Ere the sun swings his noonday sword
  Must say goodbye to all of this!
By all delights that I shall miss,
  Help me to die, O Lord.

As the British troops moved up towards the front line, many passed through the heavily bombarded town of Albert. For several centuries Albert had been a centre of Catholic pilgrimage. A golden statue of the Madonna and Child crowned the magnificent basilica and was visible for several miles around. It was said to have been found in the Middle Ages by a shepherd while he was watching his flocks, and it drew pilgrims from all over France. In 1898 Pope Leo XIII called Albert 'the Lourdes of the North'.

When the basilica was hit by German shellfire in January 1915, the base of the statue was badly damaged, but the statue did not fall to the ground. Instead, it remained at a lurching, 120-degree angle at the top of the spire. To the troops coming up into the line it seemed as if the Virgin was about to hurl the baby Jesus into the rubble below. Many soldiers believed that the war would end when the statue fell to the ground. To prevent undue expectations, British Army engineers, working stealthily at night, wired the lurching statue firmly to the spire.

Throughout June 30, the British troops moved forward through Albert, fanning out along the trenches that led up towards Usna Hill, Tara Hill, the village of Bécourt, and the Queen's, Bonté and Maple Redoubts that were to be among the main starting points of the attack. It was slow going. In an article published in the *Westminster Gazette* four months later, thirty-six-year-old Sergeant R. H. Tawney – a teaching assistant at the University of Glasgow before 1914 – recalled the walk forward. 'It was a perfect evening,' he wrote, 'and the immense overwhelming tranquillity of sky and down, uniting us and millions of enemies and allies in its solemn, unavoidable embrace, dwarfed into insignificance the wrath of man and his feverish energy of destruction. One forgot the object for which we were marching to the trenches. One felt as though one were on the verge of some new

47

and tremendous discovery; and the soft cheering of the knots of men who turned out to watch us pass seemed like the last faint hail of landsmen to explorers bound for unknown seas. Then the heat struck us, and at the first halt we flung ourselves down, panting like dogs.'

Tawney added, 'It was a tiresome job getting up the trenches. I don't know anything more exasperating then walking one to two miles with a stoppage every ten or twenty yards, especially when you're one of a long string of tired men and have a rifle and other traps hitched on to you. It was some wretched machine-gun section which inflicted this torture on us. Either because they hadn't learned how to carry their beastly instruments, or because they would go nosing up every wrong turning, they made us spend nearly two hours in getting through trenches that we'd known for five months as well as their native population of rats — fat old stagers to whom men meant grub.'

That evening the British divisional commanders issued their battle orders. In a dugout on the outskirts of Carnoy, Second Lieutenant Kenneth George Mappin, 4th Battalion, North Staffordshire Regiment, received, like all the troops awaiting the assault, the 'Special Order' of the day. This one, from Brigadier General Jackson, commanding 55th Brigade, read, 'I wish it to be impressed on all ranks the importance of the operation about to commence. Success will mean the shortening of the war, failure means the war prolonged indefinitely. Success or failure depend on the individual efforts and fighting spirit of every single man. The Germans are now out-numbered and out-gunned and will soon go to pieces if every man goes into the fight tomorrow determined to get through whatever the local difficulties may be. I am confident that the 55th Brigade will distinguish itself in this its first battle. Let every man remember that all England and all the world is watching him. GOOD LUCK. WE WILL MEET AGAIN IN MONTAUBAN.'

The Special Order read out to the 22nd Battalion, Manchester Regiment — the 7th Manchester Pals — included a warning: 'The use of the word retire is absolutely forbidden, and if heard can only be a ruse of the enemy and must be ignored.'

Battle was about to begin: a joint Anglo-French attempt to break through the German lines by means of artillery bombardment and infantry assault that would create the conditions in which cavalry could then ride forward to exploit the breakthrough. Three German sets of trench lines, the first two deeply dug and powerfully defended, the second under construction, faced the attackers. 'What the actual result will be, none can say,' Rawlinson wrote in his diary on June 30, 'but I feel pretty confident of success myself, though only after heavy fighting. That the Boche will break and that a debacle will supervene I do not believe, but should this be the case I am quite ready to take full advantage of it.' That 'advantage' might lead the British forces well beyond Bapaume, as far north and east as the Canal du Nord, with Douai – twenty-eight miles from the starting point – and Cambrai – just over twenty miles – as ultimate objectives.

Of the twenty-two-mile-long sector of trenches that was to serve as the launching points for the Battle of the Somme, eight miles were under French and fourteen under British command. The main German strength faced the British sector. The French Sixth Army under General Fayolle would attack with eight divisions – a force much reduced, because of French needs at Verdun, from the original plan to use forty divisions along a twenty-eight-mile front. The British would have two armies in action: General Rawlinson's Fourth Army and General Gough's Reserve Army, with a total of thirteen divisions in the first line and six divisions in close reserve.

Facing this combined force was the German Second Army: eight German divisions under General Otto von Bedow, with three divisions in reserve. Man for man, 200,000 British and French troops faced 150,000 German troops in the front line. But, if required, up to twice that number of German soldiers could be brought from the Eastern Front and, more importantly, from Verdun – something the French commanders at Verdun so desperately hoped for, and the British accepted as one of the main purposes of the attack.

In all, 158 British battalions were to be heavily involved in the attack on the Somme on July 1. Of these the majority, 88 battalions – almost 90,000 men – were the volunteers of Kitchener's New Army, men who had not been in action before. There were also 43 Regular Army battalions and 27 Territorial battalions. 'Never before', wrote Brigadier General Sir James Edmonds in the official history, 'had the ranks of a British Army in the field contained the finest of all classes in the nation, in physique, brains and education. And they were volunteers, not conscripts.' At 5.15 a.m. all 158,000 men were in place. 'If ever a decisive victory was to be won,' Edmonds added, 'it was to be expected now.'

3

The first day of the battle: 'Dead men can advance no further'

A T FIVE IN the morning of 1 July 1916, the first British air reconnaissance of the day took place over German lines. Before the battle
on the ground began, British aircraft were bombing German railway
yards, cuttings and bridges far behind the lines. Béthune and Cambrai
were both targeted. Each bomber carried two 112-pound bombs.

Then, starting at 7 a.m., nearly a quarter of a million shells were
fired at the German positions in just over an hour. This was an average
of 3,500 shells a minute. So intense and so loud was the barrage that
it was heard on Hampstead Heath in north London, almost two
hundred miles away. It was an astonishing sound, as guns of all calibres fired simultaneously. In some parts of the line British soldiers sat
on their parapets cheering at each explosion, but their enthusiastic
shouts were lost in the thunder of the guns. The sound was so intense
that if a man screamed at the top of his voice into another man's ear,
he could not be heard. One officer tried to count the detonations by
his watch, but this proved impossible. Instead, he tried chattering his
teeth, which he could click about six times a second. This was not
enough to keep up with the rate of fire.

With the sound of the shellfire an unbroken roar, the sound of individual shells bursting was lost. The few Germans who ventured into
the storm observed through periscopes a mass of British troops in the
front lines. Along the whole length of the British line, trench ladders
were fixed into place. Officers looked over and over again at their
watches as the hands moved steadily round towards zero hour, 7.30 a.m.

At 7.20 a.m., ten minutes before zero hour, a massive mine at
Hawthorn Ridge, on the approach to the German-held village of
Beaumont-Hamel, was exploded. The mass of earth being hurled into
the air was captured by a film camera. A frame from the film became

one of the iconic photographs of July 1. Eight minutes later, at 7.28 a.m., two minutes before zero hour, the British sappers exploded sixteen more mines under the German trenches.

In order to enable British troops to reach and occupy the mine crater at Hawthorn Ridge, the British artillery on that sector halted its bombardment of the German front-line trenches as soon as the mine was detonated – eight minutes before the other mines, and ten minutes before the attack itself. Although three sections of the German 119th Reserve Regiment were killed in the explosion, the early detonation of the mine gave the Germans in the adjacent trenches ten minutes to man their defences and bring their machine guns out of their dugouts, unhindered by the hitherto relentless pounding of the guns.

The largest of the mines exploded under the German front-line trenches was in front of the village of La Boisselle. It used two charges, one of 36,000 pounds and the other of 24,000 pounds of ammonal, 60 feet apart, both 52 feet below the surface. Earth was thrown 4,000 feet into the air. The resulting crater, known to the attackers as the Lochnagar Crater, measured as much as 450 feet across and 95 feet deep. Nine German dugouts and the men inside them were obliterated. The nearby Y Sap mine, under the German trenches overlooking Mash Valley, used 40,000 pounds of ammonal.

The artillery barrage was also halted on the sectors facing the other mines, and concentrated on the rear German defences further back. This also gave these defenders ten minutes before the assault during which their forward positions were not under intense artillery bombardment. The British planners had gravely underestimated the German capacity to survive in their deep dugouts, and then to emerge with their fighting ability unimpaired and their machine guns ready to open an intense and unremitting fire into the lines of the advancing infantry.

At 7.30 a.m., British troops attacked along the whole fourteen-mile front. The weather, recalled Second Lieutenant Siegfried Sassoon, 'after an early morning mist, was of the kind commonly called heavenly'. A tin triangle was pinned on each man's back, so that, flashing in the morning sun, it would indicate to the Allied artillery observers just how far forward they had reached, enabling the artillery to fire beyond them.

As they went over the top, most British soldiers carried with them sixty-six pounds weight of equipment. This consisted of a rifle with fixed bayonet, between 170 and 220 rounds of small-arms ammunition, two Mills grenades, a waterproof cape, two sandbags, a steel helmet, two gas helmets in a satchel, a pair of goggles against tear gas, a first-aid field dressing, and iodine. In place of the standard soldier's pack, each soldier also carried a rolled waterproof groundsheet, a filled water bottle and a haversack. In the haversack were a mess tin, a towel, shaving kit, extra socks, a message book, the uneaten portion of that day's ration, extra cheese, one preserved ration and one iron ration. In addition, at least 40 per cent of the men would carry shovels, and 10 per cent would carry picks – strapped to their backs. In at least one battalion, one soldier was given a tin of grey paint to add to his burden, in order to paint the unit's identification on any German artillery pieces it might capture.

To add to what they were already carrying, each battalion distributed among its thousand men a total of 1,600 flares, to indicate to the Royal Flying Corps observers where the battalion had reached, 512 haversacks containing the extra ammunition for the Lewis guns, 64 bundles of five-foot wooden pickets to serve as trench supports, a minimum of 10 trench bridges – each ten foot long, to be carried by two men – and 16 sledgehammers.

Other men were detailed to take, as well as their standard equipment, rifle grenades, seven-foot trench ladders, and buckets in which to carry bombs. In addition, in order to cut the enemy wire where the artillery bombardment had failed to do so, 640 men in each battalion carried, to add to their existing burdens, barbed-wire cutters, and 33 men per battalion carried the twenty-foot-long steel Bangalore Torpedoes.

As a result of these extra burdens, some men were carrying as much as seventy-six pounds of equipment.

The soldier-historian General Edmonds wrote, in the British official history, that the weight of this equipment made it 'difficult to get out of a trench, impossible to move much quicker than a slow walk, or to rise and lie down quickly'. The British military historian Peter Liddle commented on this, 'In the event, many thousands of men offering so bulky and slow-moving a target would crumple to the ground quickly enough but would not rise at all, never mind quickly.'

The officers, who carried only gas masks, ammunition pouches, pistols and sticks, wore the same uniform as the men, to avoid the Germans picking them out. As, however, the officers inevitably led their men forward, they were conspicuous enough for special attention.

The mines, exploded deep under the German front-line trenches, were intended to stun and confuse the Germans two minutes before the assault, enabling the heavily-laden attackers to cross No-Man's Land before the Germans could man their trenches and set up their machine guns. But because the mines were set off between 100 and 900 yards from the British lines, German troops were able to occupy the rims of the craters before the advancing troops were able to reach them. When the Germans reached the rim nearest them, they immediately set up machine guns that poured a devastating fire on the attackers, still many yards away.

The official historian of the German 119th Reserve Regiment, which was opposite the 29th Division at Beaumont-Hamel, wrote of the explosion of the mine under Hawthorn Ridge: 'This explosion was a signal for an infantry attack, and everyone got ready and stood on the lower steps of the dugouts, rifles in hand, waiting for the bombardment to lift. In a few minutes the shelling ceased, and we rushed up the steps and out into the crater positions. Ahead of us, wave after wave of British troops were crawling out of their trenches and coming towards us at a walk, their bayonets glistening in the sun.'

Lieutenant Stefan Westmann later recalled, 'Then the British Army went over the top. The very moment we felt their artillery fire was directed against the reserve positions, our machine-gunners crawled out of the bunkers, red-eyed and dirty, covered in the blood of their fallen comrades, and opened up a terrific fire.'

The nineteen mine craters, in most of which so many British soldiers were trapped and killed by the German machine-gunners, became a hated feature of the battlefield. In *The Golden Virgin*, Henry Williamson described the group of craters known as the Glory Hole, which on July 1 had been blown immediately behind the German forward trenches in front of La Boisselle, where the opposing trenches were especially close.

It was 'a bone yard without graves', Williamson wrote, with British and German corpses and unexploded British shells, making 'a gap of five hundred yards in the British line, an abandoned No-Man's Land of choked shaft and subsided gallery held by a series of Lewis gun posts'.

The blowing of the Lochnagar, Y Sap and Glory Hole mines at La Boisselle was witnessed by the pilots who were flying over the battlefield to report back on British troop movements. One of these pilots, Cecil Lewis, described the early morning scene in his book *Sagittarius Rising*: 'We were to watch the opening of the attack, co-ordinate the infantry flares (the job we have been rehearsing for months) and stay over the lines for two and a half hours.' It had been arranged that continuous overlapping patrols would fly throughout the day. Lewis's patrol was ordered 'to keep clear of La Boisselle' because of the mines that were to be blown. As he watched from above the village of Thiepval, almost two miles from where the mines exploded, Lewis saw a remarkable sight. 'At Boisselle the earth heaved and flashed,' he wrote, 'a tremendous and magnificent column rose up into the sky. There was an ear-splitting roar, drowning all the guns, flinging the machine sideways in the repercussing air. The earthly column rose, higher and higher to almost four thousand feet.' Lewis's aircraft was hit by lumps of mud thrown out by the explosion.

Battle had begun along the British front line from Foncquevillers in the north to Maricourt in the south. The most northerly sector, facing Foncquevillers, lay two miles north of the main battlefield; the attack was intended as a feint. But it was no less determined a battle than along the main sectors. The task of the diversionary attack was to capture the German-held village of Gommecourt, pinning down the opposing German troops and thus preventing them going to the aid of the German defenders further south.

The feint worked, but at a high cost, as the 46th and 56th Divisions, part of General Allenby's Third Army, moved forward without any massive prior artillery bombardment. 'We went over the top and eventually arrived in the German trenches,' Rifleman Aubrey Rose, of the Queen's Westminster Rifles, a Territorial battalion, recalled in 1983 in an interview with the author Paul Reed. 'The smoke barrage was so thick you could not see where you were going and we did not know it was a trap. They had withdrawn all their troops from the front line and left only a few. Many of these were either dead or dying. They had deep dugouts and had set traps in them.' In the first dugout there were German helmets, which the men thought 'would do nicely as souvenirs. But as they touched them they were blown up. The word soon got around after that; when we came to a dugout, we didn't ask who was down there – it was just "take that Fritz!" with a hand grenade.'

Rifleman Rose's company officer, twenty-two-year-old Captain Hugh Mott, was killed by a shell, together with his batman – 'blown to pieces', Rose recalled 'I had the job afterwards of going to his parents and telling them what had happened.' Captain Mott's body was never identified. His name is inscribed on the Thiepval Memorial.

An estimated 2,765 British troops were killed in the diversionary attack at Gommecourt. More than twice that number were wounded. In Foncquevillers Military Cemetery are the graves of 125 of those killed on July 1 whose bodies were identified. They include men from all regiments and units of the 46th (North Midland) Division that took part in the assault: the South and North Staffordshire Regiments, the Sherwood Foresters (Notts and Derby), the Leicestershire, Lincolnshire and Monmouthshire Regiments, the Machine Gun Corps, the Royal Engineers, and the Royal Army Medical Corps – the doctors and orderlies who were trying to save the lives of the wounded. The bodies of some of these men were recovered from No-Man's Land and the German wire only after the German Army withdrew from the whole Somme area in the spring of 1917.

There are also two British war cemeteries in the former British front line at Gommecourt. Of the 749 graves in the Gommecourt Wood New Cemetery, 456 are of soldiers whose bodies were never identified. In Gommecourt British Cemetery No. 2 are more than a hundred graves of men killed on July 1. In Gommecourt Park, shell craters are visible ninety years after the battle.

The German losses in this northern sector were a quarter those of the British: 400 killed and just over 800 wounded. Because of their losses, the British troops were sent the following week to what was called a 'quiet sector' of the front far from the Somme. Gommecourt remained within the German trench lines for the rest of the year.

The ebb and flow of the attacks at Gommecourt, as of each battle that day, and of each day's battle in the months ahead, were seen from the air by Royal Flying Corps pilots and the observer flying with each pilot. The airmen were witness to the struggle below them. Their task was to signal back to their base by wireless each time they saw the red flares that the British troops had been instructed to fire to indicate where they had reached. Where no flares were seen, the aerial observers would try to work out what had happened by flying low enough to be able to make out the colour of the uniforms. They would be met by rifle and machine-gun fire from the ground if the troops they were trying to identify were wearing German grey, rather than British khaki. Several planes were so badly shot up that, once they were brought back safely to their base at Vert-Galant, they were unable to return to their tasks; but none was shot down behind German lines on July 1, and no pilots were killed.

South of Gommecourt, on its fourteen-mile front, the Fourth Army had as its objective on the first day of battle the line of villages Serre–Beaumont-Hamel–Thiepval–Pozières–Contalmaison–Montauban, and the German strongpoints – the redoubts – that were defending them. Much depended on the ability of the British artillery to destroy the German barbed wire and to pulverize the German trenches and dugouts. Except in the southern sector facing Montauban, this was not achieved. Many shells fell short, and many others failed to explode. An officer with III Corps reported seeing, after the advance into Sausage Valley, 'a dud shell every two or three yards over several acres of ground'. Sausage Valley was named after a German observation balloon that sometimes flew over it. Inevitably the British soldiers called the nearby valley Mash Valley: as in sausage and mash.

At the northern edge of the main attack, in the area held by VIII Corps, the 11th Battalion, East Lancashire Regiment – the Accrington Pals – one of ninety-seven New Army battalions that were in action on July 1, emerged from its front-line trenches facing the village of Serre. A few of the signallers whose job was to work in their own trenches watched the attack from behind a mound of earth. 'We were able to see our comrades move forward in an attempt to cross No-Man's Land, only to be mown down like meadow grass,' Lance Corporal H. Bury later recalled. 'I felt sick at the sight of this carnage and remember weeping. We did actually see a flag signalling near the village of Serre, but this lasted only a few seconds and the signals were unintelligible.'

As many as a hundred German machine guns, most of them hidden in armoured emplacements which had protected them during the bombardment, opened fire as the infantry moved forward from their trenches. Many of the attackers were killed as they bunched together to push through the unexpectedly narrow gaps in their own barbed wire.

On many sectors of the front a problem arose regarding the interpretation of the flares used by the infantry to indicate their positions. This caused particular uncertainty during the attack by the 4th Division between Serre and Beaumont-Hamel. The signal warning that a unit had been 'stopped at uncut wire' was a single white flare. The signal announcing the good news 'objective gained' was three white flares. In the confusion of battle, with shells exploding and unclear time lags, it was not possible to distinguish one from the other. This made it difficult to know what commands to give, or where to direct the artillery.

On the site of the four small copses that saw the fiercest fighting that day in the attack on Serre, a Sheffield Memorial Park was established twenty years after the battle, where the shellholes and trench lines have been preserved. Inside the park are memorial plaques that commemorate the men who were killed there: members of the Accrington, Barnsley, Chorley and Sheffield Pals. There is also a wooden cross in memory of twenty-two-year-old Private Albert Bull, a Sheffield Pal, killed on July 1, whose body was not found until 13 April 1928. He is buried in Serre Road Cemetery No. 2.

Outside the wall of Serre Road Cemetery No. 2 is a private memorial to Lieutenant V. A. Braithwaite, Somerset Light Infantry, who had served at Gallipoli as aide-de-camp to his father, the Chief of the General Staff there. The young Braithwaite had won one of the first Military Crosses of the war, at Mons. He was killed on July 1 while attacking the German stronghold known as the Quadrilateral, together with his commanding officer, his adjutant and fourteen other officers in the battalion. Braithwaite's body was never identified; his name is on the Thiepval Memorial.

At Château Val Vion, half an hour after the attack began along the whole fourteen-mile front, Haig noted in his diary, 'Reports up to 8 a.m. most satisfactory. Our troops have everywhere crossed the Enemy's front trenches.' This was not so. The red flares that the infantry were meant to send up when they reached the German front-line trenches, and which the Royal Flying Corps pilots were then to report back to base, had in some cases failed to go off. In many more cases the soldiers carrying the flares had been killed long before reaching the first German trench line. Where small groups of men did reach the German trenches, and a report of it was sent back, the subsequent failure to hold the positions gained was often not reported. In many cases there was no one left to report it.

At nine o'clock Haig was told that his troops had 'in many places' reached the line fixed for them to reach an hour and twenty minutes after the start. What was not known was that most of these men were even then being pinned down in the German wire, or driven back. Haig was then told that the 31st Division was moving into Serre village. This was afterwards proved to be incorrect. Another false report reaching Haig at Val Vion stated that the attacking troops were entering the village of Thiepval.

South of the village of Serre, the 2nd Battalion, Essex Regiment, was in action on July 1, hoping to cut off Beaumont-Hamel from the north by seizing the strongly held Munich Trench. The regimental history describes how, as the attackers moved forward, German artillery batteries behind Serre 'placed a barrage along the British front trench, which effectively prevented the advance of supports to those who had broken through the German front defences. The ground between the support trench and the Munich trench was pitted with craters caused by the British bombardment, and using these as a protection, the German counter-attack developed rapidly. Working forward from front and flanks, the Germans ran from crater to crater, gradually forcing back the invaders, most of the fighting being with hand grenades.'

British accounts that day told of how the Germans fought with remarkable obstinacy and courage, barricading themselves at every step and showing fight to the last. Without supports, however, their supply of bombs and ammunition ran short and they were compelled to withdraw to the Heidenkopf Crater by midday. Hand-to-hand fighting in the crater continued throughout the afternoon, and it was not until dusk that the Germans succeeded in regaining the line of their front trench.

Among those attacking with the Essex Regiment was Second Lieutenant Gilbert Waterhouse. Before the attack he had written, in his poem 'Bivouacs', using a generic name for the wood:

> In Somecourt wood, in Somecourt wood,
> The cuckoo wakened me at dawn,
> The man beside me muttered, 'Hell!'
> But half a dozen larks as well
> Sang in the blue – the curtain drawn
> Across where all the stars had been
> Was interlaced with tender green,
> The birds sang, and I said that if
> One didn't wake so cold and stiff
> It would be grand in Somecourt wood.

At the end of July 1, Gilbert Waterhouse was among the thousands of men reported 'missing, presumed killed'. His grave lies today in Serre Road Cemetery No. 2, one of 7,127 soldiers buried there, of whom 4,944 were never identified: 'Known unto God' in the words – devised by Rudyard Kipling – of the inscription on many gravestones. Others state with equal simplicity, 'A Soldier of the Great War'.

Serre Road Cemetery No. 2 is located in what was, on July 1, the German defensive system known as the Quadrilateral. Among those fatally wounded during the fighting there that day was forty-seven-year-old Brigadier General Charles Prowse, Somerset Light Infantry, the commander of 11th Brigade. Taken to a casualty clearing station in Doullens, he died there and is buried in Louvencourt Military Cemetery.

Also in action near Serre on July 1 was twenty-two-year-old Second Lieutenant Henry Field, before enlistment a student at the Birmingham School of Art. 'Thank God I don't flinch from the sound of the guns,' he had written to his mother four months before the battle. His battalion, the 6th Battalion, Royal Warwickshire Regiment, reached its objective, but after coming under unbroken German machine-gun fire from both flanks was forced to fall back to its original line.

On the first Christmas of the war, in December 1914, Henry Field had written:

> Through barren nights and fruitless days
> Of waiting when our faith grows dim,
> Mary be with the stricken heart,
> Thou hast a Son, remember him.
>
> Lord Thou hast been our refuge sure,
> Thy everlasting Arms are wide,

Thy words from age to age endure,
Thy loving care will still provide.

Vouchsafe that we may see, dear Lord,
Vouchsafe that we may see,
Thy purpose through the aching days.

Of the 836 men who set out with Henry Field in the attack, 520 were killed and 316 wounded. Before the attack Field had written:

Above the shot-blown trench he stands,
Tall and thin against the sky;
His thin white face, and thin white hands,
Are the signs his people know him by.
His soldier's coat is silver barred
And on his head the well-known crest.
Above the shot-blown trench he stands,
The bright escutcheon on his breast,
And traced in silver bone for bone
The likeness of a skeleton.

Field never finished the poem. He is buried in Serre Road Cemetery No. 2. Of his battalion's destruction, its official historian wrote, 'July 1st – Ill-fated day. Wounds and death were the fruit of it, and to those who outlived it an accursed memory of horror. Imperishable courage inspired every fighting man, but, where, where was Victory?'

Among those in the attack on the village of Serre – which was entered by a few of the attackers, who quickly had to pull back – was John Streets, a company sergeant in the 12th Battalion, York and Lancaster Regiment, the Sheffield City Battalion, also known as the Sheffield Pals. As he went back for medical help, he was told that a soldier in his platoon was too seriously wounded to return to the dressing station on his own. Streets returned towards the front line to bring the soldier back, and was never seen alive again. His grave is in Euston Road Cemetery, Colincamps, not far from where he was killed. Troops going through Colincamps on July 1 on their way to the front line passed the mass graves that had been dug there, in anticipation of the battle losses. Streets had earlier written, in his poem 'A Soldier's Funeral':

No splendid rite is here – yet lay him low,
Ye comrades of his youth he fought beside,
Close where the winds do sigh and wild flowers grow,
Where the sweet brook doth babble by his side.
No splendour, yet we lay him tenderly
To rest, his requiem in artillery.

Another poet serving with the Sheffield Pals on July 1 was Corporal Alexander Robertson, a thirty-four-year-old lecturer in history at the University of Sheffield. Before the battle in which he was killed, he wrote:

Soon is the night of our faring to regions unknown,
There not to flinch at the challenge suddenly thrown . . .

Corporal Robertson's body was never found. His name is inscribed on the Thiepval Memorial.

Among those serving on July 1 with a field ambulance unit, at a dressing station in the basilica at Albert, was John Streets's brother Harry. He later described how the wounded 'flooded in on foot, or were brought by stretchers, wheelbarrows, carts – anything. Their wounds were dressed, and then they were laid out on the floor to await evacuation.' Those who were not expected to survive were put on one side and left. 'It was very hard to ignore their cries for help', he wrote, 'but we had to concentrate on those who might live.'

In several parts of the line facing Beaumont-Hamel, the attacking troops reached the German front-line trenches. On the edge of Y Ravine, on the southern approach to Beaumont-Hamel, a twenty-four-year-old Scottish drummer, Walter Ritchie, of the 2nd Battalion, Seaforth Highlanders, stood on the parapet of a captured German trench under heavy machine-gun fire, and, in order to rally the men of several units who had lost their officers and were beginning to waver and pull back, sounded the 'charge' again and again. The men moved forward. Ritchie spent the rest of the day carrying messages over the fire-swept ground. He was awarded the Victoria Cross, the highest British military honour.

Ritchie survived the war. On 25 November 1916 he was presented with his Victoria Cross by King George V. In 1917 he was wounded, and in 1918 he was gassed and wounded twice. Even after bugles ceased to be employed on the battlefield, he carried his until the end of the war. In July 1921 he joined the 1st Battalion, Seaforth Highlanders, was promoted to sergeant and appointed drum major. He left the army in 1929, later becoming a recruiting officer in Glasgow. He died in Edinburgh in 1965, ten days before his seventy-third birthday.

July 1 was a dire day for Ritchie's battalion. Of the thousand officers and men who attacked that morning, 120 were killed, and twice that number wounded.

While trying to penetrate the German lines, the Seaforth Highlanders received two messages, neither of which had a time of dispatch on it, and both of which arrived with the same runner. One said 'the battalion must hold on at all costs', the other ordered it to return to its original front line. As German machine-gun fire intensified, the decision was made to retire.

The British troops who attacked on July 1 were from particular areas of Britain, predominantly the industrial North and the Midlands. Yorkshire provided the largest force, twenty-nine battalions, followed by twenty-two from Lancashire, twenty from Ireland – mostly Ulster – seventeen from Tyneside, fourteen from the Midlands, and thirteen from London.

There was one Dominion force fighting on the Somme on July 1, the 1st Battalion, Newfoundland Regiment, which formed part of the second wave of attackers against the village of Beaumont-Hamel. Because their own front-line trenches were clogged with bodies and debris from the first assault, and as the advance of the Essex Regiment on their right flank was delayed because the trenches in front of it were likewise clogged with the dead of the first wave of attackers, the Newfoundlanders had to cross 750 yards of exposed front without flank support. Many were killed as they clambered out of their trenches. Few reached even to the line of their own barbed wire, which lay 250 yards beyond their starting point.

Those Newfoundlanders who did reach their own wire – four well-laid belts of wire in all – had to follow the zigzag lanes between pre-cut, highlighted gaps, which had been exactly pinpointed by the German machine-gunners. Those who managed to emerge through these gaps in the wire discovered that at least five hundred yards of open ground lay between them and the first line of the German defences. That open ground lay on a downward slope, exposed to German fire from positions on the facing hill. Near a particular tree halfway down the slope, known to the Newfoundlanders as the Danger Tree, German shellfire was especially accurate and fatal. Today the remains of that tree serve as a stark memorial to those who were killed around it.

Some of the Newfoundlanders were able to get close enough to the German line to hurl their hand-held bombs into the enemy trenches, but most had been struck down long before that point. The official Newfoundland historian writes, 'Where two men had been advancing side by side, suddenly there was only one – and a few paces farther on he too would pitch forward on his face. A young subaltern looks around him in vain for men to lead. Defiantly he brandishes his field telephone at the German trenches; then putting down his head he charges to his death. The leading man of a pair carrying a ten-foot bridge is hit, and as he falls he brings down with him bridge and partner. Without hesitation the latter gets up, hoists the bridge on his head, and plods grimly forward until machine-gun bullets cut him down.'

Those few Newfoundlanders who reached the German wire were shot down as they tried to cut their way through it with their wire-cutters. By ten in the morning every officer who had gone into battle less than an hour and a half earlier was either killed or wounded.

A British soldier, Private Byrne, who was in the next wave of attackers, recalled his first sight of his predecessors: 'Ahead of me were two Newfoundland blokes – one on the left-hand side was lying well up to the German wire and the other, about twenty five yards to his right, was spread-eagled over the German wire itself. They were quite dead, there was no doubt.'

Of the 810 Newfoundlanders in action that morning, 310 were killed and more than 350 wounded. Only sixty-eight escaped serious injury. Captain Eric Ayre was one of four members of a leading Newfoundland family to be killed on July 1, including his only brother, Captain Bernard Ayre, who was serving with the Norfolk Regiment near Maricourt, at the other end of the Fourth Army front. Eric Ayre, aged twenty-seven, is buried in the Ancre Military Cemetery. His brother, aged twenty-four, is buried at Carnoy. Their cousins, twenty-four-year-old Second Lieutenant Gerald Ayre and twenty-one-year-old Second Lieutenant

Wilfrid Ayre were also killed at Beaumont-Hamel on July 1. Gerald's body was never found: his name is on the Newfoundland Memorial to the Missing. Wilfrid is buried in Knightsbridge Cemetery at Mesnil-Martinsart. Unrelated, and from humbler Newfoundland stock, nineteen-year-old Lance Corporal Edward Ayre was also killed on July 1. He is buried in Y Ravine Cemetery.

During the afternoon, on the Beaumont-Hamel sector as elsewhere, wounded men trying to crawl back across No-Man's Land to their own lines did not know that their tin triangles, meant to be identification for their own artillery during the advance, were flashing continually as they moved painfully across the open ground, signalling their position to the German snipers and machine-gunners. The Newfoundland Regiment's twenty stretcher-bearers worked all day under fire to bring wounded men back. When they found Lieutenant Bert Dicks propped up in a trench and prepared to put him on a stretcher, he insisted, 'Take those who are in greater need, I can stick it out,' and he did. Many of the Newfoundlanders who reached the safety of their own lines had only one question: 'Is the Colonel satisfied? Is the Colonel pleased?'

When the battle was over the commanding officer of the 29th Division, General de Lisle, informed the Prime Minister of Newfoundland, 'It was a magnificent display of trained and disciplined valour, and its assault only failed of success because dead men can advance no further.'

The ferocity of the fighting on July 1 was relentless. In a letter home three days later, Second Lieutenant Eric Miall-Smith wrote of the 'glorious victory' on that first day of battle, 'I know I accounted for four Germans so I have done my bit.' And he added, 'I saw parties of Germans during the attack fire on our fellows until they were within a few yards of them; then, as soon as they found out that there was no hope for them they threw down their arms and rushed forward to shake our men by the hands. Most of them got their deserts and were not taken prisoner. Some of the wounded Germans were shooting men in the back after they had been dressed by them. They are swine – take it from me – I saw these things happen with my own eyes.'

Another officer, Lieutenant J. Capper, later recalled a German soldier clasping his knees and thrusting a photograph of his wife and children at him. 'I remember feeling inward amusement at adopting a "tough guy" approach towards so comparatively harmless and frightened an individual when I was myself having to make a great effort at disguising my own "windiness".'

A British medical officer, Captain G. D. Fairley, himself wounded, wrote in his diary of how, as he made his way along the trenches with stretcher-bearers, looking for wounded, 'We came across a case of "shell-shock". An emotionally distraught soldier was going back, cowering, cringing and gibbering with fright at the shellfire.' Shell shock − so recently identified as an aspect of battle − was to exact a heavy toll, as the nerves of men under sustained artillery fire were shattered under the strain.

Even behind the front line the casualties from the German artillery barrages were severe. In the attack towards Beaumont-Hamel each battalion had held back a dozen men whose job was to be clearing out the captured German dugouts and escorting back German prisoners. As no dugouts or prisoners were secured, these men remained all day in the rear trenches. There, a quarter of them were killed or injured by the persistent German artillery fire.

While waiting for orders to go over the top in the second wave, Second Lieutenant Edward Brittain's men had been unnerved by the large numbers of wounded from the first wave coming back and crowding in the trench. Then a battalion in front of them in No-Man's Land had panicked. 'I can't remember just how I got the men together and made them go over the parapet,' Brittain told his sister, Vera Brittain, a few weeks later. 'I only know I had to go back twice to get them, and I wouldn't go through those minutes again if it meant the VC.'

When he was about seventy yards into No-Man's Land, Brittain was hit in the thigh. He tried to continue to lead his men forward, but was unable to do so and found refuge in a shellhole. There a shell fragment pierced his arm. In the shellhole were two other men. 'One was badly wounded,' he told his sister, 'but the other wasn't hurt at all − only in a blue funk.'

Brittain managed to crawl back to the British trenches. 'I don't remember much about it except that about half way across I saw the hand of a man who'd been killed only that morning beginning to turn green and yellow. It made me feel pretty sick and I put on a spurt.' For his courage that morning, Second Lieutenant Brittain was awarded the Military Cross.

Among the soldiers in action on July 1 along the River Ancre and the heights on either side of it were more than fifteen thousand Irishmen, including the Royal Dublin Fusiliers and thirteen battalions of the 36th (Ulster) Division, including the Royal Inniskilling Fusiliers, the Royal Irish Rifles and the Royal Irish Fusiliers. At seven in the morning they were issued with rum, although many of them were teetotal. Thirty minutes later, as they went 'over the top', many were mown down by German machine-gun fire.

The Royal Inniskilling Fusiliers were in action that day on the left bank of the Ancre. The 1st Battalion reached the German front-line trenches, but could not break through the wire. When it called for reinforcements, no reserves were brought up. The regimental historian, Sir Frank Fox, a former Staff Officer at Haig's headquarters, commented, 'In that field of fire nothing could live.' The battalion then fell back to the trench from which it had moved for the attack – 'or rather one-third of it did: the rest were casualties.' The battalion's commanding officer, Lieutenant Colonel Pierce, was among the 280 men killed, and is buried in the Ancre Military Cemetery.

In all, more than half of the men who had gone into action were dead or wounded. This was also the casualty rate for the 9th, 10th and 11th Battalions. 'The losses of that day made mourning in many Ulster homes,' writes Sir Frank Fox, 'but with the mourning there was pride that the Province had once again proved the steadfastness of its loyal courage.'

In the attack along the left bank of the Ancre, towards Beaucourt Station, the 1st Battalion, Royal Dublin Fusiliers, left their trenches at nine in the morning, but were trapped in their own barbed wire. The 2nd Battalion attacked in the second wave. They too were stopped by intense German machine-gun fire. The combined casualties were 479, with many others missing. Captain George Stanton, a medical officer, whose brother Robert had been killed at Gallipoli, died in Ireland a few months later from his wounds. He is buried in St Finbarr's Cemetery, Cork. Robert Stanton's name is one of 20,837 on the Helles Memorial to the Missing, a tall obelisque overlooking the Aegean Sea.

Within two hours of the start of the attack, many of the Irishmen were dead, the precise details of their deaths unknown. The fate of twenty-one-year-old Rifleman Robert Carson, 12th Battalion, Royal Irish Rifles – the Central Antrims – is typical. He was in the advance on the left bank of the Ancre, from the village of Hamel. His body was never found. Robert Thompson, the author of *Bushmills Heroes*, the story of the soldiers from a single Ulster parish who were killed in action, writes, 'It seems likely that he got into the German front-line defences and was taken prisoner there, or was killed. In any case he was never seen again and by November 1917 his parents were still waiting news of him.' His name is on the Thiepval Memorial, 3,000 yards from the No-Man's Land he had crossed.

Nineteen-year-old Rifleman William Eason was also killed in the fighting east of Hamel. In *Portrush Heroes, 1914–1918*, Robert Thompson, who also wrote a history of the ten soldiers from the Ulster parish of Portrush who were killed on the Somme that day, writes, 'As the men emerged from their trenches a withering fire met them. It must have been awful for boys of eighteen or nineteen to have to face up to this, knowing that they faced almost certain death from the enemy if they went forward and just as certain death from their own side if they went back.'

From the parish of Ballymoney, twenty-eight Ulster lads were killed that day. So many Ulstermen were killed or injured on July 1 that the 12th Battalion, Royal Irish Rifles, was withdrawn from the battle on the following day, and sent far from the Somme for reorganization. Not all those killed were immediately registered as dead. It was only in May 1917 that Annie Verner was officially notified that her husband, Rifleman James Verner, from Ballymoney, was believed to have been killed 'on or about' July 1. Verner, a noted local footballer, had four children; the youngest, Jane, whom he had never seen, was born six months before he was killed. After he had been posted missing at the beginning of July, Chaplain Andrew Gibson wrote to Annie Verner, 'I write to offer you our deepest sympathy in your suspense and anxiety, and to express the hope that you may have word of him from some reliable quarter, as it is to be feared that many of the "missing" have laid down their lives on the field of battle.'

Andrew Gibson added, 'Today there are many homes in Ulster where sorrow is and many hearts prostrate with grief. Ulster's sons fought a great fight and covered her name with glory. We are confident that you at home will meet our losses bravely and patiently, and will walk the hard path with unwavering faith, as those who have fallen would wish us to do. Let us comfort ourselves in the hope that beyond this world of sorrow and loss is God's world & He has gathered our own safely Home. Brave and courageous in life they are honoured among the fallen sons of the Empire and with their comrades they rest content "until the day break and the shadows flee away".'

Rifleman Verner's body was never found. He is commemorated on the Thiepval Memorial. There are two other Verners on that memorial, killed on July 1: Private Adrian Verner and Private Richard Verner, both of the York and Lancaster Regiment, which was in action a mile to the north.

Some of the hardest fighting in which the Irishmen were involved was in the swampy ground along the banks of the Ancre – now a placid water meadow. This was the scene of action for the 9th Battalion, Royal Irish Fusiliers (Armagh, Monaghan and Cavan), and the 12th Battalion, Royal Irish Rifles (Central Antrim). Even while advancing through their own wire they suffered heavy casualties from German machine-gun fire, the most persistent and the most deadly coming from a hidden emplacement on the high bank of the Ancre. This machine-gun fire devastated the attempt to cross the 600-yard width of No-Man's Land.

Fifty yards short of the German wire, hardly any men were left able to advance further. In an artillery observation post behind the British lines, a young artillery officer asked his major, 'Why do they stop there? Why don't they move?' To which the major replied: 'They will never move more.'

The main objective of the 36th (Ulster) Division on July 1 was the Schwaben Redoubt, a German strongpoint that contained a fortified bunker more than twenty feet deep, in which the German defenders had sheltered throughout the initial bombardment. For the German soldiers facing the Ulstermen, the defence of the Schwaben Redoubt was onerous in the extreme. Captain Herbert von Wormb, Bavarian 8th Reserve Infantry Regiment, recalled how, at about five o'clock in the afternoon, Major Beyerköhler, 'the commander of our group, had one on ahead. Suddenly a member of his staff called out, "Herr Major, a British soldier!" "What's that you say – a British soldier?"

replied the commander. "Pass me a rifle!" He aimed at a British soldier who was very close to him, but that man was a second quicker than he.'

Captain von Wormb's account continued, 'Mortally wounded, the kindly Beyerköhler slumped to the ground. His batman was quick to avenge him by shooting this assailant with his master's bloodstained rifle, but the regiment mourned the passing of this outstanding battalion commander ever after. One morning earlier as I was returning from the Schwaben redoubt with him, he had said to me: "When the war is over, I am going to take my pension. You young men must carry on the work." All too soon and far from home they had to bury him here.'

By midday the Ulstermen had overrun the Schwaben Redoubt, had taken 500 prisoners, and were holding a line beyond its eastern edge; but by nightfall they had been driven back to the German front-line trenches. A few Ulstermen succeeded during the morning in reaching Stuff Redoubt, in the German second line, almost a mile from their starting point. They found the redoubt undefended, but before they could enter it they were caught by a massive British artillery barrage and had no means of signalling back that they were already there.

Sergeant Felix Kircher, of the German 26th Field Artillery Regiment, one of the few German soldiers in Stuff Redoubt, was a witness to this furthest Ulster advance. He later recalled someone shouting down to him in amazement, 'The Tommies are here.' He rushed up, 'and there, just outside the barbed wire, were ten or twenty English soldiers with flat steel helmets. We had no rifle, no revolver, no grenades, no ammunition, nothing at all; we were purely artillery observers. We would have had to surrender but, then, the English artillery began to fire at our trench; but a great deal of the shells were too short and hit the English infantrymen as they began to fall back.' Kircher added, 'If the English could have got through, they would have only met clerks, cooks, orderlies and suchlike.'

For those few moments, for several hundred yards to left and right of Stuff Redoubt there were no German soldiers, but the few Ulstermen so far forward had no chance once their own artillery opened up on them. 'It was just Hell,' recalled Corporal G. A. Lloyd, West Belfast Volunteers: 'the British artillery were at us, the German artillery were at us, and rifle and machine-gun fire as well.' Those who survived their own shells beat a swift retreat.

In all, 5,500 Ulstermen – more than one quarter of all the British fatalities – died on July 1 in the area overlooked today by the Ulster Tower, a memorial honouring the dead of the 36th (Ulster) Division. Many of the dead lie today in the two nearest Commonwealth War Graves cemeteries: Connaught Cemetery, located on what had been the British front line along the edge of Thiepval Wood, and Mill Road Cemetery, overlooked by the tower, on the site of the Schwaben Redoubt. Because of the underground workings of the redoubt – a maze of deep, fortified tunnels and dugouts on July 1 – even after ninety years the ground continues to shift and subside. For that reason, many of the gravestones have been placed flat on the ground, to avoid tilting and lurching.

Four Victoria Crosses were awarded to men of the Ulster divisions for their courage on July 1. The first – indeed the first of all fifty-one Victoria Crosses of the Battle of the Somme – was awarded to Rifleman William McFadzean, from Belfast, who saved the lives of several colleagues when he placed his body on two bombs that had been thrown into his trench. He was killed outright. Several accounts report that when his remains were being carried away on a stretcher a shell blew them to pieces. The stretcher men removed their helmets in salute of a brave man, and wept. His name appears on the nearby Thiepval Memorial, half a mile from where he was killed.

Another of the four Ulstermen who won the Victoria Cross on July 1, Captain Eric Bell, was killed while rallying and reorganizing groups of infantrymen who had lost their officers. He had won his Victoria Cross a few hours earlier standing on a trench parapet and using his rifle to halt a German counter-attack. Lieutenant Geoffrey Cather, who won his award for bringing in wounded men from No-Man's Land, was killed on the following morning while trying to bring in more.

Thirty-year-old Private Robert Quigg, 12th Battalion, Royal Irish Rifles, was the only one of the four Ulster Victoria Cross winners on July 1 to survive the battle. Hearing a rumour that his platoon commander, Second Lieutenant Sir Harry Macnaghten, a twenty-year-old baronet and the local squire, was lying wounded in No-Man's Land, he went out seven times to look for him under heavy shell and machine-gun fire. Unable to find him, he returned each time with another wounded man, the last of whom he dragged back on a water-proof sheet from within a few yards of the German wire. Then, completely exhausted, he accepted that Macnaghten would never be found. Nor was he; his name is on the Thiepval Memorial

Having served throughout the war, Quigg was then declared as not meeting army physical requirements. After presenting him with the Victoria Cross, King George V described him as 'a brave wee man'. Quigg, who never married, lived in Bushmills, Ulster, until his death in 1955, at the age of seventy.

A mile south of the Schwaben Redoubt, in a salient between Thiepval Wood and Authuille Wood, was another German strongpoint, Leipzig Redoubt. Among those who fought for its capture on July 1 was fifty-four-year-old Lieutenant Colonel Percy Machell, a veteran of the Nile Expeditionary Force of 1884–5. He was killed leading his battalion's attack. He is buried in Warloy-Baillon Communal Cemetery, five miles west of Albert.

Leipzig Redoubt resisted capture, as did the salient it protected. Neither tenacity nor courage could prevail against the determination of the German defenders. Sergeant James Turnbull of the 17th Battalion, Highland Light Infantry – a Pals battalion, the Glasgow Commercials – held a crucial post in the salient for sixteen hours, hurling bomb after bomb at the Germans in a strongpoint flanking the German trench the Scotsmen had captured. A fine cricketer, he could throw a bomb further than any man in his battalion. After most of the men with him were exhausted, he continued throwing bombs. During a momentary lull in the fighting, Turnbull was killed by a German sniper. Posthumously awarded the Victoria Cross, he is buried in the Lonsdale Cemetery at Authuille.

Thiepval village, with its dominating position over the whole northern sector of the battlefield, resisted all attempts to capture it. Every gap made by the British artillery in the German wire was covered by German machine-gunners. Another Pals battalion, the 16th Battalion, Northumberland Fusiliers – the Newcastle Commercials – had been told by its brigadier, 'You will be able to get over the top with a walking stick, you will not need rifles. When you get to Thiepval you will find the Germans all dead, not even a rat will have survived.' The men, who advanced behind the drop kick of a leading North Country footballer, did not even reach the German wire, but were overwhelmed by machine-gun fire while still in No-Man's Land.

In what is now the Thiepval Anglo-French War Cemetery, soldiers of the German 99th Reserve Regiment stood on their parapet and taunted the men who could advance no further. 'It was said, with some truth,' wrote General Edmonds, 'that only bullet-proof soldiers could have taken Thiepval on this day.'

The failure to capture Thiepval gravely impeded the British advance further south, across Nab Valley. During the attack, one battalion of 70th Brigade, the 9th (Service) Battalion, York and Lancaster Regiment, a Kitchener battalion of South Yorkshire miners, was overwhelmed by German enfilading machine-gun fire directed against its flank from the Thiepval spur less than 800 yards away; 423 men were killed. Almost none reached the German front-line trench. Their historian, J. B. Montagu, wrote with pathos, 'So ends the Golden Age.'

In this attack by 70th Brigade, two of the four commanding officers, Lieutenant Colonel B. L. Maddison and Lieutenant Colonel A. J. B. Addison, were killed, and the other two wounded. Maddison's grave is in Blighty Valley Cemetery, Addison's in Bécourt Cemetery.

The British assault trenches closest to the town of Albert were along Usna Hill and Tara Hill, facing the German-held villages of Ovillers and La Boisselle. The attack on the German front line at Ovillers lay across Mash Valley, 800 yards of No-Man's Land. South of La Boisselle, at Sausage Valley, the No-Man's Land was almost as wide.

The men of the 8th Division who tried to cross Mash Valley were easy targets for the German machine-gunners, who waited until the British soldiers had crossed more than 600 yards of No-Man's Land and then opened a relentless barrage of machine-gun and artillery fire. About seventy men from several different battalions managed to enter the German front-line trench along a 300-yard section, but no reinforcements could reach them. Organized by the unfortunately named Lieutenant Colonel Bastard, a veteran of the Boer War, the commanding officer of the 2nd Battalion, Lincolnshire Regiment, they held the German trench until, with many wounded and their supply of bombs exhausted, they were driven out by German counter-attacks. Falling back into No-Man's Land, they found the ground – in the words of General Edmonds – 'covered by dying and wounded men'.

Many who were killed in Mash Valley are buried today in Ovillers Military Cemetery at the head of the valley, just before the village they failed to take. Lieutenant Colonel Bastard survived, but two other battalion commanders, both in their early forties, were killed as a result of the fighting in Mash Valley. Lieutenant Colonel C. C. Macnamara, 1st Battalion, Royal Irish Rifles, and Lieutenant Colonel A. M. Holdsworth, 2nd Battalion, Royal Berkshire Regiment, both of whom died several days later of their wounds. Macnamara, who was taken back to hospital in England, is buried in his home village of Chorleywood. Holdsworth, who was taken to hospital in Etaples, is buried in the military cemetery there.

Among those in the attack on the village of La Boisselle, on the high ground between Mash Valley and Sausage Valley, was Lieutenant Bernard White, of the 20th (1st Tyneside Scottish) Battalion, Northumberland Fusiliers. He was twenty-nine years old. A fellow officer, Lieutenant Frederick Nixon, later wrote, 'His platoon was the first to leave the trenches, and he himself was responsible for the direction of the attack. He led his men right across No-Man's Land – here eight hundred yards broad – and was last seen standing on the parapet of the German trenches throwing bombs. He then disappeared, and for a short time was missing. Then his body was found and buried, with one or two other officers, who fell beside him . . . His death has left a very empty place in my life, for he was an exceptional man in many ways, so brilliant and full of life.'

Although Lieutenant White's body was found and buried immediately after the battle, its location was utterly destroyed in the shelling and fighting in the weeks that followed. Today his name is on the Thiepval Memorial.

Beyond the 500-yard No-Man's Land of Sausage Valley, several sections of the German front line were overrun, but the casualties were as high there as on every sector of the front, with at least 40 per cent of the attacking troops being killed or wounded. A group of men who tried to take the Sausage Valley Redoubt by storm were burned to death by German flame-throwers as they reached the parapet. Two battalion commanders were also killed in Sausage Valley, forty-year-old Lieutenant Colonel William Lyle and fifty-four-year-old Lieutenant Colonel Charles Sillery, both of the Northumberland Fusiliers. Both are buried in the Bapaume Post Military Cemetery, just north of Albert.

The German forces facing the British assault across Sausage Valley, defending the approach to the village of Contalmaison, watched with amazement and fear as the British mines blew up with such massive force. At what is now Lochnagar Crater, almost a complete company of the German 5th Reserve Infantry Regiment was destroyed, and twelve battalions of the British 34th Division were able to cross No-Man's Land and enter the German front-line trenches. But the German machine-gunners who emerged from their deep dugouts took up positions in front and on the flank of the British attack. Their fire was to be devastating.

One witness on the German side was Lieutenant Colonel Kienitz, of the Machine Gun Company of the 110th Reserve Infantry Regiment. 'Silently our machine guns and the infantrymen waited until our opponents came closer,' Kienitz wrote. 'Then, when they were only a few metres from the trenches, the serried ranks of the enemy were sprayed with a hurricane of defensive fire from the machine guns and the aimed fire of the individual riflemen. Standing exposed on the parapet, some individuals hurled hand grenades at the enemy who had taken cover to the front. Within moments it seemed as though the battle had died away completely. But then, initially in small groups, but later in huge masses, the enemy began to pull back towards Bécourt, until finally it seemed as though every man in the entire field was attempting to flee back to his jumping-off point. The fire of our infantrymen and machine guns persuaded them, hitting them hard; whilst some of our men daringly charged the British troops, capturing prisoners. Our weapons fired away ceaselessly for two hours, then the battle died away.'

In the attempt to reach Contalmaison, the 16th Battalion, Royal Scots Fusiliers – McCrae's battalion of footballers – pushed deep into the German trench lines from their starting point in Sausage Valley. Among them were eight well-known players: the inside forward Teddy McGuire, the midfield player Ernie Ellis, the retired midfielder Jimmy Hawthorn, a member of the youth team, Jimmy Hazeldean, the full back Annan Ness, the left back Duncan Currie, the forward Harry Wattie, and the right back Pat Crossan.

Of the moment when the battalion moved forward into No-Man's Land towards the German fortified positions, the historian of the McCrae Battalion, Jack Alexander, writes, 'By now the German field guns had joined in. Teddy McGuire was struck in the arm by flying shrapnel. As he fell, a machine-gun round grazed his head. Ernie Ellis and Jimmy Hawthorn took a bullet in the thigh. Annan Ness saw Duncan Currie hit in the right shoulder. He also noticed Harry Wattie fall. Crossan was racing forward . . . when a shell exploded in front of them. There was nothing left but a crater and some khaki.'

The bodies of Sergeant Currie and Privates Ellis, Hawthorn and Wattie were never identified. Their names appear on the Thiepval Memorial. In all, 6 officers and 327 men of McCrae's thousand-strong battalion were killed that day, including 59 missing, their bodies never found.

The footballers and their fans – united on the field of battle as in the football stadium – had come to within a mile of Contalmaison before they were driven back. But the attacks on Contalmaison – the first day's objective on this sector – did penetrate the German defences to a depth of a thousand yards, one of the deepest penetrations of the German trench lines that day.

It was to take forty-eight hours before all the British wounded on the Mash Valley–Sausage Valley sector could be brought back to the main dressing station. In the first twenty-four hours after the battle, more than five thousand wounded men were taken back; the numbers were too great for the stretcher-bearers to carry them back any faster. Once the attack died down, however, the Germans in this sector – unlike in most others – offered no opposition to the work of the stretcher-bearers, who operated as far forward as the third German trench. The journey from there took two and a half hours across the shattered terrain. From the dressing station, where the wounds could be identified, basic attention be given, and labels be affixed to each wounded man to indicate his medical needs, the men had to make a further journey to the casualty clearing stations.

More than two hundred officers and four thousand men were killed in this same sector. Thirty were taken prisoner by the Germans.

★

Cecil Lewis, the airman who had witnessed the explosion of the mine at La Boisselle, had the task of reporting back to headquarters where the attacking troops had reached. Two methods of indicating an advance were used by the troops: the placing of groundsheets on the fields, and the firing of flares. In his logbook for July 1, Lewis wrote, 'From our point of view an entire failure. Not a single ground sheet of Battalion or Brigade Headquarters was seen. Only two flares were lit on the whole of both Corps fronts.'

His afternoon air patrol fared no better: 'Again a complete failure. No flares or any ground signals seen. Nothing whatever to report to the Corps.' The only reports he sent in that afternoon were of 'movements on roads, limbers, ammunition, etc.' behind Pozières moving up to Contalmaison. Lewis added, 'Many active enemy batteries seen and though all information was wirelessed to "M", our batteries did not reply on the co-ordinates given. There must be colossal lack of organization somewhere. Our patrol was n.b.g.': no bloody good. M was the signals officer at Vert-Galant, the headquarters of 60 Squadron.

Lewis concluded, 'I was bitterly disappointed. For months we have been preparing, hoping and believing that at last the air could do something valuable and definite for the wretched men who were carrying forward the line, and in effect it was a complete washout, with no co-operation from the very men we were there to help.'

Another British objective on July 1 was the village of Fricourt, just south of that morning's advance towards Contalmaison. Among those attacking it at 7.30 that morning, in four waves, were the 10th Battalion, West Yorkshire Regiment. After they had advanced to the German first-line trench and overran it, they were trapped in the open ground between it and the next German trench. Their position was precarious in the extreme: a slope in full view of German machine-gunners well hidden in the ruins of Fricourt 200 yards away. Within an hour and a half of setting off, more than half of the battalion were killed.

Among the dead was twenty-two-year-old Private Henry Webster. His body was never found. His name is on the Thiepval Memorial, and, as with almost all those British and French soldiers killed on the Somme, it is also on the war memorial in his home town, Pudsey, near Leeds. On the war memorial at nearby Headingley is the name of

Second Lieutenant Thomas Willey, also killed on July 1, and also listed on the Thiepval Memorial to the Missing.

Also killed in the advance towards Fricourt was the Cambridge University graduate, barrister and poet, twenty-nine-year-old Lieutenant Alfred Ratcliffe. In his poem 'Optimism', written while he was in the trenches, he declared:

> At last there'll dawn the last of the long year,
>   Of the long year that seemed to dream no end;
> Whose every dawn but turned the world more drear,
>   And slew some hope, or led away some friend.
> Or be you dark, or buffeting, or blind,
> We care not, Day, but leave not death behind.
>
> The hours that feed on war go heavy-hearted:
>   Death is no fare wherewith to make hearts fain;
> Oh, we are sick to find that they who started
>   With glamour in their eyes come not again.
> O Day, be long and heavy if you will,
> But on our hopes set not a bitter heel.
>
> For tiny hopes, like tiny flowers of Spring,
>   Will come, though death and ruin hold the land;
> Though storms may roar they may not break the wing
>   Of the earthed lark whose song is ever bland.
> Fell year unpitiful, slow days of scorn,
> Your kind shall die, and sweeter days be born.

Ratcliffe is buried in Fricourt New Military Cemetery, on the site of the battlefield where he was killed. Alongside him are the graves of 159 members of the West Yorkshire Regiment who lost their lives in the same attack, among them the curiously named Private Gaiety. Fifty-one others are buried elsewhere, or have no known grave. One of those in the cemetery is nineteen-year-old Second Lieutenant Francis Joseph Hicking. Almost eighty-nine years later, on 19 June 2005, a group of boys from Bramcote School, Scarborough, left two photographs at the graveside, one of Hicking as a schoolboy in his cricket cap, and one of him in his military uniform, and a note with the words 'proudly remembered'.

Another note left in the Fricourt New Military Cemetery, addressed to 'Uncle John', reads: 'You ended your life here 1.7.16. You will never be forgotten.'

Not only West Yorkshiremen were buried that day at what became Fricourt New Military Cemetery. Also in the cemetery are the graves of Captain John Rutledge of the East Yorkshire Regiment and Lieutenant Colonel A. Dickson of the South Lancashire Regiment. In all, twenty-seven lieutenant colonels were killed on July 1 while leading their battalions into action, or died soon afterwards of their wounds.

A mile to the east of Fricourt, at Casino Point, where one of the large mines had been exploded, General Horne's XV Corps succeeded in driving the Germans from the village of Mametz. During the struggle, 159 men of the Devonshire Regiment advanced towards Mansel Copse. As they approached it they were killed by a single German machine gun, which was built into the base of a crucifix at the edge of Mametz village. They had advanced 400 yards from their starting point.

The British officer who led the attack on the copse, Captain D. L. Martin, had predicted that the machine gun at the crucifix would be a fatal hazard if it survived the preliminary British artillery bombardment. He was killed with his men as they advanced into the uninterrupted fire. They were buried in a trench in the copse, and a notice was put above their grave: 'The Devonshires held this trench. The Devonshires hold it still.' Today that trench is the site of the Devonshire Cemetery.

Among the officers buried in that trench was the poet William Hodgson, 'Smiler', the battalion's bombing officer. When bringing a supply of bombs up to the trench, he was killed by a bullet in the throat. His body was found with that of his batman dead at his side.

A British officer recorded in his diary the information about the attack on Mametz he was given by a chaplain who had reached the front line ten days after the attack of July 1. 'His news was ghastly – everyone I care for gone: all four officers of my company killed: dear Harold died most splendidly before the German lines. He was shot through the stomach and Lawrence killed behind him by the same shot. Iscariot was shot through the heart below Mansel Copse and all his staff killed around him; Smiler killed about the same place, getting his bombs up. No single officer got through untouched. The men did grandly – going on without officers and reaching all objectives.'

Among those in the attack on Mametz was Captain Charles May, 22nd Battalion, Manchester Regiment – the 7th Manchester Pals. He was twenty-seven years old. In the early hours of the morning he found a few moments to write in his diary a letter to his wife. 'I must not allow myself to dwell on the personal,' he wrote. 'There is no room for it here. Also it is demoralising. But I do not want to die, not that I mind for myself. If I have to go I am ready, but the thought I may never see you or our darling baby again turns my bowels to water. I cannot think of it with even a semblance of equanimity. It may well be that you only have to read these lines as ones of passing interest. On the other hand they may well be my last message to you. Know for all of your life that I love you and baby with all my heart and soul; that you two sweet things were just all the world to me. I pray God I may do my duty, for I know you would not have it otherwise.'

Captain May was killed in the attack. His grave is in Dantzig Alley British Cemetery, near where he fell.

Sergeant Tawney of the 22nd Manchesters also took part in the attack on Mametz. In his October article in the *Westminster Gazette* he reported, 'We crossed three lines that had once been trenches and tumbled into the fourth, our first objective. "If it's all like this it's a cake-walk," said a little man beside me, the kindest and bravest of friends, whom no weariness could discourage or danger daunt, a brick-layer by trade, but one who could turn his hand to anything, the man whom of all others I would choose to have beside me at a pinch; but he's dead. While the men dug furiously to make a fire-step, I looked about me. On the parados lay a wounded man of another battalion, shot, to judge by the blood on his tunic, through the loins or stomach. I went to him, and he grunted, as if to say, "I am in terrible pain; you must do something for me; you must do something for me." '

Tawney tried, but without much success, to ease the wounded man's equipment, and then thought of getting him into the trench. 'But it was crowded with men and there was no place to put him. So I left him. He grunted again angrily, and looked at me with hatred as well as pain in his eyes. It was horrible. It was as though he cursed me for being alive and strong when he was in torture. I tried to forget him by snatching a spade from one of the men and working fiercely on the parapet.'

Looking round, Tawney 'saw the men staring stupidly, like calves smelling blood, at two figures. One was doubled up over his stomach, hugging himself and frowning. The other was holding his hand out and looking at it with a puzzled expression. It was covered with blood – the fingers, I fancy, were blown off – and he seemed to be saying: "Well, this is a funny kind of thing to have for a hand." Both belonged to my platoon; but our orders not to be held up attending to the wounded were strict. So, I'm thankful to say, there was no question what to do for them. It was time to make our next objective, and we scrambled out of the trench.'

Tawney and his men crossed into No-Man's Land. German soldiers shot at them from their parapet, and they shot back. The Germans who had not been killed or wounded got back into their trenches. 'I stopped firing and looked about me. Just in front of me lay a boy who had been my batman till I sacked him for slackness. I had cursed him the day before for being drunk. He lay quite flat, and might have been resting, except for a big ragged hole at the base of his skull where a bullet had come out. His closest friend, also a bit of a scallywag, was dead beside him . . . My platoon officer lay on his back. His face and hands were as white as marble. His lungs were labouring like a bellows worked by machinery. But his soul was gone. He was really dead already; in a minute or two he was what the doctors call "dead".'

Tawney went off in search of the men who might still be alive on the right flank, in the hope that they could reinforce his small group of survivors. 'One couldn't believe that the air a foot or two above one's head was deadly. The weather was so fine and bright that the thought of death, had it occurred to me, which it didn't, seemed absurd.' Seeing 'a knot of men' lying down away to his right, Tawney did not know if they were dead or wounded, so he waved to them, while calling out 'reinforce'. When they did not move he knelt up and waved again. Then he was hit.

Feeling the ground beside him, Tawney's fingers closed on the nose-cap of a shell. 'It was still hot, and I thought absurdly, in a muddled way, "This is what got me." I tried to turn on my side, but the pain, when I moved, was like a knife, and stopped me dead. There was nothing to do but lie on my back.'

After a few minutes two men in Tawney's platoon 'crawled back past me at a few yards' distance. They saw me and seemed to be laughing, though of course they weren't, but they didn't stop. Probably they were wounded. I could have cried at their being so cruel. It's being cut off from human beings that's as bad as anything when one's copped it badly, and, when a lad wriggled up to me and asked, "What's up, sergeant?" I loved him. I said, "Not dying, I think, but pretty bad," and he wriggled on. What else could he do.'

Tawney raised his knees to ease the pain in his stomach, 'and at once bullets came over, so I put them down. Not that I much minded dying now or thought about it. By a merciful arrangement, when one's half-dead the extra plunge doesn't seem very terrible. One's lost part of one's interest in life . . . Though the rational part of me told me to lie flat, my stomach insisted on my knees going up again, in spite of the snipers, and it didn't bother me much when they began shelling the trench about sixty to eighty yards behind me, with heavies. One heard them starting a long way off, and sweeping towards one with a glorious rush, like the swift rustling of enormous and incredibly powerful pinions. Then there was a thump, and I was covered with earth.'

After about the thirtieth thump, 'something hit me in the stomach and took my wind. I thought, "Thank heaven, it's over this time," but it was only an extra heavy sod of earth. So the waiting began again. It was very hot. To save what was left of my water, I tried one of the acid-drops issued the night before, the gift, I suppose, of some amiable lunatic in England. It tasted sweet, and made me feel sick. I drank the rest of my water at a gulp. How I longed for the evening! . . . I began to shout feebly for stretcher-bearers, calling out the name of my battalion and division, as though that would bring men running from all points of the compass. Of course it was imbecile and cowardly. They couldn't hear me, and, if they could, they oughtn't to have come. It was asking them to commit suicide.'

Then, Tawney recalled, a man was standing beside him. 'I caught him by the ankle in terror lest he should vanish.' It was a corporal in the Royal Army Medical Corps. In answer to the corporal's shouts a doctor came. 'Then the corporal and the doctor went off, to attend to someone else, they said, and would be back in a minute. I thought they were deceiving me – that they were leaving me for good.' But they returned, and as soon as the doctor spoke to his orderly 'I knew he was one of the best men I had ever met. He can't have been more than twenty-six or twenty-seven; but his face seemed to shine with love and comprehension, not of one's body only, but of one's soul.'

The doctor listened 'like an angel' while Tawney told him 'a confused, nonsensical yarn about being hit in the back by a nose-cap. Then he said I had been shot with a rifle-bullet through the chest and abdomen, put a stiff bandage round me, and gave me morphia. Later, though not then, remembering the change in his voice when he told me what was amiss, I realised that he thought I was done for. Anyway, there was nothing more he could do. No stretcher-bearers were to hand, so it was out of the question to get me in that night. But, after I had felt that divine compassion flow over me, I didn't care. I was like a dog kicked and bullied by everyone that's at last found a kind master, and in a grovelling kind of way I worshipped him. He made his orderly get into a trench when I told him they were sniping, but he wouldn't keep down or go away himself.'

After thirty hours in No-Man's Land, Tawney was taken back to a casualty clearing station. He survived the war, to become a distinguished socialist thinker and teacher.

The most easterly part of the British attack was against the village of Montauban. It began three minutes before 7.30 a.m. with the explosion of two mines, one of 5,000 pounds, the other of 500 pounds, at Casino Point, at the eastern end of the front to be attacked. As the British troops crossed No-Man's Land, flame-projectors set up by the Germans on one edge of the larger crater caused heavy casualties. So did a German machine-gunner firing along No-Man's Land from the smaller crater. The attackers persevered, German shrapnel shells burst high, and the German front-line positions were overrun.

The 55th Brigade was among the forces attacking Montauban. On the sector of the front on which the 8th Battalion, East Surrey Regiment, was to advance, Captain Wilfred Nevill gave each of his four platoons a football, to encourage them forward. His idea was that the platoons should compete to see which would be the first to dribble their ball up to the German front line. On the leather was written: 'The Great European Cup-Tie Final – East Surreys versus the Bavarians'.

Nevill kicked off one of the balls, but was killed during the advance. He is buried in Carnoy Military Cemetery, half a mile from where he fell.

Despite strong German resistance, the attack on Montauban was the most successful British attack that morning. Artillery support was effective; the strongly fortified trenches and two formidable strongpoints, Pommiers Redoubt and Glatz Redoubt, were overrun. Four German artillery pieces were captured, as were 12 machine guns, 4 trench mortars and 500 prisoners. 'We consolidated and held the positions against a counter-attack,' noted Second Lieutenant Kenneth Mappin, who was among those who entered the village, but he added, 'Our losses too were very heavy.'

General Edmonds, the official historian of the first day of the Battle of the Somme, has described how, although the trench outside the southern edge of Montauban was well sited, 'the Germans made no effort to defend it, and the village was entered by the Manchesters and Scots Fusiliers at 10.05 a.m. without opposition. It was deserted − except for a fox − and a scene of complete devastation, although, the houses having been small, the alignment of the main streets was quite plain. The front line pressed on through the ruins, with the second line hurrying up close behind from the determination of the men to be in at the finish.' Fifty-five minutes later, at 11 a.m., 'as the last of the smoke cloud dispersed, the part of Montauban Alley beyond the northernmost houses, the second and last objective, was entered. The Germans still there, some hundred in all, mostly surrendered without a fight.'

The next phase of the struggle in and around Montauban was for the brickworks of La Briqueterie, the chimney stacks of which were being used by the Germans as observation points with a clear field of vision over the whole battlefield. At 12.34 p.m. the buildings of the brickworks, which had suffered severely in the British artillery bombardment, were rushed, and, in the words of General Edmonds, 'many German dead were found; but no opposition was encountered until the far side was reached. There a machine gun was being hurriedly brought into action from a dugout, and a few casualties occurred before resistance was overcome. A number of officers and men in the deep dugout nearby surrendered.' These included the headquarters colonel and adjutant of the German 62nd Regiment and two artillery officers, the commander and his observer, of No. 2 Group, German 21st Field Artillery Regiment. Two machine guns and a quantity of documents, regimental orders and material were also taken.

★

In the capture of Montauban, 76 British officers and 1,664 other ranks had been killed. By late afternoon, in the words of General Edmonds, it was 'extraordinarily quiet'. The British artillery bombardment had ceased, 'and only a single German 5.9-inch gun shelled Montauban Alley at extreme range slowly and inaccurately'. From the air, British observers saw some of the attacking infantry advancing between Trones Wood and Bernafay Wood. As for Montauban, 'There was no difficulty in getting up supplies or removing wounded. The Germans being fully occupied by the attacking troops, the clearance of the wounded, indeed, had been begun soon after the first advance, and was carried on steadily all day across the open, motor ambulances coming up as far as Carnoy. All wounded were evacuated within twenty-four hours. Once Montauban had been reached, the long slope between it and the old front line was dotted with groups of carrying parties, and of engineers repairing the roads and the light railway, which was made available for pushing trucks by hand. Even the field batteries trotted forward without molestation.'

The view from the captured heights was remarkable. In the evening light, General Edmonds later wrote, the outposts of XIII Corps, looking across Caterpillar Valley to the broad southern slopes of the Ginchy–Pozières plateau, could see the villages of Longueval, with Delville Wood on its eastern side, Bazentin-le-Grand and Contalmaison, half hidden and separated by the Bazentin and Mametz woods, and, further behind, High Wood. 'The names of these localities, when discovered from the map, meant nothing to the watching groups, though all were soon to become for ever memorable in the annals of the British Army.'

Edmonds added, 'As the light failed, all fighting ceased; even the British guns which had been shelling fugitives were silent. Activity behind the front line, however, increased and intensified: the machinery by which food, water and ammunition reached the troops was soon in full swing, and aided by reinforcements, the work on defences and improvement of communications was redoubled.' An attempt made at 9.30 p.m. by a small party of Germans to approach Montauban from a quarry in Caterpillar Valley north of it 'was driven off by fire, and night fell with XIII Corps in solid occupation of its conquests'.

★

Along the River Somme, and south of the river, in the eight-mile French sector of the front, the French forces moved forward at 9.30 a.m., two hours after the British. The American poet Alan Seeger was among those who prepared to advance that day, although not in the first wave. A Harvard graduate, he was serving in the French Foreign Legion as Legionnaire No. 19522. Also in action that day with the French forces were many thousands of black troops from the French African colonies.

A friend who was with Seeger that day later wrote of how, at eight in the morning, 'there was roll call for the day's orders and we were told that the general offensive would begin at nine without us, as we were in reserve, and that we should be notified of the day and hour that we were to go into action. When this report was finished we were ordered to shell fatigue, unloading 8-inch shells from automobile trucks which brought them up to our position.'

Seeger's friend's account continued, 'All was hustle and bustle. The Colonial regiments had carried the first German lines and thousands and thousands of prisoners kept arriving and leaving. Ambulances filed along the roads continuously. As news began to arrive we left our work to seek more details; picking up souvenirs, postcards, letters, soldiers' notebooks, and chatting all the time, when suddenly a voice called out: "The company will fall in to go to the first line."'

At four o'clock the order came to get ready for the attack. 'None could help thinking of what the next few hours would bring. One minute's anguish and then, once in the ranks, faces became calm and serene, a kind of gravity falling upon them, while on each could be read the determination and expectation of victory. Two battalions were to attack Belloy-en-Santerre, our company being the reserve of battalion. The companies forming the first wave were deployed on the plain. Bayonets glittered in the air above the corn, already quite tall.'

Alan Seeger's section formed the right and vanguard of the company, his friend's section formed the left wing. 'After the first bound forward, we lay flat on the ground, and I saw the first section advancing beyond us and making toward the extreme right of the village of Belloy-en-Santerre. I caught sight of Seeger and called to him, making a sign with my hand. He answered with a smile. How pale he was! His tall silhouette stood out on the green of the cornfield. He was the tallest man in his section. His head erect, and pride in his eye, I saw him running forward, with bayonet fixed. Soon he disappeared and that was the last time I saw my friend.'

The detachments of the Foreign Legion in this attack included several dozen Americans. Seeger's unit was led by a Swiss baron, Captain de Tscharner. During their attack on the strongly fortified village of Belloy-en-Santerre, the legionnaires were caught by fire from the flank by six German machine guns.

Lying mortally wounded in a shellhole, Seeger was heard crying out for water, and for his mother. Earlier that year he had written in his poem 'Rendezvous':

> I have a rendezvous with Death
> On some scarred slope or battered hill,
> When Spring comes round again this year
> And the first meadow-flowers appear.
>
> God knows 'twere better to be deep
> Pillowed in silk and scented down,
> Where love throbs out in blissful sleep,
> Pulse nigh to pulse, and breath to breath,
> Where hushed awakenings are dear.
>
> . . . . . .
>
> But I've a rendezvous with Death
> At midnight in some flaming town,
> When Spring trips north again this year,
> And I to my pledged word am true,
> I shall not fail that rendezvous.

By nightfall Belloy-en-Santerre was in the Foreign Legion's hands, but 25 officers and 844 men had been killed or seriously wounded – a third of the attackers' total strength. Seeger is thought to be buried – as one of the many unknown soldiers – in the French National Cemetery at Lihons. There is a memorial bell to him in the church at Belloy, the town near where he was killed, and where a square is named after him.

Elsewhere south of the Somme, General Fayolle, commanding the French Sixth Army, used a combination of superior artillery resources and skilful infantry tactics to push the less well-defended Germans back along the whole eight-mile length of his army front.

An underlying weakness on July 1 for the attacking force was the lack of counter-batteries: the artillery needed to bombard the German artillery positions behind the German lines. After the Battle of Loos, General Rawlinson had stressed the harm done by the failure of the counter-batteries to knock out the German artillery. 'The success of an operation depends largely upon keeping down the fire of hostile artillery' were his words then. On the Somme however, on July 1, his priorities were different: he directed more than 1,000 of his guns to cut the German wire, which they were often unable to do; 233 heavy howitzers to bombard the German trenches; and fewer than 180 guns to serve as counter-batteries and target the German artillery. Of the 180 guns used to strike at the German artillery batteries, 32 were obsolete and far from accurate in their fire.

In all, 598 German field guns and 246 howitzers survived the British artillery fire. It was they that were able to direct a devastating barrage of fire on the advancing British troops. In the words of the Heavy Artillery War Diary of X Corps, whose troops on the River Ancre failed to take Saint-Pierre-Division, the Schwaben Redoubt or Thiepval, but did take Leipzig Redoubt, 'Our superiority in artillery was not used to destroy the enemy's heavy artillery with heavy howitzers, and there was not much counter-battery work.' Studying the reports from all the British sectors during the first day of the battle, Haig commented that on such a long front of attack 'varying fortunes must be expected.'

In some sectors the advance was more successful than others. A major factor in this was the relative availability of artillery support. Greater success was achieved in the southern sectors, where adequate guns and shells were available to support the advancing infantrymen. In the northern sector, this support was less strong.

After lunch at Val Vion on July 1, Haig was driven to Querrieu, where Rawlinson gave him a mixed report. The German defenders at Ovillers and Thiepval 'have held our troops up'. The strongly fortified Schwaben Redoubt, on the ridge north of Thiepval, had been captured and a German counter-attack driven back. The Montauban–Mametz spur and the villages of Montauban and Mametz had been taken, but the Germans were still in Fricourt.

North of the River Ancre, VIII Corps under General Hunter-Weston had entered the German defences but had then been driven back to the German front line. Haig noted scathingly in his diary: 'I am inclined to believe from further reports that few of VIII Corps left their trenches!'

Rawlinson, although sceptical of the report that Serre had been captured, still hoped that it might be possible to send the cavalry forward that afternoon, and secure the planned-for breakthrough. But it was not to be. Realizing the seriousness of the situation, at five o'clock that afternoon, driving from Querrieu to the headquarters of II Corps in reserve at Villers-Bocage, eight miles away, Haig ordered two reserve divisions, the 38th and 23rd, to march in two hours' time 'nearer to the front', as the Fourth Army was 'getting through its reserves'.

During July 1 more than five hundred of the British attackers were taken prisoner by the Germans. The town of Bapaume, less than ten miles from the starting point, was never reached, either that day or in five months of renewed assaults. The scale and intensity of the British attack had, however, achieved what the French wanted of it, forcing the Germans to transfer sixty heavy guns and two infantry divisions from Verdun to the Somme, and seriously impeding the possibility of a German victory at Verdun.

The first day of the Battle of the Somme was the 132nd day of the Battle of Verdun, from whose tormented defenders it was drawing more than twenty thousand German troops. French attacks on the Somme further south made larger gains than the British, but they, too, failed to get anywhere near their first day's objective, the town of Péronne. They did, however, take 3,000 German soldiers prisoner and capture 80 German guns.

There was one British success on July 1 that gave particular cause for satisfaction. Shells from a heavy-artillery gun, mounted on a railway carriage behind Albert, hit the headquarters of the German XIV Corps in Bapaume, thirteen miles away, forcing the headquarters to move to Beugny, three and a half miles further east.

The human cost of the fighting on July 1 was higher than on any other single day of battle in the First World War. In all, 19,240 men had been killed and large numbers seriously wounded; the Royal Army Medical Corps recorded that from six in the morning of July 1 to six the following morning, British field ambulances collected 26,675 wounded men. Several thousand more were lying in No-Man's Land, beyond the reach of succour or rescue.

The heroism of the infantrymen and the horrors they faced were undoubted. The reason for failure did not lie in any lack of zeal. The men who went over the top were determined to succeed, and had been instilled with a fierce hatred of the enemy. On all but the southern sector of the front, however, they had been let down by the inability of their own artillery to make sufficient breaches in the German wire, or to destroy the deepest German dugouts, or to use its counter-battery fire to undermine the German artillery power.

The Battle of the Somme had only just begun, as had the creation of the cemeteries that are today a sombre, defining feature of the landscape. Twelve miles behind the German front line, at Villers-au-Flos, one of several German cemeteries was begun on that first day of battle. Today it holds the remains of 2,449 men, their names in pairs under black crosses. In the British war cemeteries and on the Thiepval Memorial to the Missing are the names of 118 boys aged seventeen or under who died on that first day. Reading reports of the battle, Florrie Iles wrote to her sixteen-year-old brother, Horace, urging him to come home. Her letter was returned from France stamped on the envelope with the words 'Killed in Action'.

Private Horace Iles, 15th Battalion, West Yorkshire Regiment – the Leeds Pals – had been killed during the attack on Serre. His grave is in the Serre Road Cemetery No. 1. In the letter he never received, his sister had written, 'You have no need to feel ashamed that you joined the "Pals" now, for by all accounts they have rendered a good account of themselves, no one can call them "Featherbed Soldiers" now.'

Of the 143 British battalions in action on the first of July, 32 had more than 50 per cent losses in killed and wounded. By far the largest number of those so severely affected – twenty in all – were Kitchener's New Army battalions. Seven were Regular Army battalions, four were Territorial battalions, and one was an Empire force, the 1st Battalion, Newfoundland Regiment.

Throughout the night of July 1, stretcher-bearers toiled backwards and forwards in No-Man's Land to find the wounded and bring them back. Where possible, weapons and equipment were salvaged. Abandoned trenches and large shellholes were used as multiple burial grounds. At dawn, with the ground again visible to the German snipers and machine-gunners, the work of rescue was suspended. Several thousand wounded men had to lie out in the hot sun for another day. Many hundreds, unreachable under the vigilant eyes of the German defenders, died of their wounds. Their screams of pain and cries for help, heard in the facing trenches of friend and foe, rent the day and night.

4

The first full week of battle:
'It looked like victory'

THE GERMAN SECOND Army had prevented the British and French from achieving their objectives on 1 July 1916. But the Germans had also suffered heavily – so much so that General Grünert, the Second Army Chief of Staff, agreed to a request from his subordinate General Pannewitz for a partial withdrawal in the southern, French, sector. On July 2 the German Commander-in-Chief, General Falkenhayn, visiting Second Army headquarters at Saint-Quentin, was outraged at the thought even of a tactical withdrawal, and removed General Grünert from his command.

Among the British troops being gathered on July 2 to be transferred to the Somme was an American citizen, Second Lieutenant Harvey Augustus Butters, who had volunteered to fight with the British forces, and had been serving with the Royal Field Artillery for more than a year. Butters was one of 32,000 Americans who had circumvented the British army regulations that listed, among the categories of those 'not to be allowed to enlist or re-enlist under any circumstances', the category '(vi) A foreigner'.

In anticipation of returning to the front, Butters wrote home on July 2, 'Already – although the sound of a shell still sends my heart action up to approximately a thousand a minute – I am beginning to take a more normal view of things. The moments of depression come farther apart – and the rest of the time I see things in a much more endurable light. I realize that I must be philosophical about it. Steady is the word – and we'll see the great work through to the end yet. (And no doubt live to brag about it!)'

Battle was renewed on July 2 with a determination to secure the first day's objectives. 'A day of ups and downs!' Haig noted in his diary that evening. A German counter-attack at dawn against the forces holding Montauban had been driven off. 'This was good,' Haig noted, 'but the Enemy was still in Fricourt', as well as in La Boisselle and Thiepval. Four battalions of British troops were reported cut off, two in the Schwaben Redoubt and two in the village of Serre.

Lieutenant Cecil Lewis took his aircraft up again on July 2. That morning, he later wrote, 'we started a practice which was to become a habit during the next few months – going down low enough to see the men in the trenches with accuracy, and getting our reports this way.' As Lewis described it in his logbook, 'We circled above the trenches at a thousand feet, saw the infantry crossing the old No-Man's Land above Fricourt, saw many Hun dead round the mine-craters, saw the communication trenches running from Mametz to Montauban full of troops, noted it all on scraps of paper, put them in a message bag, and came back, swooping low to drop it on the brigade headquarters ground sheet, then up and back again for more information.'

From the air it was possible to see 'to what extent the great offensive had succeeded. There did seem to be a definite advance all along the front of the 15th and 3rd Corps, except at Boisselle and Fricourt; but there was evident disorder, hesitation, and delay, due probably to the enemy resistance at these two points, which spoiled the outline of the offensive. Still, it was early to be depressed. Perhaps the objectives aimed at for the second and third days of the offensive would be realised and the initial hold-ups compensated for.'

Lewis and his number two, 'Pip', 'after doing all we could to report on the state of the line', then flew eastward: 'We wandered farther over to see what the Hun was doing behind it. Was he bringing up supplies or reinforcements? On the main road from Bapaume to Pozières, five miles beyond the line, we saw two horse-drawn limbers. They were coming up at the gallop, bringing ammunition to their batteries, their six horses stretching out, the riders crouching low over their necks, the wagon rolling and swaying along the awful road. We dived. At a thousand feet Pip opened fire with the Lewis gun. Whether he killed or wounded the leading horse of the first limber I shall never know. Perhaps it was just panic; but the horse crumpled up, and the others, with their tremendous momentum, overran him, and the whole lot piled up in the ditch, a frenzied tangle of kicking horses, wagons, and men. The second limber, following close behind the first, swerved, but could not avoid its leader; its wagons overturned, wheels spinning, and split. Shells rolled over the road. We returned elated. We had helped to win the war.'

It being Sunday, Haig went to church in Beauquesnes on the morning of July 2. He then drove to Querrieu to see Rawlinson. 'I directed him to devote all his energies to capturing Fricourt and neighbouring villages, so as to reduce the number of our flanks, and then advance on Enemy's second line.'

Haig also visited two casualty clearing stations at Montigny on July 2, one under Major Thomas, the other under Colonel Macpherson. 'They were very pleased at my visit,' he noted. 'The wounded were in wonderful good spirits.' When details of the casualty figures reached Val Vion on July 2, they had been tallied to more than forty thousand in dead and wounded. Haig noted in his diary that such a figure 'cannot be considered severe in view of the numbers engaged, and the length of the front attacked'. It was reported from Bernafay Wood that the Germans had only a few patrols there 'and that they were surrendering freely'. That night, Haig noted, the situation on the battlefield 'was much more favourable than when we started today!'

At Querrieu, General Rawlinson was likewise undismayed about continuing the battle, noting in his diary on July 2 that, although the casualties had been 'heavy', there were 'plenty of fresh divisions behind'.

The main impediment to a renewed offensive on July 2 came from General Sir Hubert Gough's Reserve Army. Gough reported at midday that in the sector held by his VIII Corps, facing Serre and Beaumont-Hamel, the dead and wounded from the first day's attack were still choking all the communications trenches, and that to remove them would mean a suspension of military operations for some days. As a result, operations were focused on the southern part of the line. Here a success was secured when it was discovered that the Germans had evacuated the exposed Fricourt Salient. This was secured.

A young South African officer, Hugh Boustead, was among the infantrymen who went into the attack north of Sausage Valley that day. 'Our brigade crossed the scarred fields through the stricken squadron,' he later wrote. 'Dead and dying horses, split by shellfire with bursting entrails and torn limbs, lay astride the road that led to battle. Their fallen riders stared into the weeping skies. In front, steady bursts of machine-gun fire vibrated on the air. Caught by a barrage, these brave men and fine horses had been literally swept from the Longueval road.'

Horses were an ever-visible feature of the battlefield. The highest British animal fatalities on the Western Front were the horses, of whom 58,274 were killed during the course of the war, at least 5,000 on the Somme, mostly by artillery fire.

On July 3 the British forces attacked again, but failed to capture their objective, the villages Ovillers and La Boisselle in the German line. South of the Somme, the French made greater progress, so much so that a German general's order that day stated directly, 'I forbid the voluntary evacuation of trenches.' But by nightfall on July 4 the French had taken 4,000 Germans prisoner and had broken through the German line on a six-mile front.

The Germans knew that the British would not give up, and did not relish the continuing assaults on their heavily bombarded positions. On July 3 the commander of the German Second Army, General von Below, issued a stern Order of the Day. 'The outcome depends', he wrote, 'on Second Army being victorious on the Somme. Despite the current enemy superiority in artillery and infantry we have got to win this battle. The large areas of ground that we have lost in certain places will be attacked and wrested back from the enemy, just as soon as the reinforcements that are on the way arrive. For the time being, we must hold our current positions without fail and improve on them by means of minor counter-attacks. I forbid the voluntary relinquishing of positions. Every commander is responsible for making each man in the army aware about this determination to fight it out. The enemy must be made to pick his way forward over corpses.'

The German reinforcements so badly needed on the Somme by General von Below were being transferred from Verdun, as the French had anticipated, and craved.

Aerial reconnaissance and aerial combat were continuous throughout the first days of the battle, the pilots on both sides doing their utmost to photograph the opposing trench lines and troop movements, and to prevent the 'enemy' pilots from doing the same. On July 3 Maurice Baring visited the British aerodrome at Vert-Galant and, he later wrote, 'saw Ferdy Waldron go up. But this time he did not come back.' Major Francis Fitzgerald Waldron, 11th Hussars, attached to the Royal Flying Corps, was killed that day in aerial combat behind the German lines. He was twenty-nine years old. His grave is in the Ecoust-Saint-Mein Cemetery, six miles north-east of Bapaume.

Lieutenant Cecil Lewis also went up on July 3, his third successive day in the air. His friend Pip was with him. 'We wanted to drop a bomb,' he later wrote. 'It was not strictly our business, and our machines were not fitted with bomb racks; but there were bombs in the store, and we felt that they should be dropped.' The target for their bomb was a house beyond Pozières, a possible German supply dump. 'We climbed up to the lines,' Lewis recalled. 'When we got over the spot, I turned and nodded. Pip pulled out the pin and dumped the baby overboard. We circled and watched it falling. Then we lost sight of it and looked at the house. It was still there. Then – a flash and a cloud of dust about a hundred yards away. We returned home, strangely elated . . . For days on patrol we used to look for the crater it had made. It seemed a friendly crater. Then we forgot it; but we never bothered to drop another bomb.'

At three in the afternoon of July 3, General Joffre together with General Ferdinand Foch, commanding the French Northern Army, arrived, at their own request, at Val Vion. Haig was not pleased by Joffre's suggestions, recording the encounter in his diary: 'Joffre began by pointing out the importance of our getting Thiepval hill. To this I said that in view of the progress made on my right, near Montauban, and the demoralised nature of the Enemy's troops in that area, I was considering the desirability of pressing my attack on Longueval. I was therefore anxious to know whether in that event the French would attack Guillemont.'

When Haig said this, Joffre 'exploded in a fit of rage. He could not approve of it.' He 'ordered me to attack Thiepval and Pozières. If I attacked Longueval, I would be beaten, etc., etc. I waited calmly till he had finished. His breast heaved and his face flushed! The truth is the poor man cannot argue, nor can he easily read a map. But today I had a raised model of the ground before us.'

Haig added, 'When Joffre got out of breath, I quietly explained what my position is as regards him as the "Generalissimo". I am *solely* responsible for the action of the British Army; and I had approved the plan, and must modify it to suit the changing situation as the fight progresses. I was most polite. Joffre saw he had made a mistake, and next tried to cajole me. He said that this was the "English Battle" and "France expected great things from me." I thanked him but said I had only one object, viz. beat Germany. France and England marched together, and it would give me equal pleasure to see the French troops exploiting victory as my own!'

'I soothed old Joffre down. He seemed ashamed' – of his outburst – 'and I sent him and Foch off to Amiens. All present at the interview felt ashamed of Joffre . . . However, I have gained an advantage through keeping calm! My view has been accepted by the French Staffs.'

Haig still hoped that a further attack could succeed over a wide area of the front. Driving in the early afternoon of July 3 from Val Vion to Querrieu to see Rawlinson, Haig 'impressed on him' the importance of taking Trones Wood to cover the right flank of the attack on Longueval, and Mametz Wood and Contalmaison to cover the left flank. Haig was certain that the German strength was diminishing and the enemy reserves were worn down. He therefore ordered Rawlinson and Gough 'to continue the operations relentlessly and allow the Enemy no respite'. He also asked Rawlinson 'to insist on his divisions patrolling widely, especially after a counter-attack had been beaten back'.

On the night of July 3, renewed attacks were made on Ovillers and La Boiselle by British troops of the 12th (Eastern) Division. This was the first assault on the Somme that was made at night, in the hope of achieving surprise. Even so, the Germans drove the attackers off, inflicting heavy casualties. At La Boiselle, British troops entered the village, but German snipers were hiding in the dugouts among the ruins, and there were not enough hand grenades to flush them out. The attacking troops fell back, almost to their start line. As many as a thousand were killed or wounded. The divisional history ascribed part of the failure to 'the flanking machine-gun fire, which was unmolested, and raked the excessive distance between the opposing front lines over which supports had to cross'.

Another reason for the failure, in the words of the divisional history, was that the attack had been carried out in the dark 'by troops who were hurried into the fight without being well acquainted with the terrain, leading to loss of cohesion'. The British artillery bombardment destroyed the German wire and trenches yet failed 'to reach the deep dugouts, which remained unharmed', while the recent storms made the shellholes and trenches 'in places almost unpassable'.

There was one success on the night of July 3: the final capture of Bernafay Wood by the 9th (Scottish) Division. It was not a moment too soon. Heavy rain the next morning culminated in a thunderstorm that lasted all afternoon. In the words of Captain Wilfrid Miles, the official historian, 'the troops were soaked, the trenches filled with water, and the ground became inches deep in clinging mud which balled on the feet of horse and man.' It was a foretaste of what was to come in vexatious measure.

Travelling throughout July 4, amid rain and thunder, Haig exhorted his commanders to greater effort. At the headquarters of XIII Corps at Corbie he saw its commander, General Congreve – who had won the Victoria Cross in South Africa in 1899 – and his Chief of Staff, General Greenly. 'I complimented them on their work but urged greater rapidity.'

Having called en route at the casualty clearing stations at Heilly, Haig reached the nearby headquarters of XV Corps, where he learned that General Horne was 'dissatisfied' with the 17th Division under General Pilcher and 'could not get it to advance quickly'. Driving on to the headquarters of III Corps at Montigny, which he reached at five that afternoon, Haig urged General Pulteney and General Romer 'to press their advance, because by delaying, the Enemy was given more time to strengthen his second line'. The 34th Division, under Major General Ingouville-Williams, had fought 'splendidly' and, despite 'severe' losses, was anxious to remain with III Corps. The 8th Division, under Brigadier General Hudson, had been withdrawn.

During the day, Haig learned from his Royal Artillery chief, Major General Headlam, who had visited the captured German trenches at Fricourt, that some of the dugouts were thirty feet below the ground, 'and in places double tier!' There were also places in the German dugouts 'arranged for shooting upwards from below at anyone in the trenches'.

Going forward on July 4 along a former German communication trench north of Mametz was Second Lieutenant Siegfried Sassoon,

Royal Welch Fusiliers. He later recalled passing 'three very badly-mangled corpses lying in it: a man, short, plump, with turned-up moustaches, lying face downward and half sideways with one arm flung up as if defending his head, and a bullet through his forehead. A doll-like figure. Another hunched and mangled, twisted and scorched with many days' dark growth on his face, teeth clenched and grinning lips.' Then, at noon, closer to the front line, Sassoon passed 'thirty of our own laid out by the Mametz–Carnoy road, some side by side on their backs with bloody clotted fingers mingled as if they were hand-shaking in the companionship of death. And the stench undefinable.'

Thirty-year-old Sassoon wrote about this scene in one of his war poems:

> The road goes crawling up a long hillside,
> All ruts and stones and sludge, and the emptied dregs
> Of battle thrown in heaps. Here where they died
> Are stretched big-bellied horses with stiff legs,
> And dead men, bloody-fingered from the fight,
> Stare up at caverned darkness winking white.
>
> You in the bomb-scorched kilt, poor sprawling Jock,
> You tottered here, and fell, and stumbled on,
> Half dazed for want of sleep. No dream would mock
> Your reeling brain with comforts lost and gone.
> You did not feel her arms about your knees,
> Her blind caress, her lips upon your head.
> Too tired for thoughts of home and love and ease,
> The road would serve you well enough for bed.

The British war correspondent Philip Gibbs, also going forward on July 4, to the German trenches at Fricourt that had been overrun two days earlier, recalled how 'It looked like victory, because of the German dead that lay there in their battered trenches and the filth and stench of death over all that mangled ground, and the enormous destruction wrought by our guns, and the fury of fire which we were still pouring over the enemy's lines from batteries which had moved forward. I went down flights of steps into German dugouts astonished by their depth and strength. Our men did not build like this. This German industry was a rebuke to us – yet we had captured their work, and the dead bodies of their labourers lay in those dark caverns, killed by our bombers who had flung down hand-grenades. I drew back from those fat corpses. They looked monstrous, lying there crumpled up, amidst a foul litter of clothes, stick bombs, old boots, and bottles. Groups of dead lay in ditches which had once been trenches, flung into chaos by that bombardment I had seen. They had been bayoneted. I remember one man – an elderly fellow – sitting with his back to a bit of earth with his hands half raised. He was smiling a little, though he had been stabbed through the belly, and was stone dead.'

Gibbs commented, 'Victory! . . . Some of the German dead were young boys, too young to be killed for old men's crimes, and others might have been old or young. One could not tell because they had no faces, and were just masses of raw flesh in rags of uniforms. Legs and arms lay separate without any bodies thereabouts.'

Another eyewitness to the fighting on July 4 was Reserve Lieutenant Gruber, of the Machine Gun Company of the 6th Bavarian Reserve Infantry Regiment. 'A direct hit crushed the dugout where one of my machine guns, the one commanded by Corporal Krämer, was kept for safety,' he later wrote. 'Several men of the infantry battalion were killed, some were buried alive and the gun was put out of action by earth and sand. Ignoring the continuing heavy fire, Krämer and his men set about rescuing the buried men. In this they were successful, then, despite the fire, they stripped down their machine gun, cleaned it and set about getting ready for action. After a few hours they were able to report that it was back in working order, which delighted us all, because we felt that the enemy would soon be coming.'

The German will to fight seemed unbreakable. The British will to fight was equally strong. It was a struggle that would go on without respite or hesitation.

The first of the wounded from the Battle of the Somme began to arrive in London on July 4. Vera Brittain, nursing at a hospital in Camberwell, later recalled 'the immense convoys which came without cessation for about a fortnight, and continued at short intervals for the whole of that sultry month and the first part of August'. The distance from the battlefield was no protection against extreme distress. 'Day after day I had to fight the queer, frightening sensation – to which, throughout my years of nursing, I never became accustomed – of seeing the covered stretchers come in, one after another, without knowing, until I ran with pounding heart to look, what fearful sight or sound or stench, what problem of agony or imminent death, each brown blanket concealed.'

Among the wounded who reached Vera Brittain's hospital was, by complete chance, her brother Edward. He was to remain in England, and in intense pain, for many months.

At the front, there was no pause. During the night of July 4, heavy rain prevented the continuing task of seeking out wounded men in No-Man's Land – many of them were casualties from the fighting on the first day.

On July 5, during an unsuccessful attempt to capture La Boisselle, Lieutenant Thomas Wilkinson, of the Loyal North Lancashire Regiment, rescued a group of men whose machine gun had failed them while they were pulling back. Then, seeing another group of men trapped behind a mound of earth over which the Germans were throwing bombs, Wilkinson mounted a machine gun on the parapet and drove the Germans off. Later that day he was shot through the heart. He was posthumously awarded the Victoria Cross. His body was never identified. His name is inscribed on the Thiepval Memorial.

A second Victoria Cross was won that day, by Second Lieutenant Donald Bell, 9th Battalion, the Green Howards, a Yorkshire regiment. He had been the first professional footballer to enlist in the British Army. He won his Victoria Cross for attacking a German machine-gun post that was enfilading his battalion after it had captured a German trench between La Boisselle and Mametz Wood. Rushing the gun position under heavy fire, Bell shot the gunner with his revolver.

Bell's colonel later described how, 'Laden by steel helmet, haversack, revolver, ammunitions and Mills bombs in their pouches, he was yet able to hurl himself at the German trench at such speed that the enemy could hardly believe what their eyes saw.' Modestly, Bell wrote to his mother two days later, 'I must confess that it was the biggest fluke alive and I did nothing.' Five days after his heroic action he was killed carrying out a similar act during an attack on Contalmaison. He was buried where he fell. Today his grave is in Gordon Dump Cemetery. There are also memorials to him in St Paul's Church, Harrogate, and in Contalmaison – unveiled on 9 July 2000.

In writing to Bell's mother, his batman, Private John Byers, sent her 'a Prussian helmet, bayonet and pair of boots' that Bell had acquired from the German trench after his Victoria Cross action.

That night, July 5, on the front facing Beaumont-Hamel, a soldier was seen crawling in from No-Man's Land. When challenged by a sentry he identified himself as a Newfoundlander. He had been lying out in No-Man's Land, badly wounded, for five days. Having reached the front-line trenches only on the eve of battle, he had received no briefing about the lie of the land, and could not work out, in his shellhole, the direction of the opposing trench lines. Then, 'fed up', as he later described it, with his environment, he decided to crawl in any direction. He was lucky to have chosen the correct one.

On July 6, a month after Lord Kitchener had drowned, Lloyd George succeeded him as Secretary of State for War. For the next five months Lloyd George and the Chief of the Imperial General Staff, General Sir William Robertson, were the two men on whom responsibility for the conduct of the war would fall. But they had no desire to interfere with Haig's command or judgement.

The battle on the Somme became a daily struggle for woods and villages. On July 6, the village of La Boisselle was captured. That day, at Val Vion, Foch and his Chief Staff Officer, Colonel Weygand – who on 17 May 1940 became the Supreme Commander of the French forces in retreat and defeat – agreed with Haig to co-ordinate the French attack on the following day with the British. Foch would support the British attack with his counter-batteries.

The Newfoundlanders, who had suffered so heavily on July 1, were sent back into reserve on July 6. In the five days they had been at the front, their former reserve billets at Englebelmer had been pounded by German shellfire, and the village itself was reduced to ruins. It had also become the site of a field ambulance station for men brought back on July 1. Fifty-one of these died before they could be sent back to field hospitals. The first, Lance Corporal Denning, Royal Engineers, died on July 5. On July 8, Private James Foley, Monmouthshire Regiment, died. Because there were several artillery batteries around the village, many gunners are also buried in Englebelmer Cemetery, the first, on July 9, being Sergeant Frederick Styles, Royal Field Artillery. He was twenty-seven years old. Gunner William King, who died six days later, was thirty-five.

After two days under continual shellfire at Englebelmer, the Newfoundlanders were sent back further, to a tented camp in Mailly Wood. Ten days later they went back to billets at Acheux, five miles behind the trenches where they had fought with such heavy losses. It was to be more than three months before they were considered sufficiently recovered and reinforced to be able to return to the battle.

Fighting continued throughout July 7. That day, Lieutenant Cecil Lewis was again in the air. 'My most valuable piece of work to date,' he wrote in his logbook. 'Attack had proceeded at Quadrangle trench; but there was a party in Quadrangle support whose identity was unknown. Came down to 800 feet to see. Several Huns bent down showing their grey coats and helmets. Corps acted on our information and put up a two-hour heavy bombardment. Quadrangle was attacked and carried later in the evening.'

The ebb and flow of battle did not always favour the attackers. The village of Contalmaison, captured by the British on the morning of July 7, was lost that evening. Also on July 7, a British attack on Mametz Wood was driven off. Driving to Reserve Army headquarters at Toutencourt, Haig learned from General Gough that 'his troops had not yet captured the whole of Ovillers' – one of the villages that had been an objective on the first day of battle. That evening, however, back at Val Vion, Haig learned from Lord Esher, the War Office representative with the French High Command, who had just arrived from Paris, that the French were 'very pleased with the work of British Army. Our success has just made the difference of the French continuing the war, if necessary, for another winter.'

By the end of the first week of battle the doctors and medical orderlies at the two casualty clearing stations at Heilly were struggling to cope with the large numbers of wounded men. Because of a shortage of hospital trains, many of the men had to remain there for several days, and many died of their wounds before they could be moved to the army hospitals near the coast.

In that first week, about 260 wounded men died at Heilly; a plot of land was set aside for their burial. The number of deaths was such that two, and sometimes even three, soldiers were buried in a single grave. Private Walter Horton, from the Lincolnshire village of Mareham-le-Fen, who had fought with the 7th Battalion, Lincoln-shire Regiment, is buried in the same grave as Acting Lance Corporal Charles Bingham, of Bradford, Yorkshire, who had fought with the 8th Battalion, King's Own Yorkshire Light Infantry. Both men died of their wounds on July 5.

At the end of the first week of battle the 1st Battalion, Royal Welch Fusiliers, were among the soldiers who, having fought continuously for a week, were pulled out of the line. The 7th Division, of which they were a part, had fought with tenacity in front of Mametz Wood, but had failed to gain even a foothold. The division was sent to billets at Dernancourt, three miles behind the line. It took six hours for the 12,000 men to leave the line. The Royal Welch Fusiliers were among the first. That night Second Lieutenant Siegfried Sassoon, who was with them, recalled how the distant gunfire 'crashed and rumbled all night, muffled and terrific with immense flashes, like waves of some tumult of water rolling along the horizon'. Then, an hour before dawn, 'there came an interval of silence in which I heard a horse neigh, shrill and scared and lonely'.

The procession of returning troops continued. 'The camp-fires were burning low when the grumbling, jolting column lumbered back,' Sassoon recalled. 'The field guns came first, with nodding men sitting stiffly on weary horses, followed by wagons and limbers and field kitchens. After this rumble of wheels came the infantry, sham-bling, limping and straggling and out of step. If anyone spoke it was only a muttered word, and the mounted officers rode as if asleep.' The soldiers carried their emergency water in petrol cans, 'against which bayonets made a hollow clink; except for the shuffling of feet, this was the only sound. Thus, with an almost spectral appearance the lurch-ing brown figures flitted past with slung rifles and heads bent forward under basin helmets.'

A short while later, 'as if answering our expectancy, a remote skirl-ing of bagpipes began, and the Gordon Highlanders hobbled in'. Then they dispersed on the hillside and fell asleep. It was daylight, 'which made everything seem ordinary', Sassoon wrote. 'None the less I had seen something that night which overawed me. It was all in the day's work – an exhausted Division returning from the Somme Offensive – but for me it was as though I had watched an army of ghosts. It was as though I had seen the war as it might be envisioned by the mind of some epic poet a hundred years hence.'

5

The last three weeks of July:
'Boys of the Bull Dog Breed'

O N 8 JULY 1916, British forces captured most of Trones Wood, but heavy German shelling, followed by a German counter-attack, forced them out. Rawlinson was not deterred, putting to Haig his plan to break through the German second line near Bazentin-le-Grand. Haig was sceptical. 'I pointed out the necessity for having possession of Mametz Wood before making any attempt of the kind. The moment for taking the Enemy by surprise had passed, and the fighting in the Mametz Wood showed that the Enemy's "morale" was still good. I therefore gave Rawlinson an order to consolidate his right flank *strongly* in the south end of Trones Wood, and to capture Mametz Wood and Contalmaison before making any attempt to pierce the Enemy's second line. This was later confirmed in writing.'

Hundreds were killed in these attacks, and thousands wounded. Hugh Boustead later recalled the moment when he and his men were caught in a German shell barrage. 'Although a shell pitched practically in the middle of the section,' he later recalled, 'the three of us in the centre escaped any hurt other than a tremendous shock and blast which blew the equipment off our shoulders, our steel hats away, and poured tear gas in great clouds all over the trench. Coughing and spitting and weeping and blinded by the tear gas we could hear those of our comrades who were wounded moaning under the debris. Six of the section, three on either side of us, were utterly destroyed, torn to pieces, and six more were wounded.'

On the Somme, as in each of the great battles where artillery tore up the bodies of the living and then the corpses of the dead, proper identification was impossible for hundreds of thousands. Those are the men who are recorded on the monuments and in the cemeteries as having 'no known grave'. Four years after the Battle of the Somme,

Boustead received a letter from the War Office in London 'asking if I could throw any light on the grave of Number 5100, Private Hugh Boustead of the South African Scottish, the cross of which had been erected in Montauban valley in 1916 during the Somme Battle'. He was able to assure the authorities that he was alive and well.

After eight days of continuous battle, the Germans had been pushed back a mile in some places, nearly two miles in others. 'The troops are fighting very well,' Haig wrote to his wife on July 8, 'and the battle is developing slowly but steadily in our favour. In another fortnight, with Divine Help, I hope that some decisive results may be obtained. In the meantime we must be patient and determined.'

Part of that determination involved removing senior officers whose work was judged unsatisfactory. When Haig visited XV Corps headquarters at Heilly on July 9 he learned that General Horne, the corps commander, had removed General Pilcher, commander of the 17th Division, and General Phillips, commander of the 38th (Welsh) Division. Haig was shocked to be told that in the case of the 38th Division, attacking Mametz Wood, 'although the wood had been most adequately bombarded the division never entered the wood, and in the whole division the total casualties for the 24 hours are under 150! A few bold men entered the wood and found little opposition. Deserters also stated Enemy was greatly demoralised and had very few troops on the ground.'

The account Haig was given of Welsh timidity does not accord with the detailed accounts of the harsh and determined fighting. Indeed, on the following day, July 9, two brigades of the 38th (Welsh) Division entered Mametz Wood, and two battalions, as Haig noted in his diary, 'were pushing in and clearing it'.

The attack on Mametz Wood was renewed on July 10. Six months later, Private Richard Thomas of the Transport Section, 14th Battalion, Welsh Regiment – the Swansea Pals – wrote a jingle about the efforts that day of 'the gallant lads of little Wales, and good old Swansea town'; it ended:

Into the wood we went, Sir, and met the German horde,
We showed them the way the Welshman fights, and stuck to his new
abode.

Throughout the long hours of the night, Sir, we stuck like British
    Sons,
Faithful and true to that dear old flag, and our Pals behind at the
    Guns.

Counter attack at night, Sir, by Hun and Bavarian Creed,
But we were boys of the Good old Stock, boys of the Bull Dog
    Breed.

The fighting in Mametz Wood was severe. Twenty-four hours later
the Swansea Pals were sent to rest for a month far behind the
battlefield.

Among those who fought in Mametz Wood was Lance Corporal
Harry Fellows, Northumberland Fusiliers, a survivor of the fierce
fighting at Loos in September 1915. He had also survived the failed
attack on Fricourt on July 1. In Mametz Wood he buried many of his
comrades-in-arms. The horrors of the fighting in the wood never left
him. He survived the Somme, but was wounded in the head a year
later while still on the Western Front. On several visits to the Somme
after the Second World War he revisited the wood. When he died in
1987, at the age of ninety-one, his ashes were buried in the wood, in
a small glade, among his friends. His is one of nine private British
memorials erected on the Somme battlefield since 1919. On the headstone above his ashes is a verse he wrote:

> Where once there was war
> Now peace reigns supreme
> And the birds sing again
> In Mametz.

On July 10 the British recaptured the pulverized ruins of Contalmaison village, 2,000 yards from the front-line trenches of July 1. In
a letter to his wife, Haig reported with satisfaction, 'The battle is being
fought out on lines which suit us. That is to say the Enemy puts his
reserves straight into battle on arrival, to attack us, thereby suffering
big losses.'

Above the battlefield, British and German airmen did their utmost
to observe the troop movements and trench patterns of their adversary.
The opposing aviators were swift to try to fight off each intruder. On
July 10 Lieutenant Arthur Preston White watched such an encounter

from the reserve trenches of the 1st Battalion, Northamptonshire Regiment. 'Towards evening I saw a fight between aeroplanes, seven Germans attacking one of ours,' he wrote to his sister. 'Our fellows had pluck enough for fifty and put up a real good fight, but in the end down they came. I think the pilot was hit and lost control for a moment, but he regained control and came down behind our lines. Both he and the observer, I heard afterwards, were alive, though one was badly wounded and the other slightly. This incident left a bad taste in our mouths. We discussed in a puzzled way how it had happened, but as nobody seemed to have watched the preliminary stages we were not much wiser at the end.'

That evening White's battalion was to relieve another in the front line. 'I went up in advance, just before sunset. I was just estimating where I should make the boundary between two platoons when I noticed another aerial duel. This time it was two English to one German. We watched with some interest. Finally down came the Bosche headlong. He fell heavily about 600 yards in front of our line and burst into flames. Then we behaved in a way which is common enough in illustrated papers, but unusual at the front, i.e. we yelled and cheered like maniacs for about three minutes. Pilot and observer were both dead.'

On the night of July 10 the Germans launched their final attempt to take Fort Souville, and reach Verdun. The attack began with shelling with a new gas, Green Cross, a suffocating agent. But in the two and a half weeks that had elapsed since then, French soldiers had been issued with gas masks that were effective against it. Later in the attack, the German use of flame-throwers eliminated a whole battalion. Thirty-five French officers and 1,300 men were either killed or captured.

By nightfall, 2,400 French soldiers had been taken prisoner, and Fort Souville's garrison had been knocked out by artillery fire. On the following day a small group of no more than thirty German soldiers reached the outer wall of the fort and raised their flag. Two miles away they could see the twin towers of Verdun cathedral. Sheltering in the fort were sixty French soldiers and a lieutenant, Kléber Dupuy. Leading his men out of the fort, Dupuy regained the walls, taking ten of the Germans prisoner. The rest were either killed, or fled. Verdun was secure.

★

1. The 1st Lancashire Fusiliers being addressed by their divisional commander, General de Lisle, at Mailly-Maillet, June 29, 1916

2. A British twelve-inch howitzer in action, July 1, 1916

3. Empty eighteen-pounder shell cases, used by a British artillery in the bombardment of Fricourt, July 1, 1916

4. Men of Tyneside Irish Brigade attacking La Boisselle, July 1, 1916

5. Three fifteen-inch shells ready to be dispatched by men of the Royal Marine Artillery, marked in chalk "TO CAPT. FRYATT'S MURDERERS," Bécourt, August 3, 1916

6. King George V watches a practice trench attack by Australian troops at the 5th Australian School near Sailly, August 14, 1916

7. David Lloyd George, then Secretary of State for War, emerges from a captured German dugout, September 12, 1916. Within three months he was to become Prime Minister.

8. British tanks make their first appearance on the battlefield, Le Flers, September 15, 1916. This one was the Mark I Tank.

9. British cavalry on the march near Hardecourt Wood, September 18, 1916

10. German soldiers in a military hospital at Beelitz, in Silesia. Adolf Hitler, wounded on the Somme in October 1916, is in the top row, one from the right.

11. German graves, ninety years after the battle: part of the German military cemetery at Fricourt. More than 17,000 German soldiers are buried in this one cemetery. Only 5,000 were ever identified. The rest are unknown soldiers, most of them buried in four mass graves.

12. British and French graves, ninety years after the battle, at the Commonwealth War Graves Cemetery at Ovillers. The French graves, 121 in all, are marked by crosses. Buried or commemorated in the cemetery are 3,439 Commonwealth Servicemen of the First World War; 2,479 of the burials are unidentified, the headstones marked "Known to God."

On the Somme, French forces suffered heavily in a failed attempt to capture the village of Barleux. Haig noted in his diary that 'to encourage the French, we must keep on being active.' On July 12, Mametz Wood was finally taken. The number of Germans captured had risen to more than seven thousand. Among those gravely wounded that day, in the trenches facing Contalmaison, was the pianist, painter, actor and writer Captain Richard Dennys, of the 10th Battalion, Loyal North Lancashire Regiment. Taken to the British General Hospital at Rouen, he died twelve days later. In one of his last poems he wrote:

> Better far to pass away
>   While the limbs are strong and young,
> Ere the ending of the day,
>   Ere Youth's lusty song be sung.
> Hot blood pulsing through the veins,
>   Youth's high hope a burning fire,
> Young men needs must break the chains
>   That hold them from their heart's desire.
>
> My friends the hills, the sea, the sun,
>   The winds, the woods, the clouds, the trees –
> How feebly, if my youth were done,
>   Could I, an old man, relish these!
> With laughter, then, I'll go to greet
>   What Fate has still in store for me,
> And welcome Death if we should meet,
>   And bear him willing company.
>
> My share of three score years and ten
>   I'll gladly yield to any man,
> And take no thought of 'where' or 'when',
>   Contented with my shorter span.
> For I have learned what love may be,
>   And found a heart that understands,
> And known a comrade's constancy,
>   And felt the grip of friendly hands.
>
> Come when it may, the stern decree
>   For me to leave the cheery throng
> And quit the sturdy company
>   Of brothers that I work among.

No need for me to look askance,
   Since no regret my prospect mars.
My day was happy – and perchance
   The coming night is full of stars.

The daily life of the front-line soldier was full of incident. In a letter to his sister, Lieutenant Arthur Preston White recounted how, on July 11 behind Contalmaison, 'A wounded Hun on a stretcher drew quite a crowd . . . I doubt whether the fellow had ever been so lionised before.' As for the hazards of war, 'The guns continued to make the deuce of a noise, but very few German shells came our way. They loosed off at our batteries from time to time, but made bad shooting.'

The next day White was with a group of four hundred men taking stores up to Contalmaison. He wrote to his sister, 'Was it a Roman Emperor who said that no smell was sweeter to him than that of a dead enemy? I don't agree with him; I smelt a lot of dead enemies that night – very, very dead some of them, and it nearly turned me sick. On our second journey, we passed the line of men carrying Bosche wounded back from the cellars of the village. We had to halt by one stretcher on which a Bosche was raving in the most horrible fashion. I think that fellow got on my nerves more than anything else.'

On July 12, Lieutenant Cecil Lewis was again in the air. 'Tonight we hear that twelve Hun battalions are being rushed down to support the Third Line,' he wrote in his logbook. 'The Second Line is to be relinquished and the Third held. Therefore we expect to work four machines with the cavalry and destroy the Third Line at any cost. We shall see what we shall see!' Lewis was right to be sceptical.

That day, at Monchy-le-Preux, the British experimented with a new gas combination, hydrogen mixed with 12 per cent carbon disulphide. Known as Double Red Star, this gas was highly inflammable. Indeed, as soon as the Germans began shelling the British front-line trenches, the gas that was to have been released from them caught fire, and heavy casualties were sustained by the special companies whose task was to deploy gas. Another gas being used, White Star, had a toxic phosgene component that caused severe injuries. It was frequently used against the Germans, but often, in accidents, caused serious injury among those whose job was to release it.

On the day after the Monchy experiment had failed, there was consternation at Helfaut, the headquarters of General Foulkes, the head of the Special Brigade, which prepared, distributed and operated the gas, when the London *Evening Standard* reported, 'Battle of the Cylinders. Dosing the Hun with his own medicine. Thrilling story of a British gas attack.' Much inside information, albeit only of the most positive kind, was divulged in the article. A search was made to find the culprit, but he was never identified.

The appearance of gas as a regular feature of the battle from mid-July had one unexpected effect. Following each gas attack, large numbers of rats were affected, and died. 'A most horrid sight,' wrote a lieutenant colonel in the London Regiment, 'but a very good riddance!' Horses were also affected, and, despite ill-fitting horse gas masks, died in large numbers during gas attacks. The mules were so frightened of gas that when they saw men in gas masks they would panic and stampede.

The British infantry commanders did not like the use of gas, and often resisted the efforts of General Foulkes to deploy it on their sectors. One story going the rounds, as recounted by Adrian Hodgkin, a technical chemist from London, was that in one British gas attack 'we gassed about three hundred of our own men and killed one German who laughed so much that he blew his gas mask off!' Some of the gas was far from toxic. One battalion commander, Lieutenant Colonel Vivian Fergusson, ridiculed the regular White Star gas. 'I don't know much about smells,' he wrote, 'but this one had none on the Bosche. They fairly snuffed it up and loved it! If we are going to descend to this sort of thing, there is no point in making ourselves ridiculous by having a sort of sneezing mixture. What we want is something to lay out the Blighters, not fill them with beans.'

On July 13 the most aristocratic of all the fighters on the Somme was killed in action. Josselin de Rohan-Chabot, duc de Rohan, a member of the French parliament, who had earlier been wounded at Verdun, was killed at Hardecourt-sur-Bois, a few yards from the German trenches, while carrying out a reconnaissance shortly before a raid he had volunteered to lead.

It was also on July 13, twelve days after the fighting at Beaumont-Hamel, that the news of that battle reached Newfoundland. Members of the clergy then began what seemed an endless succession of condolence visits. On the Somme, the remnants of the 1st Newfoundland Regiment resumed training. A support cadre, plus the traditional 10 per cent of the total strength, had been spared from taking part in the morning assault on July 1.

In all, 150 members remained of a battalion that, at its fullest strength, had contained a thousand. Reinforced with 130 new recruits, they were transferred to the Ypres Salient, then the quiet sector. Today their former trenches at Beaumont-Hamel are maintained as a memorial, dominated by the statue of a caribou, crying out in pain for the men who were killed.

After almost two weeks of battle, it seemed to Haig that the time might be imminent for the use of the cavalry, but he was cautious. Visiting Rawlinson at Querrieu on the afternoon of July 13, 'I spoke about the use of the cavalry. The divisions were not to go forward until we had got through the enemy's fortifications, except a few squadrons to take "High Wood". For this he had the 2nd Indian Cavalry Division under his orders. As soon as he judged the situation favourable the 1st and 3rd Cavalry Divisions were available.'

In the early hours of July 14, in the hope that a cavalry breakthrough might be possible on the following day, two battalions of cavalrymen, the 20th Deccan Horse and the 7th Dragoon Guards, took up positions between Longueval and High Wood. As they moved forward, at 2.30 that morning, a massive British artillery bombardment began against the German line. 'The noise of the artillery was very loud,' Haig noted at Val Vion, ten miles behind the lines, 'and the light from the explosion of the shells was reflected from the heavens on to the ceiling of my room.' Then, at 3.30 a.m., after a five-minute intensification of the cannonade, Rawlinson launched four divisions – a total of 48,000 men – on a line from west of Bazentin-le-Petit Wood to Longueval.

The Germans were caught by surprise, and fell back. At 7.40 a.m., just over four hours after the first attack, Rawlinson ordered the mounted cavalry to go forward and seize High Wood, but the ground was too slippery for the horses. Brigadier General MacAndrew, commanding the Cavalry Division, himself had two falls.

Meanwhile, the British infantrymen had taken Bazentin-le-Petit Wood and village, almost all of Longueval, and all of Trones Wood – this latter secured for the second time in six days.

As news of the continuing successes reached Haig during the morning of July 14, he contemplated a full-scale cavalry break-through. The Deccan Horse and Dragoon Guards were in place. At 10.55 a.m. his Private Secretary, Sir Philip Sassoon, MP – a second cousin of Siegfried Sassoon – sent Lady Haig a telegram on her husband's behalf: 'I hope to get cavalry through.'

As the fighting continued throughout July 14, the Germans retook Bazentin-le-Petit, and it was several hours before they could be driven out. But by nightfall more than four miles of the German second line of trenches had been captured, and 2,000 German soldiers been taken prisoner. Foch, meeting Haig at Querrieu, told him, admiringly, that the French troops 'could not have carried out such an attack'.

In an effort to exploit the successes of July 14 to demoralize the Germans, a British aeroplane was ordered to fly over the front line and to radio back, in a message that it was known the Germans would intercept, 'Enemy second line of defence has been captured on a front of 6,000 yards. British cavalry is now passing through in pursuit of the demoralised enemy.' This message, sent at 10.30 a.m., deliberately exaggerated the situation as it was known at the time. The turn of events later in the day was to give it a measure of truth, however, when cavalrymen of the 7th Dragoon Guards, charging across open ground with their lances, killed sixteen German infantrymen and took more than thirty prisoners.

'All the cavalry are much heartened by this episode', Haig wrote in his diary, 'and think that their time is coming soon.' To his wife, Haig confided that evening, 'This is indeed a very great success. The best day we have had this war and I feel what a reward it is to have been spared to see our troops so successful! There is no doubt that the results of today will be very far reaching. Our men showed that they have the superiority to the Germans in the fighting, and the latter are very much disorganised and rattled.'

But the Germans were not so disorganized as to allow the British cavalry to break through as Haig had hoped, and they allowed no gap to be made in the line sufficient to enable the cavalry to go forward. At 3.40 in the morning of July 15 the cavalrymen were withdrawn.

Sheltered by the morning mist from the Germans' observation posts, they accomplished their withdrawal without loss.

On the evening of July 14 the 11th Battalion, Lancashire Fusiliers, went into the line. They were among the troops whose task was to capture that part of the village of Ovillers that was still within the German trenches. With them was Second Lieutenant J. R. R. Tolkien, the battalion signals officer. He was twenty-four years old. Later he was to write of the 'animal horror' of the trenches, and, in the introduction to the second edition of *The Lord of the Rings* sixty years later, to reflect, 'It seems now often forgotten that to be caught by youth in 1914 was no less hideous an experience than to be involved in 1939 and the following years. By 1918 all but one of my close friends were dead.' One of those friends was Robert Gilson, who had been killed on July 1.

On the night of July 14, in preparation for the renewed attempt on Ovillers, the 2nd Battalion, Manchester Regiment, sent a bombing party forward to find out the German strength. Coming under heavy German machine-gun fire, they were forced to go back to their own trenches without reaching their objective. The attack on Ovillers went ahead. After one German trench was overrun, the Manchesters who had taken it held out against a sustained German counter-attack. Among those killed was twenty-six-year-old Lieutenant Donald Johnson, who had won the Chancellor's Medal for English Verse at Cambridge University in 1914. One of his last poems was 'Battle Hymn':

> Lord God of battle and of pain,
> Of triumph and defeat,
> Our human pride, our strength's disdain
> Judge from Thy mercy-seat;
> Turn thou our blows of bitter death
> To Thine appointed end;
> Open our eyes to see beneath
> Each honest foe a friend.
>
> Give us to fight with banners bright
> And flaming swords of faith;
> We pray Thee to maintain thy right
> In face of hell and death.
> Smile Thou upon our arms, and bless

Our colours in the field,
Add Thou, to righteous aims, success
With peace and mercy seal'd.

Father and Lord of friend and foe,
All-seeing and all-wise,
Thy balm to dying hearts bestow,
Thy sight to sightless eyes;
To the dear dead give life, where pain
And death no more dismay,
Where, amid Love's long terrorless reign,
All tears are wiped away.

Lieutenant Johnson is buried in Bouzincourt Communal Cemetery Extension, three miles from where he was killed. Ovillers was captured two days later.

Communication was becoming a torment. 'During the first fortnight of the battle,' writes the official historian of the Corps of Royal Engineers, 'the roads just managed to hold out, but after that the consignments of stone received were a very small fraction of the essential minimum, and both transport and labour being difficult to obtain, the thin crust of road metal was cut through by the heavy traffic, the rain penetrated to the chalk, the surface became a mass of liquid mud, and a nightmare situation arose.'

On July 15, Winston Churchill – who was privately critical of the Somme offensive – wrote to his younger brother Jack, who was on the staff of the Australian and New Zealand Army Corps (the Anzacs), then far from the Somme, 'You know my views about the offensive so well that I do not need to set them out on paper.' Churchill added, of the fighting men, 'The marvellous devotion and heroism of the troops exceeds all that history records or fancy had dreamed.'

The battle for Delville Wood began on July 15, when the 3,000-strong South African Brigade was ordered to attack. 'We moved forward through an orchard in single file, led by the platoon officer,' Hugh Boustead later recalled. 'Smith, the Second Lieutenant, got through but the next seven who followed him were shot dead in a circle of a few yards, picked off by clean shooting without a murmur.'

Also on July 15, north-west of Delville Wood, British troops, including members of the 100th Company, Machine Gun Corps, reached High Wood. At one point in the action a front-line carrier pigeon flew back to the British artillery headquarters behind the lines with a tagged message requesting that heavy artillery be turned on a German machine-gun emplacement in the wood. This was done.

The fight for High Wood saw an unexpected facet of trench warfare: war from the air. A Royal Flying Corps observer, Lieutenant T. L. W. Stallibrass, noted in his logbook that day, 'A large force of Hun infantry were entrenched in a road running S.S.E. from High Wood. Fortunately a British aeroplane from No. 3 Squadron spotted the infantry and descended to 500 feet and flew up and down the line strafing them with a Lewis gun.'

A Royal Flying Corps reconnaissance later in the day showed that High Wood had been only partly overrun: on the west side British troops waved flags in reply to the aeroplane's signal, but on the east side the Germans opened rapid fire. In the northern apex of the wood a strong German machine-gun position was still intact.

In the original plot of the London Cemetery to the south-west of High Wood are 107 British, 37 New Zealand and 36 Australian graves, an incomplete but permanent reminder of the cost of one day's battle. On the following morning the troops who had secured the wood withdrew: their success in taking it had created a salient too vulnerable to German attack.

The first burials at the London Cemetery were forty-seven men of the 47th (London) Division, who were buried in a large shell crater in the week after the battle. Other burials were added later, mainly officers and men of the 47th Division who were killed on September 15. At the time of the Armistice the cemetery contained 101 graves. After the war the remains of more than three thousand men were brought in from the surrounding battlefields. The original battlefield cemetery is preserved intact within the larger cemetery. The London Cemetery is today the third largest on the Somme, with 3,872 First World War burials, of whom 3,113 are unidentified.

When the fighting on July 15 came to an end, it was clear that Rawlinson had not achieved his objective. In the morning mist the Germans had been able to bring a few machine guns into the north-east corner of Bazentin-le-Petit Wood, from which they were able to fire on the flank of the troops advancing from west of High Wood towards Pozières and Martinpuich.

The battle for Delville Wood continued. On the second night Hugh Boustead wrote, 'We nearly suffered complete annihilation from our own "steel footballs"' – circular bombs on a long stick. These bombs 'went on pitching among us for hours on end, curiously causing no casualties, but they added to our terror'.

On the third day Boustead went forward with a party of snipers to try to pin the Germans down at Waterlot Farm. 'Three of us spent the afternoon there,' he wrote. 'There were already six South African Scottish lying dead in their firing places ahead of us, but we were able to effect quite a good shoot on the Germans moving from Waterlot and after a number of hits they stopped.'

A few hours later, Boustead was wounded and left the battlefield. 'My main relief was a chance to get some sleep,' he afterwards recalled. 'For five days and nights we had hardly slept at all and at times I was conscious of a longing to get hit anywhere to be able to sleep.'

A soldier who fought at Delville Wood, Lance Corporal Urquhart of the 18th Company, Machine Gun Corps, wrote to Winston Churchill later that summer while in reserve. Churchill's recent speeches in the House of Commons about the severity of the fighting on the Western Front had marked him out as 'the soldiers' friend'. Having been in the trenches 'for almost 15 months', Lance Corporal Urquhart wrote, 'I feel very much run down and the great need of a change. Is there nothing Sir for a British soldier but to carry on no matter how long until he is either killed or wounded. Going out and in the front line trenches week after week month after month under a great strain every time we hear the crash of a bursting shell would it not take effect in some way even on the strongest.' Urquhart had fought at Loos. 'Very few of the old hands are left and the most of them fell by my side in Longueval, and Delville Wood. We have been withdrawn Sir, a new detachment awaits us here, as the few worn out, depressed ones go back.'

The extent of that wearing down was clear from an account that Lieutenant Arthur Preston White sent to his sister about the evening of July 16. 'The men dug on steadily in the rain, each with his rifle slung round him,' White wrote. 'I had to postpone all idea of burying the dead lying about until the next day. There were not many to bury. One Englishman lay down by the wood, while on the road beside it a Bosche ammunition convoy had evidently been caught by our guns. Three smashed wagons, all riddled by pieces of shell, and a dead horse lay there. Amid the debris was a dead Bosche, quite young, a fine strapping fellow when alive, no doubt. His face had a calm, untroubled appearance which is not very usual in men killed suddenly. Rather impressed me, to tell the truth. Feel that I ought to write about two pages of sloppy stuff about him.'

However, White added, 'before the night was over I had something else to do besides philosophising over dead Huns. When we had dug in, I went up to bring back the two men I had sent out in front. I could not find them in the place that I had indicated to them, and had pushed on a bit further. I didn't go very far, though, as bullets began to whiz around. I had evidently come in sight of the Bosche, who could see me, though I could not see them. So I got back fifty yards or so, when I was evidently out of their line of sight, and watched them coming out of a patch of bush near which I had been, with a machine-gun – not without a certain personal interest. When the machine-gun had ceased operations, I made my way back. The two sentries were rather a mystery, but I concluded that they had probably gone west.'

On July 16 a heavy artillery bombardment was launched against the German defences along the ridge dominated by the village of Pozières. Rain and mist made any aerial spotting impossible, however, and, far from the defences being broken up, the Germans, who realized that an attack was imminent, were able to build new machine-gun emplacements. Going up the line that day to Longueval, which his guns had bombarded two days earlier, Lieutenant R. B. Talbot Kelly, Royal Field Artillery, a forward observation officer, saw the horrific detritus of the previous days' fighting. 'Through stifling heat and endless curtains of shells', he later wrote, 'my signallers and I entered the smashed trenches before the village. Here we walked for over half a mile on half-buried German dead. Every step was on ground that yielded to the foot, as the dead body below the layer of clay gave to our weight. Sometimes a boot, removing a lump of earth, disclosed the nose or hand of a corpse below us.'

On the sunken road leading into the village, Talbot Kelly noted that 'the dead were just blasted, swollen and putrid bits of men, now a rotting head, now a pair of fleshless legs hung on a tree stump. In one place I almost tripped upon the barrel of a man's torso, no legs nor arms nor skin had it, and the bowels ran out from the tunnel of the ribs to form a fly-blown horror on the road.' In one large shellhole, 'filled with blood and water, sat a dead Highlander and a dead German, gazing, with sightless yellow eye-balls, into each other's faces'.

After his return to his artillery base, Talbot Kelly sent his sister a graphic account of what he had seen. Despite the horrors of the day, 'still I was glad', he wrote, 'that I was a soldier and would not exchange my experience for anything in the world, for war is surely a terrible but wonderful thing!' Thinking it over on the following day, he realized that what he had seen 'was all unutterably horrible, but yesterday I walked on dead bodies and looked in red, red pools on the road and minded not at all, and hardly thought of sleep until I got back and found it was all I could do to stand! Thus one's job can do away with all feeling and that is the beauty of the work.'

The preliminary British infantry attack against Pozières on the morning of July 17 was driven off by machine-gun fire so intense that the next day's attack was cancelled. Haig was vexed at what he and Rawlinson saw as local failures of command. 'He is as dissatisfied as I am with the action of the 9th Division in failing to occupy the whole of Longueval,' Haig wrote in his diary on July 17. 'I also think there has been a lack of close cooperation between XIII and XV Corps.' Soldiers from both had entered parts of High Wood three days earlier, but failed to connect their trenches. However, in a letter on July 18 to the Master General of Ordnance at the War Office, Major General Sir Stanley von Donop, Haig expressed his confidence in the course of the battle. 'The events of the last fortnight', he wrote, 'have again proved conclusively that the British troops are capable of beating the best German troops. They are fully confident, and so am I, that they can continue to do so, provided we are kept supplied with men, guns, and munitions. Our present success has been gained before we have reached our full strength, and the exploitation of this success is limited only by the extent of our resources.'

The object of Haig's letter was to prevent the diversion of those resources – arms and ammunition – to Russia, in the event of an intensification of its struggle against the Germans on the Eastern Front. Everything was needed on the Somme. When the South Africans were relieved in Delville Wood on the night of July 19, after four days' intense fighting, their dead numbered 766. A quarter of the force had been killed. During the struggle, German artillery fire had reached a deadly climax of 400 shells a minute – more than 6 shells every second.

A Territorial officer, Captain Oscar Viney, of the 'Bucks' Battalion, Oxfordshire and Buckinghamshire Light Infantry, was to recall of the attack three days later from Ovillers towards Pozières, when he was wounded: 'I was lying in the open in a shallow trench about eighteen inches deep only, and about two hundred yards behind the trench D Company had captured. I was well in view of the German trenches on the higher slope beyond (about five hundred yards). I was in considerable pain and took some morphia tablets which we all carried. I could not move much. The battle died down as it always did at breakfast time. I lay in the sun, there were lots of wild flowers and the birds were singing. It all seemed very incongruous. After a little while one of our stretcher-bearers, Cripps, crawled out and put a bandage on my wound, which was not bleeding at all. I realised it was a bad place to get hit and that I had probably got a perforated intestine.'

Captain Viney's account continued: 'I was a bit drowsy with the morphia when I heard some six-inch shells coming over every minute or so, and I realised they were methodically shelling the trench in which we had assembled and in which I was lying. The shells gradually came nearer as they shortened the range and I began to count between the shots and found it was about sixty seconds, i.e. one shell a minute. One fell about ten yards away and I saw one or two bodies go up in the air. A six-inch High Explosive shell makes a good hole about six feet across. The next one fell about five yards away and I waited for the next, very frightened. I found myself counting again and I went on beyond sixty. The next shell never came.'

That evening, Captain Viney found he could move, 'so I crawled back a bit and then walked along a small road by the trench. I was not shot at as they did not waste shells on single people. I eventually found my way to battalion headquarters.'

6

Fromelles: 'A bloody holocaust'

A DIVERSIONARY ATTACK at Fromelles, forty-five miles north of
the Somme, was being planned for 19 July 1916, to be carried
out by Australian troops. The Australians, many of whom had fought
the previous summer, autumn and winter at Gallipoli, treated their
harsh new tasks with characteristic irreverence, singing, to the tune of
'The Church's One Foundation':

> We are the Anzac Army,
> The A.N.Z.A.C.,
> We cannot shoot, we don't salute,
> What bloody good are we?
> And when we get to Ber-lin
> The Kaiser he will say,
> 'Hoch, Hoch! Mein Gott, what a bloody odd lot
> To get six bob a day!'

This was to be the Anzacs' first offensive action on the Western
Front. Its aim was to prevent the Germans from moving reinforcements to the Somme. On the eve of the battle, General H. E. Elliott,
the senior Australian officer at Fromelles, alarmed by the strength of
the German position, asked a British Staff Officer, Major H. C. L.
Howard, for his estimate of how the attack would go. Howard replied,
'If you put it to me like that sir, I must answer you in the same way as
man to man. It is going to be a bloody holocaust.'

General Elliott asked Howard to report his view back to Haig. He
did so, his report coinciding with intelligence information that there
was no longer any urgency for an attack, as German troops were not
being transferred to the Somme, and did not therefore need to be
pinned down. The XI Corps commander, General Sir Richard
Haking, wanted the attack to go on, however, the headquarters record

noting that 'he was quite confident of the success of the operation, and considered that the ammunition at his disposal was ample to put the infantry there and keep them in.'

Pressed to agree to a delay in the attack, Haking was emphatic: 'The troops are worked up to it, were ready and anxious to do it'; he considered that 'any change of plan would have a bad effect on the troops now.'

Two miles south of Fromelles was the high ground of Aubers Ridge, the objective of the attack. The attack itself lay across a low, wet No-Man's Land towards the strongly fortified German salient, the Sugar Loaf, which overlooked the attackers' approach. 'I know you will do your best for the sake of our lads who are fighting down south,' Haking told the Australians on the eve of battle.

In the church tower at Fromelles, reinforced by a concrete stairwell, with a loophole specially designed for an observer, the Germans could see, throughout July 18, the preparations being made for the attack both in the front-line trenches and in those behind them.

The assault began in the late afternoon of July 19, preceded by a day-long artillery barrage. The first Anzac casualties were caused by the Australians' own shells falling short, and by some heavy German artillery fire. When the attack began, the German machine guns in the salient opened fire: the artillery had failed to silence the defending guns before the assault.

An hour after the first men had gone over the top, General Elliott reported, 'Every man who rises is being shot down. Reports from the wounded indicate that the attack is failing from want of support.'

The wounded were streaming back. A British attack on the other side of the salient was also beaten back with heavy British casualties. Then, at a point in the line a little way from the Sugar Loaf, the Australians reached a main German trench. 'The enemy was caught in the act of manning his parapets, and some bitter hand-to-hand fighting followed,' the battle's historian, Captain A. D. Ellis, later wrote. 'It terminated, as all such hand-to-hand fighting terminated throughout the war, in the absolute triumph of the Australians and the extinction or termination of the Germans.'

The Sugar Loaf salient, which General Haking had ordered to be assaulted 'throughout the night', eluded its attackers. As dawn broke, more wounded tried to get back to the Australian lines. Many of them lay out in No-Man's Land, 'trying to call back to us', Sergeant H. R. Williams later wrote, 'and in doing so made of themselves a target for the German machine gunners'. Those who managed to get back were like men 'awakened from a nightmare', Williams recalled. 'The ordeal of the night was plainly visible on all faces, ghastly white showing through masks of grime and dried sweat, eyes glassy, protruding and full of that horror seen only on the faces of men who have lived through a heavy bombardment.'

During the night, one group of Anzacs and some British soldiers had reached the outer wire of the Sugar Loaf, but were unable to push through it. The Australian official war historian, C. E. W. Bean, visiting the battlefield in November 1918, shortly after the Armistice, wrote, 'We found the No-Man's Land simply full of dead. In the narrow sector west of the Sugar Loaf Salient, the skulls and bones and torn uniforms were lying about everywhere. I found a bit of Australian kit lying fifty yards from the corner of the salient, and the bones of an Australian officer and several men within a hundred yards of it. Further round, immediately on their flank, were a few British – you could tell them by their leather equipment.'

Amid the hundreds of cemeteries on the Western Front, VC Corner Australian Cemetery Memorial, a mile north of Fromelles, the only completely Australian cemetery in France, contains the graves of 410 Australians who had fought in the battle. Not a single one of them could be identified, and there are no headstones. Half a mile east of Sugar Loaf there is now an Australian Memorial Park.

Also killed at Fromelles were at least 400 British troops. Nearly 4,000 British and Australian troops were wounded. The German dead and wounded were fewer than 1,500 in all. Four hundred Australians were taken prisoner: they were marched by the Germans through Lille, France's most important industrial city, which had been occupied by Germany from the first months of the war.

The Anzacs were withdrawn. Their casualties had been too heavy to sustain a renewed assault. Captain Wilfrid Miles, the official British military historian of the Battle of the Somme after July 1, reflected a decade later, 'To have delivered battle at all, after hurried preparation, with troops of all arms handicapped by their lack of experience and training in offensive trench warfare, betrayed a grave under-estimate of the enemy's powers of resistance.' Even if the German defences had been 'completely shattered' by the British artillery bombardment and the infantry assault had succeeded, 'it would probably have proved impossible to hold the objective under the concentrated fire of the enemy's artillery directed by excellent observation.'

7

Pozières: 'Death grinning at you from all around'

THE BATTLE AT Fromelles was a brief interlude, fought forty-five miles from the Somme, as an integral part of a vaster battle. Its aim, to keep German troops back from the Somme, had failed. On 18 July 1916 Lieutenant Arthur Preston White, on the Somme battle front, went up the line with the 1st Battalion, Northamptonshire Regiment. 'The shelling soon started again,' he wrote to his sister, 'heavy six-inch "crumps", with an occasional eight-inch. They were a bit wide of us to begin with, but I didn't like it. Still, there was nothing to be done.'

White also told his sister that a 'big observation balloon was up behind the Bosche lines', adding that there was 'a certain song which says, all too truly':

> When the airman from on high
> Sends his signal from the sky
> You'll be coal-boxed by and by
> Never mind!

Being 'coal-boxed' – shelled in dense pattern, in this case as a result of the Germans seeing the British observation balloon over their lines – did indeed happen. 'We watched the "crumps" falling,' White told his sister, 'some short of the trench, some behind it. Then came a tremendous crash in the trench just in front and to the right of us, bits flew all around, and Brown, the orderly, leapt out of the trench and ran along the road with his hand to his head, shouting and raving. He flopped down at our feet crying "I'm a soldier; I'm an old soldier." Swell looked at him; he was hit in the left ear and the side of the head, not very badly apparently. "Get him to the dressing-station" said Swell, to the stretcher-bearers. Then Noaks, who had gone to the bit of injured trench, shouted "Stretcher-bearers!" I ran over and saw a heap of men huddled together; one had no head. The stretcher-bearers came running up, when another shell burst in front. Knight fell forward on his face in the road; Noaks ran to look at him, while I got two men to carry a spare stretcher. Knight was dead; a small piece of shell had entered his head and killed him at once. Another shell burst further down to the right.'

Second Lieutenant Robert Knight, twenty-four years old, lies today in the Contalmaison Château Cemetery. Killed with him that day, and buried in the same cemetery, were Lance Corporal Bromwich and six Northamptonshire Regiment privates, two Gloucestershires, and one South Wales Borderer.

Following Knight's death, Lieutenant White told his sister, Captain Swell then ordered all the officers, 'Get to your platoons!' White admitted, 'I should very much have liked to get to mine, as it was not being shelled, but I hadn't the moral courage to do so & I told Swell that I couldn't very well bolt off out of the shelling. If I had been there to start with, I should have stayed there; I don't go looking for trouble, but as things were, it would look bad. Besides, I might have to take my platoon over the top in a few hours' time, and I didn't want them to think that I suffered from cold feet. So I waited up by Swell, who was walking up and down the road in a very unconcerned way. My walk was less unconcerned, I expect, but I stalked about with my ears pricked up for the whiz that precedes a crump. Then we got into the trench, having done our little promenade for the benefit of the men's nerves and to the detriment of our own. Later the shelling cooled down a bit, and I took the opportunity of a temporary lull to get down to my platoon, where no casualties had been sustained.' During the shelling, White added, 'I had left my haversack and mackintosh by the shelter in which I had slept the previous day. Both were riddled with fragments of shell. I got a dead soldier's overcoat from B Company.'

Captain A. E. Swell was killed in action a month later; he is buried in Bazentin-le-Petit Communal Cemetery Extension.

On July 19, Lieutenant Cecil Lewis was again in the air. 'There was an attack at dawn on High Wood,' he noted in his logbook. 'It seems to have been successful. I personally saw two Battalion ground sheets this side of the wood and flares beyond it. Men could be seen waving handkerchiefs on rifles. Damn fine the Tommy is! The war generally seems to be hanging fire. What about the general attack? Will it go through? Always tomorrow . . .'

In the air, the British had the upper hand over their German aerial adversaries. 'Today four De Havillands met eleven Fokkers,' Lewis noted. 'They downed four and the rest ran.'

Air combat had become a daily feature of the battle. On July 20 an unusual incident took place, recalled by a British army chaplain. 'It was the only occasion', he wrote, 'when we have heard troops in battle break into a spontaneous and whole-hearted cheer, when after a half-hour's single combat on July 20, 1916, a German aeroplane crashed behind our lines, with the full glory of a blood-red sky in the background. The excitement had been so intense that on both sides the gunners had stopped firing to watch.'

Also on July 20, in the struggle to complete the capture of Longueval, the Brigade Major of 76th Brigade, Major William Congreve, the son of the commander of XIII Corps, General Sir Walter Congreve, VC, was shot in the throat and killed by a sniper. He had been in action almost continuously since July 6. He was awarded a Victoria Cross, one of only three sons of Victoria Cross holders to gain it. Unusually, his award was not for one particular act of bravery, but for his having 'by his personal example' inspired those around him 'at critical periods of the operations' during two weeks of fighting.

Major Congreve had just returned from leave when the Battle of the Somme began, having married a month earlier. He had already been awarded the Military Cross in 1915 and the Distinguished Service Order in April 1916 for his actions in the Ypres Salient. On the latter occasion he had captured two German officers and seventy-two men during a rush on a mine crater. After his death, the soldiers of his brigade laid wild poppies and cornflowers on his grave. He lies today in Corbie Communal Cemetery Extension. On his grave are the words 'In memory of my beloved husband and in glorious expectation'.

Two more Victoria Crosses were won on July 20, both in Delville Wood, by Corporal Joseph Davies and Private Albert Hill, both of the 10th (Service) Battalion, Royal Welch Fusiliers. Davies had found himself with eight men surrounded by a larger number of Germans. Taking refuge in a shellhole, he then drove the Germans off, bayoneting several as they retreated. Because he had been badly wounded in the shoulder, the King had to pin the medal on his sling.

Davies and Hill both survived the war. Having been sent by his platoon sergeant to get in touch with his company, Hill was surrounded by eight Germans and drove them off. He then helped the sergeant back to the lines, and later went into No-Man's Land to bring in wounded men. He died in 1971, at the age of seventy-five. At the outbreak of the Second World War he tried to enlist again, in Canada, but was told that his work as a construction worker would be of more use to the war effort.

On July 20 the 11th Field Company, Royal Engineers, were, in the words of Captain Miles, 'pressed into the fight' for High Wood. Its official historian writes that in the ensuing struggle the Corps of Royal Engineers 'lost all its officers and was brought out of action by a corporal'. In order to dig an essential communication trench back from High Wood, to protect those being brought back, two companies of the 18th (Pioneer) Battalion, Middlesex Regiment, all of them roadworkers in civilian life, worked, in the words of one observer, 'as though they were opening up Piccadilly, and took as little notice of German shell-fire as they would have done to London traffic'.

On July 20, Lieutenant Robert Graves was ready to go into action with the 2nd Battalion, Royal Welch Fusiliers, in an attack on High Wood. While he and his men were waiting to move forward, German artillery put down a barrage on the ridge where they were gathered. A third of the battalion were killed or wounded: 'I was one of the casualties,' wrote Graves. Stretcher-bearers took him back to a former German dressing station at the north end of Mametz Wood. For more than twenty-four hours he was unconscious. On July 22 the battalion commander wrote to his mother, 'I much regret to have to write and tell you your son has died of wounds. He was very gallant, and was doing so well, and is a great loss.'

Six or seven officers of the battalion had been killed in the attack, but on July 23 Graves in fact regained consciousness and was taken by ambulance to a casualty clearing station at Heilly. The medics there did not dare lift him into the hospital train to go back to No. 8 Hospital, Rouen, for fear of starting a haemorrhage in the lung. For five days he was on the same stretcher. Then, on July 24 – his twenty-first birthday – an orderly gave him a pencil and paper and he wrote home to his mother, 'I am wounded, but alright.' That letter arrived two days after the colonel's letter announcing his death. But his parents could not tell which had been sent first.

Graves had misdated his letter July 23. 'They could not decide whether my letter had been written just before I died and misdated, or whether I had died just after writing it.' Then a telegram arrived from the Army Council confirming his death, and, Graves wrote, 'they gave me up.' It was only on July 25, when an aunt visited No. 8 Hospital to see a nephew whose leg had just been amputated, that she saw Graves's name listed on the door of the ward. It was she who then wrote to his mother with the news that he really was alive.

The telegrams and letters from the hospitals often brought heart-breaking news. On July 22, Lieutenant A. B. Cohen, West Yorkshire Regiment, who had been brought to the Red Cross Hospital in Rouen after the July 1 attacks, was buried in the nearby Saint-Sever Cemetery. His name is also on the war memorial of his home town, Headingley, near Leeds. More than eleven thousand British soldiers died in the hospitals in Rouen during the First World War.

The attack on Pozières was to be renewed on July 22. In a letter home four days earlier, a young Australian schoolteacher, Private Jack Bourke, had written, 'Why go to war with one another? With these men we have no quarrel.' A German soldier, writing on July 21, headed his letter 'In Hell's Trenches', and added, 'It is not really a trench, but a little ditch shattered with shells – not the slightest cover and no protection. We have lost fifty men in two days and life is unendurable.'

Even before any new assault, the death toll was unremitting. Among those killed on July 21 was Lieutenant Henry Webber. Sixty-eight years old, he is believed to be the oldest soldier killed on the Somme, or indeed on any of the war fronts. His grave is in Dartmoor Cemetery, just outside Albert. A member of the Surrey Stag Hunt, and a good horseman, he had persuaded the War Office in London to let him enlist. As first-line transport officer of the 7th Battalion, South Lancashire Regiment, he was returning from taking rations up to Mametz Wood when he was killed by a shell – while talking to his commanding officer. Three of his sons were serving in the army. All three survived the war.

★

For the British forces to maintain the offensive required a vast movement of men and supplies. The records kept by Traffic Control at
Fricourt for the twenty-four hours starting at nine in the morning of
July 21 show, with all the precision of British military officialdom, that
26,536 soldiers went through the control point, as did more than 5,000
horses and riders, 3,000 horse-drawn wagons, 813 motor lorries, 617
motor cycles, 568 motor cars and 330 motor ambulances. Because of
German shelling with tear gas, gas masks had to be worn from ten that
evening until four in the morning.

The renewed attack on Pozières began on July 22. German troops
had used the six days since the previous attack to place a network of
machine-gun posts in shellholes in front of their main defences. The
British night-time artillery bombardment, seen from afar, turned the
whole skyline into what an Australian soldier called 'one flickering
band of light'. As the newly arrived Australian Corps went into action
there was little time or mood for mercy. One Australian officer,
Lieutenant E. W. D. Laing, later recalled a German soldier who 'tried
to give himself up as soon as he saw our chaps on him. "Come out,
you . . .", yelled one of my men. I heard him, rushed back shouting
at the chap to shoot the swine or I would – so he got him.'

Six Germans were killed in that sweep, and eighteen captured. 'The
men had great sport chucking bombs down any hole they saw,' Laing
remembered. In the corner of one dugout, Private Bourke found
some gift boxes of cake addressed in a child's handwriting. 'In another
corner was a coat rolled up,' he wrote in a letter home. 'I opened it
and found it stained with blood. Right between the shoulders was a
burnt shrapnel hole, telling a tragic tale. The owner of the coat was a
German and some might say, not entitled to much sympathy. Perhaps
he was not, but I could not help thinking sadly of the little girl or boy
who had sent him the cakes.'

This was the second Australian action on the Western Front in
three days. Contemporary letters and later recollections all testify to
the severity and cruelty of the fighting. Lieutenant Colonel Iven
Makay recalled how, as the Australians advanced, many Germans
'remained in their dugouts, terrified and had to be bombed or bayoneted out. Some never came out. A number of the German prisoners would not, through pure fright, cross No-Man's Land. They had
to be killed.'

Among those killed on July 22, more than a mile behind the British front line, was the commander of the 34th Division, Major General Ingouville-Williams, known to his men as Inky Bill. He had been reconnoitring the area to the south of Mametz Wood and was walking back to his car when he was hit by a shell. He was fifty-four years old. He is buried in the Warloy-Baillon Communal Cemetery Extension.

During the fighting on July 22, one of Second Lieutenant J. R. R. Tolkien's best friends, Lieutenant Ralph Payton, Royal Warwickshire Regiment, was killed in action. Two days later Tolkien went up to the trenches for the second time. His task as signals officer was to run communications to the brigade command post a mile and a half away.

Coming out of the line on July 25, Lieutenant Arthur Preston White, after writing to his sister of his battalion's heavy losses, told her that during the previous few weeks he had worn '(a) My best Burberry, originally someone else's, lost while on the move . . . (b) A government mackintosh, riddled with bits of shell and replaced by (c) A dead officer's overcoat, later exchanged for (d) A wounded officer's mackintosh'.

The assault on Pozières was renewed before dawn on July 23. The official historian Captain Miles noted that, as the German artillery bombardment had cut all the signal wire, the Australian troops 'had to rely for information upon pigeons, runners, and when morning came, the reports of low-flying aeroplanes'. Soon after dawn the Royal Flying Corps pilots located the position of the German forward troops, 'taking great risks in the process'.

Two Australian soldiers, twenty-three-year-old Second Lieutenant Arthur Blackburn and twenty-year-old Private John Leak, were awarded the Victoria Cross for their actions at Pozières. Blackburn led the capture of 120 yards of German trench, and then a further 120 yards, enabling communications to be established with another battalion. Leak seized a German bombing post, and then, when driven out, was the last to withdraw, still throwing his bombs. In the words of his citation, 'His courage had such an effect on the enemy that when reinforcements arrived, the whole trench was recaptured.' Both men survived the war, and died in Australia: Blackburn in 1960, Leak in 1972.

The battle for Pozières continued without abatement. Among those killed on July 25 was thirty-three-year-old Second Lieutenant Henry Teed, a British artist of distinction. Three months later, in London, his works were a feature of the autumn exhibition of the Royal Society of British Artists. His body was never found; his name is on the Thiepval Memorial. Also in action that day, Lance Corporal E. Moorhead later recalled how, after his company had entered a deserted German trench, a captain 'filled to the neck with rum' ordered the men to continue 'and dashed ahead again. Finally the survivors came back in a panic, calling out we must retreat, we're all cut up, the Germans were on us etc etc. The Captain had been shot through the heart on the barbed wire.'

Not long afterwards the Germans attacked, but the impetus of their thrust was broken by the Australian artillery. 'When the Huns came into view over the crest in twos and threes or singly, some with packs, probably filled with bombs, others with fixed bayonets,' Corporal Moorhead wrote, 'we lined the parapet like an excited crowd and blazed like hell at them, knocking them over like rabbits, not a man getting away so far as I could see. The range was about 400 yards, and as each man appeared he got 100 bullets in him. One officer appeared and waved his men forward in a lordly way, and then collapsed like a bag, filled with our lead. I fired about thirty rounds and did my share.'

A little while later there was a moment of black humour. 'One unfortunate Boche,' Moorhead recalled, 'having run the gauntlet of our rifle fire, was getting away apparently only slightly wounded when one of our shells burst on him as though aimed, and he went up blown to pieces. Well, we cheered and laughed at the happening as though it was the funniest thing in the world.'

Not so humorous was the experience of an Australian officer, Captain W. G. M. Claridge, who was wounded that day and sent to hospital in England. 'I am not going to tell a lie and say I wasn't afraid,' Claridge wrote to his parents two weeks after the battle, 'because I was and who wouldn't be with Death grinning at you from all around and hellish 5.9 inch shells shrieking through the air and shrapnel dealing death all round. I don't know how long I stood it without breaking.' He had been buried three times by earth thrown up by the shelling, and was 'very thankful to get my wound as it got me out of the firing line for a rest'.

In the Pozières British Military Cemetery is a memorial to 14,691 soldiers of the Fourth and Reserve (later Fifth) Armies killed while attacking the ridge in 1916, 1917 and 1918, and who have no known grave. There are also 690 named Australian headstones.

On the night of July 25, after Haig had visited the headquarters of the Australian Corps at Contay, he wrote in his diary, 'The situation seems all very new and strange to Australian HQ. The fighting here and the shellfire is much more severe than anything experienced at Gallipoli! The German, too, is a very different enemy to the Turk!' Haig added, in explanation of the setbacks on July 25, 'The hostile shelling has been very severe against Pozières today, and owing to clouds observation was bad, and our counter-battery work could not be carried out effectively.'

General Rawlinson, commenting in his diary that night on a documentary film of the battle that had just been compiled, wrote, 'Some of it very good but I cut out many of the horrors in dead and wounded.' Other 'horrors' were to be stressed and widely publicised: these were any actions by the Germans that made the fight against them seem justified.

That this was a 'just war' was self-evident to each of the combatants − it gave them their cause and their zeal − but nevertheless it helped to be able to stress the point whenever possible. On July 27 the Germans, who a year earlier had executed a British nurse, Edith Cavell, in Brussels, gave further powerful ammunition to their enemies. That day, in Bruges, they executed a captured British merchant-navy officer, Captain Charles Fryatt. While in command of the Great Eastern Railway steamer *Brussels*, Fryatt tried to ram a German submarine. His exploit made him a hero in Britain. Ten weeks later the Germans boarded the *Brussels* and seized Fryatt during one of his steamer's regular twice-weekly crossings from Harwich to Hook of Holland (Holland being neutral). Accused of being a 'pirate' for trying to ram the German submarine, he was found guilty and shot. The fact that Germany had already occupied Belgium for two years was cruelly stressed by Fryatt's execution being held on Belgium's national day.

On the Somme, British Royal Marine gunners painted a slogan on the base of their heaviest, fifteen-inch, shells: 'To Captain Fryatt's murderers'.

8

The battle continues: 'A little uneasy in regard to the situation'

O N 27 JULY 1916 the British forces made one final attempt to drive the Germans from the north end of Longueval and from their stronghold at the edge of Delville Wood, neither of which had been captured in the attack on July 14. By evening the Germans had been forced to abandon both positions. Haig was particularly pleased that the soldiers driven out of Delville Wood were 'the famous 5th German Division (Brandenburgers)'.

On the following day, July 28, the Brandenburgers were driven out of their positions north of Longueval. Two German counter-attacks on Delville Wood that day were driven off. Three German officers and 158 men were captured. 'They said they were the only survivors,' Haig noted in his diary. 'They were greatly depressed and said "Germany is beaten." This is the first time we have taken German officers who have arrived at that opinion.'

Writing to his parents on July 28, a young infantryman, George Leigh-Mallory, described life in the trenches as 'as harrowing as you can imagine when one sees the dead and the dying and hears of regiments being cut up by machine guns'. He added, 'I am not one of the optimists about the war and shall be quite surprised if it ends before Xmas. I suppose we may at any moment hear very good news from Russia – but it's a very long time coming and the German war machine must be far from run down if he can put up the fight he has done.' Both on the Russian Front and on the Somme, the Germans were fighting with tenacity.

George Leigh-Mallory disappeared while climbing Mount Everest in 1924. His brother Trafford, a First World War pilot, and a leading airman in the Second World War (becoming Commander-in-Chief of Fighter Command), was killed in an air crash in November 1944 while on his way to take up a Far Eastern command.

★

On the evening of July 28, a few hours before the next attack was to start, Haig was told by General Birch, his artillery chief, that the Australians would move forward without artillery support as 'they did not believe machine-gun fire could do them much harm'. Haig commented in his diary, 'The Australians are splendid fellows but very ignorant.'

Shortly after midnight on July 28/29, following an intense artillery bombardment the previous day, with the darkness lit by flares and star shells, the 2nd Australian Division attacked the German trenches between the village of Pozières and the Pozières windmill. The village was captured, but the three lines of German trenches beyond it were not. Some of the Australians entered the first line of trenches, and two companies pushed forward into the second trench, but the only battalion to reach the objective had to pull back because it had no support from the battalion that was meant to be alongside it.

The failure of the Australians to reach their objective was a cause for concern at Val Vion. 'From several reports,' Haig noted the next morning, 'I think the cause was due to want of thorough preparation.' He then set out four reasons for the failure:

1. The attacking troops were not formed up square opposite their objective. Troops started from the railway line and attacked against three fronts . . . Gaps occurred between the flanks of the three attacks. This must happen unless special detachments are made to fill the larger front.
2. The advance was made in the dark for a distance of 700 yards (over ground covered with shellholes and Enemy had thrown out 'knife rests' of wire) and then the men were expected to charge home against the Enemy's trench. Our experience is that about 150 yards is the limit for a successful charge. In this case it was hoped to advance unobserved in the dark to that distance and form up prior to the charge.
3. One of our brigades had spent the day two miles in rear and only marched up to Pozières after dark so, although the officers had reconnoitred their objective, the bulk of the troops were quite ignorant of the task before them.
4. The artillery bombardment was only for 'one minute' before the attack, which was made soon after midnight.

Visiting the headquarters of the Reserve Army at Toutencourt on July 29, Haig urged General Gough and his senior General Staff Officer, Lieutenant Colonel Neil Malcolm, 'that they must supervise more closely the plans of the Anzac Corps'. Some of the corps' divisional generals, Haig added, 'were so ignorant and (like many Colonials) so conceited' that they could not be trusted to work out a plan of attack.

From Reserve Army headquarters, Haig went on to the Australian Corps headquarters at Contay, where he saw General Birdwood and his Chief Staff Officer, General Brudenell White. 'The latter seems a very sound capable fellow,' Haig noted in his diary, 'and assured me that they had learned a lesson, and would be more thorough in future. Luckily, their losses had been fairly small considering the operation and the numbers involved.' There had been about a thousand dead and wounded 'for the whole twenty-four hours'.

The capture of Pozières could not be belittled; but, while he was at Contay, Haig pointed out to Birdwood that this success was 'thanks to a very thorough artillery preparation' – by the Royal Artillery the previous day. Haig added that the French had often spent a fortnight in capturing such villages. 'Still, the capture of Pozières by the Australians would live in history! They must not however underestimate the Enemy or his power of defence, machine guns etc.' Haig added that he had given Birdwood 'a very experienced and capable' artillery commander, a British officer, Brigadier General Napier – hitherto the General Officer Commanding the Heavy Artillery of XV Corps, 'and he must trust him'. Haig added, 'Birdwood was very grateful for my visit and my remarks.'

On his return to Val Vion on the evening of July 29, Haig found awaiting him a letter from London, from General Sir William Robertson, Chief of the Imperial General Staff. Robertson warned Haig, as Haig noted in his diary, that ' "The powers that be" are beginning to get a little uneasy in regard to the situation.' The concern was 'Whether a loss of say 300,000 men will lead to really great results, because if not, we ought to be content with something less than we are now doing.' These same powers that be, Robertson informed Haig, 'are constantly enquiring why we are fighting and the French are not. It is thought that the primary object – relief of pressure on Verdun – has to some extent been achieved.'

Haig had no doubt that the Somme offensive should continue. 'In another six weeks,' he replied, 'the Enemy should be hard put to find men. The maintenance of a steady offensive pressure will result eventually in his complete overthrow.' That 'steady offensive pressure' continued, but with no decisive result, and a steady mounting up of British casualties.

On July 29, near Rawlinson's headquarters at Querrieu, British cavalry practised bringing a heavy machine gun into action. The hopes for a cavalry breakthrough could not be set aside; they were an integral part of the battle plan from its inception.

That night, near Bazentin-le-Petit, the forty men of Sections Three and Four of the 82nd Field Company, Royal Engineers, who were laying barbed wire, came under intense German shell and machine-gun fire. Six men were killed, their names being listed on a memorial that was set up in their honour seventy three years after the battle. Also commemorated on the memorial are the six Royal Engineers killed the previous night. Nineteen men were wounded. The bodies of all but two of the dead disappeared in the later fighting; their names are listed on the Thiepval Memorial.

Also never found were seven of the nine Royal Engineers who were killed after they had volunteered to build a strongpoint in front of Bazentin-le-Petit village when the infantrymen working on its construction were withdrawn to prepare for the next assault. A private memorial to 'Nine Brave Men', erected in 1917, survives to this day. The men – who were killed between July 29 and 31 – were R. F. Choat, a carpenter from Moulsham, C. W. Vernon from Wakefield, J. Joiner from Maidstone, J. Higgins from Glasgow, W. Haviland from Birmingham, A. Robotham from London, F. Blakeley from Preston, C. D. Ellison from Hednesford in Staffordshire, and Private F. Tredigo, a Cornishman living in Nottingham. All but Ellison and Higgins are remembered on the Thiepval Memorial; Ellison is buried in Caterpillar Valley Cemetery near where he was killed, and Higgins in Bécourt Military Cemetery just outside Albert.

On July 30, four British battalions, among them three Liverpool Pals battalions, attacked the village of Guillemont, which had resisted a similar attack a week earlier. The dense fog made the preliminary British artillery preparations almost valueless, as many German soldiers left their trenches unseen, and took shelter in No-Man's Land. As the attackers went forward the fog did not protect them, however. The German machine-gunners knew in which direction the attack must come, and fired into the advancing men, who could not see from where their adversary's fire came. One group of Pals, reaching the German front line, found more than sixty Germans in the bottom of a trench, apparently sheltering from the bombardment. Only one prisoner was taken. This was presumably so that he could be interrogated for the purposes of intelligence.

Letters written by the attackers immediately after the unsuccessful battle for Guillemont gave a picture of the randomness of death. Lance Corporal H. Foster described how 'Our sergeant had just given us our rum ration and gone to the shellhole where the gun team were, and here, unfortunately, one gas shell found its mark, landing in the centre of the gunners. Poor lads, it wiped the whole of them out.'

Corporal G. E. Hemingway wrote an account of the death of his friend Lance Corporal J. Quinn, in one of the many hundreds of thousands of letters sent home during the war to describe to a wife or parent the fate of his or her loved one: 'About half way across No-Man's Land, whilst waiting in a shellhole for one of our own barrages to lift, I became aware of the fact that Joe was in the next hole to mine, and we smiled encouragement to each other. Enemy machine guns were sweeping the whole place with explosive bullets, and there was a fearful noise, and speech was impossible. The streams of death whistled over our shellholes, coming from the left flank, and Joe's hole being the left of mine, he received the bullet in his side. He slipped away quietly – just a yearning glance, a feeble clutching at space, and then a gentle sinking into oblivion, with his head on his arm.'

The twenty-six-year-old James Quinn is buried in the war cemetery at Warloy-Baillon.

Among the members of the Liverpool Pals killed at Guillemont on July 30 was Lance Corporal Stephen Atherton. His grave is in Guillemont Road Cemetery. For fifteen years before the war, Atherton had been a player and then groundsman for the Oxton Cricket Club in Birkenhead. Although a married man, he had been among the first to volunteer. He left a widow and four daughters, the eldest seven years old, the youngest two and a half. On his behalf the club made a special appeal for funds 'to tide the Widow over the next six years' or until her children 'are in a position to assist her by their own earnings'.

Five hundred men of the 2,500-strong Liverpool Pals battalions were killed that day, plunging Merseyside into deep mourning. Many of the bodies of the dead lay, unrecoverable, in machine-gun-raked No-Man's Land, until they were reduced to skeletons by the depredations of rats and the intensity of the August sun. Some, submerged and buried under the continually shell-shattered earth, were not discovered until more than a decade after the war.

That summer there was violent activity on every European war front – on the Russian Front, on the Italian Front and at Salonika – but no decisive change in the battle lines. On the Somme, as at Verdun, the German Army, far from marching from triumph to triumph, was being bled to death. Haig's conviction that continued British assaults would lead to Germany's 'overthrow' led him to continue to try, by steady stages, to reach the objectives he had set for the first day of battle on July 1.

On July 31 Haig received encouraging news from General Trenchard, the General Officer Commanding the Royal Flying Corps. Trenchard reported that the Germans had concentrated their aircraft on the Somme front, so that 'very few' were available to harass the French at Verdun. Even on the British front, Trenchard noted, British planes had made 431 separate flights over the German lines, while only 8 German planes crossed the British lines. British aircraft were also operating towards Ghent and Brussels, forcing the Germans to detach aircraft from the battle area to guard their important munitions and supply depots in the rear.

Slowly, despite repeated counter-attacks, the Germans were being pushed back across the Somme battlefield. On July 31, at his desk in Berlin, the head of the German Raw Materials Board, Walther Rathenau, wrote in his diary that the 'delirious exaltation' he had witnessed in the streets two years earlier had seemed to him even then 'a dance of death', an overture to a doom that would be 'dark and dreadful'.

That day at Bazentin-le-Petit, twenty-six-year-old Private James Miller of the 7th Battalion, King's Own (Royal Lancaster) Regiment, set off under shell and rifle fire with a message, instructed to bring back the reply 'at all costs'. Almost immediately a German rifleman shot him in the back, the bullet exiting from his stomach. In spite of this, Miller compressed the gaping wound with one hand, delivered the message, and staggered back with the answer. He died at the feet of the officer to whom he delivered it. He was awarded the Victoria Cross. His body lies today on the Somme, in Dartmoor Cemetery, with the insignia of the Victoria Cross engraved on the tombstone below his regimental badge.

In schools throughout Britain, July 1916 ended with a renewed sense of loss. From St Edward's School, Oxford, a preparatory school, twelve former students were killed on the Somme, five on July 1, among them twenty-five-year-old Lieutenant Thomas Houghton, Royal Irish Rifles, who was killed by machine-gun fire leading his platoon. Three officers and his batman were wounded trying to help him. He is buried in Hamel Military Cemetery.

At the annual speech day at King Edward's School, Birmingham, there was a minute's silence for the forty-two Old Edwardians who had been killed in the previous year. Among those killed on the Somme were Robert Gilson and Ralph Payton, close schoolfriends of Tolkien and of another young officer then at the front, G. B. Smith. On learning of the death of Gilson, the first of the four friends to be killed in action, Smith wrote:

> Let us tell quiet stories of kind eyes
>   And placid brows where peace and learning sate:
> Of misty gardens under evening skies
>   Where four would walk of old, with steps sedate.
>
> Let's have no word of all the sweat and blood,
>   Of all the noise and strife and dust and smoke
> (We who have seen Death surging like a flood,
>   Wave upon wave, that leaped and raced and broke).
>
> Or let's sit quietly, we three together,
>   Around a wide hearth-fire that's glowing red,
> Giving no thought to all the stormy weather
>   That flies above the roof-tree overhead.
>
> And he, the fourth, that lies all silently
>   In some far-distant and untended grave,

Under the shadow of a shattered tree,
  Shall leave the company of the hapless brave,

And draw nigh unto us for memory's sake,
  Because a look, a word, a deed, a friend,
Are bound with cords that never a man may break,
  Unto his heart for ever, until the end.

During the struggles of July 1916, more than half of the bodies of those killed were never identified; many were never found. Among those with no known grave was the second of Tolkien's four friends, Ralph Payton. His name is inscribed on the Thiepval Memorial to the Missing.

9

Criticism and commitment: 'Under no circumstances must we relax our effort'

O N 1 AUGUST 1916 the War Committee in London had before it a memorandum by Winston Churchill, commenting critically about the first month of fighting on the Somme. Churchill had been without government office for nine months, and his effort was submitted to the committee by his friend F. E. Smith, recently brought into the Cabinet as Attorney General, who suggested in a covering note that Churchill's views 'would interest my colleagues and enable them to apply their minds to the situation which develops from day to day with both the official and a critical view before them'.

Churchill's critical view was outspoken. 'We have not conquered in a month's fighting as much ground as we were expected to gain in the first two hours,' he wrote. 'We have not advanced three miles in the direct line at any point. We have only penetrated to that depth on a front of 8,000 or 10,000 yards. Penetration upon so narrow a front is quite useless for the purpose of breaking the line. It would be fatal to advance through a gap of this small size, which could be swept by a cross fire of artillery.'

In four weeks the British forces had advanced less than a mile. Unless a gap of at least twenty miles could be opened, Churchill argued, 'no large force could be put through.' Even then it would have to fight a 'manoeuvre battle', for which neither its training nor the experience of its staffs had prepared it.

Churchill was convinced that it was a mistake to continue the Somme offensive. The month that had passed since the start of the battle had enabled the enemy to make 'whatever preparations behind his original lines he may think necessary'. Those defences would be formidable. 'He is already defending a 500-mile front in France alone, and the construction of extra lines about ten miles long to loop in the small sector now under attack is no appreciable strain on his labour or trench stores. He could quite easily by now have converted the whole countryside in front of our attack into successive lines of defence and fortified posts.'

Churchill, who had served for almost five months on the Western Front, from January to May 1916, had first-hand experience of the well-fortified German trench system. He also knew the power of artillery in the defensive. 'A very powerful hostile artillery has now been assembled against us,' he wrote, 'and this will greatly aggravate the difficulties of further advance.'

Another point that Churchill made concerned the objective of the battle. The Allied armies on the Somme, he wrote, were not making 'for any point of strategic or political consequence'. The retention of Verdun 'at least would be a trophy – to which sentiment on both sides has become mistakenly attached. But what are Péronne and Bapaume, even if we were likely to take them?' He went on to warn, 'The open country towards which we are struggling by inches is capable of entrenched defence at every step, and is utterly devoid of military significance.'

Surprise had been lost. There had been no 'overwhelming concentration of artillery on particular points' as had characterized the German operations against Verdun. 'We are using up division after division – not only those originally concentrated for the attack, but many taken from all parts of the line. After being put through the mill and losing perhaps half of their infantry and two-thirds of their infantry officers, these shattered divisions will take several months to recover, especially as they will in many cases have to go into the trenches at once. Thus the pent-up energies of the army are being dissipated, and if the process is allowed to go on, the enemy will not be under the need of keeping so many troops at our front as heretofore. He will then be able to restore or sustain the situation against Russia.'

Like Lloyd George in his initial hesitation before the Battle of the Somme, Churchill believed that the immediate Allied need was to prevent a German victory over Russia in the East. Such a victory would release huge quantities of German troops to move against the Allied forces in the West – as was to happen with disastrous effect in March 1918. But his arguments did not deter Haig, whose friend Lord Esher commented with shrewd realism that the combination of Churchill and F. E. Smith 'can do no harm, so long as fortune favours us in the Field', and that such critics 'only become formidable during the inevitable ebb of the tide of success'.

At the meeting of the War Committee that received Churchill's criticisms, General Robertson presented a survey of the previous weeks of battle. Haig, he said, was doing all he could; he could not do more and he could not do less. British casualties had been heavy, but they included 56,000 sustained on the first day, whereas during the last week they had amounted to 18,000. He calculated – without explaining the basis for his calculation – that German losses were at least 1.25 million, 'of which 600,000 were a dead loss', as against total losses 'on our side' of 160,000. Joffre had spoken highly of the British contribution, saying that 'we had killed more Germans than the French.'

As to what these actual British and supposed German casualties had accomplished, Robertson told the War Committee, 'We had started operations to relieve Verdun, and to prevent the move of troops to Russia'. Since the opening of the campaign, 'there had been no large attacks against Verdun.' As for the Eastern Front, as a consequence of Russia's offensive the Austro-Hungarians 'were now in a bad way', whereas 'if we had not been fighting' on the Somme the Habsburg forces would have received great assistance from their German allies.

No one at the War Committee pointed to the discrepancies between the casualty balances given by Robertson and by Churchill, who had asserted, with far greater accuracy, that the figures were about equal. Nor did the War Committee question whether Robertson's extraordinarily exaggerated total of 1.25 million German casualties had been incurred against the British alone, or against the British and the French combined, or whether it applied just to the Somme, or to the entire Western Front.

When General Foch, the commander of the French forces on the Somme, visited Haig at Val Vion on August 1, he brought good news. He had appointed General Fayolle, one of the most successful army commanders of July 1, to fight alongside the British between the British right flank and the north bank of the river. This would give the British in that sector the benefit of the French heavy artillery.

Haig told Foch that, once the line Pozières–Morval–Sailly-Saillisel had been reached, the combined Anglo-French army could strike northward. For this advance he considered that the tanks, which had not yet appeared on the battlefield, 'would be most useful'. But when he asked if Foch's forces would have them, 'Foch did not seem to know about these machines.' Foch did agree, however, 'to press for them'.

On August 2, Haig informed his army commanders that the Germans had 'recovered to a great extent from the disorganisation' inflicted on them in early July. He therefore instructed them that German positions could not be attacked 'without careful and methodical preparation'. Good starting positions must be secured for a major attack in the future.

On August 5 the War Committee met again in London, to hear Robertson read out Haig's rebuttal of Churchill's criticisms. Haig was clear in the reasons why the Somme offensive had been right, and effective, and must go on: 'First: The pressure on Verdun had been relieved, and the situation was no longer regarded as serious by the French authorities. Second: The Russian front would certainly have been reinforced' – by the Germans – 'and Russia would not have got on as she had. Third: There was a general good moral effect.' In the language of the time, the word 'moral' had the same meaning as 'morale' today. Haig added, 'The moral and material results had brought the Allies forward on the way to victory. The Germans regarded the Somme operations as very serious.'

Haig was emphatic that 'Under no circumstances must we relax our effort, and we must retain the offensive. Our loss had been 120,000 in the last month more than if we had not attacked which could not be considered unduly heavy. Our troops were in excellent heart. We should maintain a vigorous offensive well into the autumn, and prepare for a further campaign next year.'

Asquith commented briefly that Haig's arguments were 'very satisfactory'. Robertson was then instructed by the War Committee to send Haig a message 'assuring him that he might count on full support from home'.

The weather was the most gorgeous summer sunshine – 'not the weather for killing people', Captain Harold Macmillan, in reserve with the 4th Battalion, Grenadier Guards, west of Beaumont-Hamel, wrote to his mother on August 2. Two days later, on August 4 – the second anniversary of Britain's declaration of war on Germany – the 13th

Battalion, Durham Light Infantry, made two attacks on the German trench facing them. The second attack, with bombs, was a success, and a hundred yards of trench was captured. During this second attack a noted composer, thirty-one-year-old Lieutenant George Butterworth, was killed. The trench was later named after him as a private memorial. 'His hastily buried body was subsequently lost,' write Major and Mrs Holt, 'and Butterworth is commemorated on the Thiepval Memorial. It is a hauntingly beautiful experience to take a small tape recorder with a cassette of one of Butterworth's works, find his name on the memorial, and quietly listen to the music under the awe-inspiring arches of Lutyens' massive creation.'

There are twenty Butterworths whose names are on the Thiepval Memorial, each of whom has no known grave. Lieutenant George Butterworth's name is on Pier 14A, Face 15C.

On the night of August 4, the Australian 2nd Division attacked north of Pozières along a 2,000-yard front. Its attack was preceded by a forty-eight-hour artillery bombardment, with, as Haig noted, 'occasional bursts of 18-pounder to make the Enemy expect an attack and man his trenches'. At nine that evening, as Haig wrote in his diary, 'an intensive barrage with 18-pounder shrapnel was opened, behind which our infantry advanced, close up to our shells, and entered Enemy's trench before he had become aware of the attack. In some cases the Enemy was engaged in repairing the damage caused by our bombardment during the day when our real attack and barrage caught him.'

Having succeeded in their objective, the capture of part of the German second line of trenches, the Australians then beat off three German counter-attacks. To the left of the Australians, the 12th (Eastern) Division seized a further thousand-yard length of the German second line.

On August 6, the day after this successful battle, General Joffre appeared at Haig's chateau. He was in a far less confrontational mood than at the time of his previous visit, and brought with him a box containing fifty Croix de Guerre – 'for me to distribute as I thought right', Haig noted in his diary. Haig added, 'I managed to get together 10 officers who had rendered "good service under fire" and he presented the crosses to them himself.'

★

The Germans were suffering considerable casualties and distress. One German officer wrote in his diary that because of the enemy artillery fire his infantry unit 'lost probably half of its men, if not more. Those who survived are at this moment not men, but more or less finished beings, fit neither to defend nor attack. Officers whom I once knew as very vigorous are openly sobbing.'

Second Lieutenant Tolkien was among the British troops going into the front line on August 6, having attended Roman Catholic Mass in the village of Bertrancourt the previous day. This was his third spell of front-line duty. The line west of Beaumont-Hamel proved to be a quiet sector. During the five days that his battalion, the 11th Lancashire Fusiliers, was in the line, four men were killed.

Further south, on August 6, there was intense activity. Although severely wounded in the foot, Private William Short of the 8th Battalion, Yorkshire Regiment, refused to go back for medical attention, and continued to bomb the enemy trenches at Munster Alley. Eventually his leg was shattered and he could not remain standing. Lying down in the trench, he continued to adjust detonators and straighten bomb pins for his comrades, until he died of his wounds. He was awarded the Victoria Cross. His grave is in the Contalmaison Château Cemetery.

On August 7, the Germans launched a sustained attack against the 4th Australian Division north of Pozières. They were driven off, much credit being given to the efforts of Lieutenant Albert Jacka, who had earlier won a Victoria Cross at Gallipoli. During the battle, Jacka was wounded seven times. One bullet went straight through his chest and out of his back. After three and a half months in hospital, first in France and then in England, he returned to his battalion, where many felt that his deeds on August 7 deserved a bar to his Victoria Cross. Instead, he was awarded a Military Cross. He survived the war, living in Melbourne, where he died in 1932, at the age of thirty-nine. His last words, to his father, were, 'I'm still fighting, Dad.'

On August 8, after making an official report on the situation at the front line, Lieutenant Arthur Preston White wrote to his sister of how 'Parties were at work everywhere clearing up the battlefield. Much of their work was done, but here and there bodies were still lying where they had fallen, the faces all blackened by this time. An occasional shell from beyond the ridge that lay in front of us served to remind us that not the whole of the Bosche army had been wiped out yet.' Going even further forward 'we ran into a bunch of shells, but we jolly soon ran out again.'

As the fighting on the Somme continued, thousands of men left the battlefield with their nerves shattered. Reporting sick and being asked what had happened, most would answer, 'Shell shock.' With some, this was clearly the case, but for the medical authorities it was not necessarily so. The British Army official medical historian states, 'To explain to a man that his symptoms were the result of disordered emotional conditions due to his rough experience in the line, and not, as he imagined, to some serious disturbance of his nervous system produced by bursting shells, became the most frequent and successful form of psychotherapy. The simplicity of its character in no way detracted from its value, and it not infrequently ended in the man coming forward voluntarily for duty, after having been given a much needed fortnight's rest in hospital.'

Still, the genuine cases of shell shock were also growing, reaching more than fifty thousand by the end of the war. It was during the Battle of the Somme that, because of the intensification of nervous break-downs and shell shock, special centres were opened in each army area for diagnosis and treatment. The view of the military authorities, as the official medical history emphasizes, was that the subject of mental collapse was 'so bound up with the maintenance of morale in the army that every soldier who is non-effective owing to nervous breakdown must be made the subject of careful enquiry. In no case is he to be evacuated to base unless his condition warrants such a procedure.'

On 8 August 1916, British forces on the Somme launched a further attack against the village of Guillemont. The attack, planned at the last moment, lacked adequate artillery preparation, and was a failure. As the soldiers left their trenches, they found that the German artillery was hitting No-Man's Land with great accuracy. As they continued their advance along the caustically named Death Valley they were met by intense German machine-gun fire. On the sector being fought over by a Liverpool Scottish battalion, 10 of their 20 officers, and 96 of their 600 men, were killed or missing. The battalion attacked three times before being forced to fall back.

That evening, in search of wounded men lying out on the battlefield, the battalion's medical officer, Captain Noel Chavasse, led a group of volunteers into No-Man's Land. 'We collected a lot of identification discs,' he wrote home, 'and so cut down the tragic missing list.' The word 'missing' meant, in virtually every case, killed without identifiable trace being found.

Among the twenty wounded men whom Chavasse brought back were three who had been lying only twenty-five yards from the German front line. Two of them died later. 'The amazing thing about this rescue exploit', one soldier recalled of Chavasse, 'was that he carried and used his electric torch as he walked about between the trenches, whistling and calling out to wounded men to indicate their whereabouts, and so be brought in. Ignoring the snipers' bullets and any sporadic fusillade, he carried on with his work of succour throughout the hours of darkness.' At one point the group of rescuers found themselves right up against a German trench. The Germans opened fire, and Chavasse was wounded in the thigh. For his work that night he was awarded the Victoria Cross.

A year later, on the Belgian sector of the Western Front, Chavasse, after being wounded while carrying a wounded soldier back to safety, continued to go out under heavy fire to search for more wounded men. He died of his wounds, and was posthumously awarded a second Victoria Cross, one of only three men in a hundred and fifty years to receive that double honour.

On August 10, the documentary film that had been made of the battle, with its sequence of the mine detonation at Hawthorn Ridge, was screened to an invited audience at the Scala Theatre in London. Eleven days later it was shown simultaneously in thirty-four London cinemas, opening in provincial cities the following week. Members of the Royal Family were given a private screening at Windsor Castle in September. It was eventually shown in eighteen Allied countries.

The film, entitled *The Battle of the Somme*, had been commissioned by the government. Two official War Office cinematographers, Geoffrey Malins and John McDowell, were given the task of compiling it. The completed film spanned five reels and lasted just over an hour. Despite being intended as patriotic propaganda, it was the most graphic portrayal of trench warfare yet shown. Dead and dying British and German soldiers were filmed, but scenes that General Rawlinson found too gruesome were cut out.

Some of the scenes of troops going 'over the top' had been staged before the battle had started, but Malins, who was near the front at Beaumont-Hamel on July 1, filmed the detonation of the massive mine beneath Hawthorn Ridge Redoubt, as well as the preparations and advance of the 1st Battalion, Lancashire Fusiliers.

Malins and McDowell had set out to make a short documentary, but, when the volume and quality of their footage were seen in London, the British Topical Committee for War Films decided to make it into a feature-length film, produced by William F. Drury and edited by Malins and Charles Urban. The film was screened for British soldiers at rest areas in France, to provide new recruits with some idea of what they were about to face. As it was a silent film, the soldiers' main complaint was its failure to capture the sound of battle. However, the titles could be remarkably forthright, describing images of injury and death. A typical sequence was titled, 'British Tommies rescuing a comrade under shell fire', with the subtitle in a bracket 'This man died 30 minutes after reaching the trenches.'

The film was shown to the British public as a morale-booster, and was for the most part favourably received. But the Dean of Durham Cathedral, the Very Reverend Herbert Hensley Henson, protested 'against an entertainment which wounds the heart and violates the very sanctity of bereavement'. Others complained that such a serious subject ought not to be shown in the same programme as the ever-popular comedies. An estimated twenty million tickets for the film were sold in Britain in two months. On this basis it remains one of the most successful British films ever screened.

Despite the success on the night of August 4 in taking part of the German second line of trenches, attrition rather than the hoped-for breakthrough had become the grim pattern of fighting for the Anglo-French armies on the Somme. The battle had become a struggle for the possession of woods, copses, valleys, ravines and ruined villages; for the possession of pulverized fields and a dense array of shellholes.

On August 10 King George V visited the battlefield, with his son Edward, Prince of Wales, and General Rawlinson. At St George's Hill, a few hundred yards south of the British front-line trenches of

July 1, he was photographed at the graveside of a Private Pennington. At least six Private Penningtons had been killed on the Somme since July 1. There seems no way of knowing which Private Pennington's grave the King saw.

Also on August 10, in the quiet sector of the front opposite Gommecourt, scene of the failed diversionary attack on July 1, eighteen-year-old Private Thomas Littler, of the 5th Battalion, Cheshire Regiment, a Territorial regiment, recorded the events of a typical day, as he worked that morning in a trench about ten yards from the billet. The Germans 'were shelling the village heavily', he wrote, 'and about 12 o'clock noon a 5.9 was dropped direct on the billet, it killed Private Joe Orme, Private Harry Percival, and Private Dick Hearne, it wounded Privates Hazelhurst, Coalthorpe, Duckworth, and Barton, and Private George Hunt (my chum) got shell-shock, losing his speech and use of his limbs, the billet took fire, but was quickly put out, and the rescue of dead and wounded went on, afterwards we had to find fresh billets in cellars which was much safer, everyone was fagged out and done, but what few were left in the Platoon had to go to work at 6 p.m. till 2 a.m. and about 8 p.m. an enemy airoplane swept us with machine gun fire.'

Privates Orme, Percival and Hearne are buried in the Hébuterne Military Cemetery, near where they were killed.

As the Anglo-French attempt to reach Péronne and Bapaume, continued, Haig was hopeful that the appearance of the new British weapon, the tank, could help effect a breakthrough. On August 11 he was disappointed to learn that the first deliveries would not be made before September 1. By contrast, the interrogation of German prisoners of war gave Haig cause for optimism. It seemed, he wrote in his diary on August 11, 'that Enemy has lost heavily in his counter-attacks since we took the German second line northeast of Pozières' a week earlier.

Haig's plan of attack remained the capture of the Pozières–Morval ridge, with the French taking part on the right flank, and then, as he explained to Gough at Reserve Army headquarters on August 11, 'a general advance northwards in close touch with one another'. The immediate objective was to capture the villages of Guillemont and Ginchy 'and assist the French to come up into line'. Meanwhile,

Gough would continue his efforts to capture Thiepval. Haig 'congrat-
ulated him on the daily progress made'.

Among those in the front-line trenches on August 11 was Captain
Charles Wilson, medical officer with the 1st Battalion, Royal Fusiliers
– later, as Lord Moran, to be Churchill's doctor in the Second World
War. The battalion had been in the trenches for two days. 'I found
myself in Longueval Alley with a score or more of trench mortar
people,' Wilson wrote in his diary. 'The Boche followed us down the
trench as if their gunners were watching all our movements. Their
shells fell so close they threw earth over the trench mortar men who
came back in a rush towards me, and then as another shell burst
behind them ran forward again like frightened cattle that push and
jostle and are harried into the fields through the open gate by
barking dogs.'

There was no officer with the trench mortar men, Wilson noted:
'they were a mob. But fear which had so often lain hidden in my
heart had gone from me. These animals given up to their brute
instincts horrified me; that wild panic only left me with a surprising
feeling of courage. Then there was a terrific noise, a smell of powder,
and we were breathing black smoke; a shell had come into the
trench, the fumes lifted and hung over the trench and drifted away
and I was alone with my servant and a man lying in the trench
without a hand.'

Captain Wilson wrote critically of the men whose panic he had
seen: 'These men were the refuse of a dozen units that had been
ordered to detail men for service with this battery, and had sent these
misfits of this time when men are men or nothing.'

Wilson's own behaviour was recorded that day in the battalion war
diary, which noted: 'Captain C. M. Wilson again distinguished
himself by rendering aid and evacuating Major Musgrove who was
wounded by shell fire.'

On August 12 King George V went to Val Vion, where he lunched
with the French President, Raymond Poincaré. The two men then
discussed the Somme battle with Haig. During their discussion,
Poincaré told Haig that 'he was most anxious before the approach of
winter, that we should have made some decisive advance in order to
keep the people of France and England from grumbling.' Haig replied

that 'we had yet at least ten weeks of good weather, probably more, and that I believe much will be done by us in that time.'

Joffre and Foch were also at Val Vion that day. Hardly had the King and the French President left than Lloyd George, Kitchener's successor as Secretary of State for War, arrived. When he asked Haig about the current scheme to negotiate a separate peace with Germany's ally Bulgaria, Haig replied that 'beat the Germans as soon as possible is our objective: so I recommended making terms with Bulgaria and bring ing in Romania on our side as soon as possible.' In the event, Bulgaria remained an active member of the Central Powers until the end of the war. Romania was within two weeks of declaring war against Germany.

The 6th Battalion, Somerset Light Infantry, was sent on August 12 to the front-line trenches in Delville Wood. After the British capture of the wood a month earlier, the Germans had counter-attacked and regained its northern and eastern sectors. Everard Wyrall, the historian of the Somerset Light Infantry, noted, 'As the battle progressed the wood was totally ravaged and the ground became littered with broken branches and tangled masses of bushes. The whole area was pock-marked with shellholes, which both sides had turned as far as possible into posts and machine-gun nests, intersected here and there by trenches and what had been roads through the wood. It was a terrible place over which to fight.'

The Somerset Light Infantry historian added, 'The stench from the decaying dead was awful, gas fumes hung about the shellholes and clung to the undergrowth, weird and ghostly in the semi-darkness were the gaunt long arms of the torn and blasted trees or all that remained of them. The uncertainty of the whereabouts of the German trenches kept the nerves of both officers and men at high tension.'

The regimental account continued, 'During the night of the 12th/13th August the Battalion sent patrols out in the wood to discover the enemy's position. The Somersets had the best of two encounters with German patrols. The Battalion was relieved on the evening of the 14th and returned to the support trenches in front of Montauban Alley. However, on the nights of the 15th and 16th August, the Battalion still had to provide working parties of 250 men to dig in the wood all night.'

★

The British attempt to capture Thiepval also continued. On August 13, Winston Churchill, who was then staying at Hurstmonceux, seven miles from the Channel coast, wrote to a friend, 'I can hear the guns here (Sussex) quite plainly thudding away.' On the following day, Haig drove to II Corps headquarters at Villers-Bocage, where he found General Jacob 'full of confidence' after having 'arranged careful plans for capturing certain parts of the trenches tonight, and a larger piece tomorrow and the next day.'

During their meeting, Haig passed on to Jacob his criticism of the Staff work at the various army headquarters. 'I have noticed lately', he explained in his diary, 'that in many divisions, the Staff does not circulate sufficiently amongst the brigades and battalions when operations are in progress.'

Gough's new offensive began on the night of August 13. French troops on the right flank took part, but, in Haig's words in his diary, 'accomplished nothing, although *The Times* says they did wonders'. They had been in the line so long, Haig noted, 'that the men had lost most of their dash'. Behind the lines on August 14, King George V watched a practice trench attack by Australian troops at the No. 5 Australian School near Sailly-le-Sec.

From the British sector of the battlefield, the British poet and painter Isaac Rosenberg wrote to a friend on August 17, 'We are kept pretty busy now, and the climate here is really unhealthy; the doctors themselves can't stand it. We had an exciting time today, and though this is behind the firing line and right out of the trenches there were quite a good many sent to heaven and the hospital. I carried one myself in a handcart to the hospital (which often is the antechamber to heaven).'

Among those killed on August 17 was Private Leonard Broadbent, West Yorkshire Regiment. His body was never found. His name is on the Thiepval Memorial, and, as with almost all those who were killed on the Somme, is also on the war memorial in his home town, Armley, near Leeds.

On August 18, German troops counter-attacked from their positions in Leuze Wood. The war correspondent Philip Gibbs saw them advance towards the British trenches, 'shoulder to shoulder, like a solid bar'. It was 'sheer suicide', he wrote. 'I saw our men get their machine-guns into action, and the right side of the living bar frittered away, and then the whole line fell into the scorched grass. Another line followed. They were tall men, and did not falter as they came forward, but it seemed to me they walked like men conscious of going to death. They died. The simile is outworn, but it was exactly as though some invisible scythe had mown them down.'

Gibbs noted that the letters written by German soldiers during those weeks of fighting 'and captured by us from dead or living men' were 'one cry of agony and horror'. One German soldier later wrote, 'I stood on the brink of the most terrible days of my life. They were those of the Battle of the Somme. It began with a night attack on August 13 to 14. The attack lasted till the evening of the 18th when the English wrote on our bodies in letters of blood: "It is all over with you." A handful of half-mad wretched creatures, worn out in body and mind, were all that was left of the whole battalion. We were that handful.'

The losses of many of the German battalions were 'staggering', Philip Gibbs reported, 'but not greater than our own, and by the middle of August the morale of the troops was severely shaken'. Captain F. C. Hitchcock, 2nd Battalion, Leinster Regiment, was a witness to the aftermath of the attack on Guillemont on August 18. 'It had been a fine sight seeing the leading battalions advancing into action,' he wrote, 'but it was a most depressing one seeing them retiring. Streams of wounded, walking and on stretchers, were now beginning to drift by; men with smashed arms, limping, and with the worst of all to see – facial wounds. They all muttered of machine guns in a sunken road, which enfiladed them and had broken up the attack.' Among the stretcher cases passing him he saw his own commanding officer, who had been badly hit in the groin, and the company sergeant major, severely hit in the head. Near an advanced dressing station, he found the padre, the Reverend Denis Doyle, making cover for the wounded. Later that day 'this fine man had his leg blown off by a shell.' He was taken back to a dressing station, but was not expected to live.

On August 19, Second Lieutenant Harvey Augustus Butters, the American volunteer serving with the Royal Field Artillery, and a Roman Catholic, wrote home, 'Father Doyle is dead – Always in the front trenches when the shelling was heaviest, he was terribly wounded three days ago, tending some of the dying that had been caught in the fierce counter-shelling that precedes the attack. They got him out the same evening, and down to the dressing station, but there was no hope of his recovery. He died the same night, after great suffering, I suppose.'

Butters added, 'The last, long rest and the reward for courage and fidelity are before him now – his suffering all behind. God will certainly rest his soul – but his regiment will miss him sorely. He was buried this morning – I was unable to get to his funeral, being up the line with ammunition.'

The Reverend Denis Doyle, Chaplain 4th Class, lies today in Dive Copse British Cemetery, near Sailly-le-Sec, less than a mile from the northern bank of the River Somme.

Reflecting a week later on the French failure during the attack on the night of August 13, Haig noted in his diary that 'the fault lay with the troops and not Foch.' After learning that Foch had been reprimanded by Joffre for the failure, Haig 'wrote and asked him to lunch. He came today and seemed grateful for my little attention. The French troops on our right are now fresh, and Foch expects great things of them when next we advance to attack.'

10

Both sides fight on: 'This fantasy of woe'

ON 18 AUGUST 1916, at an army barracks at Warley, in Essex, a
court martial took place, not of a soldier charged with desertion, but of a pacifist charged with refusing to agree to any form of
military or non-combatant service. This was twenty-six-year-old
Clifford Allen, a Cambridge University graduate and the President of
the No-Conscription Fellowship established after the government
brought in its first compulsory-service legislation at the beginning of
the year. Allen had refused his call-up papers, being convinced that
the war was wrong: that it was a violation of human brotherhood.

Allen told the officers trying him, 'I believe in the inherent worth
and sanctity of every human personality, irrespective of the nation to
which a man belongs.' He was sentenced to three months' hard labour.
After serving those three months to the last day, he was released for a
few hours, rearrested, court-martialled again, and then sentenced to a
longer period of imprisonment; this pattern was repeated until the
end of the war. All imprisoned conscientious objectors were then
deprived of their right to vote for five years.

On the day of Clifford Allen's first sentence for refusing to be conscripted, a Scottish officer, Captain Hugh Stewart Smith, was in action
with the Argyll and Sutherland Highlanders in an attack on High
Wood. A few members of his battalion entered the German trenches.
All were forced back to their own front line. Smith was killed in the
attack. In his pocket book was found a piece of light verse:

> On the plains of Picardy
> Lay a soldier, dying
> Gallantly, with soul still free
> Spite the rough world's trying.
> Came the Angel who keeps guard
> When the fight has drifted,

'What would you for your reward
When the Clouds have lifted?'
Then the soldier through the mist
Heard the voice and rested
As a man who sees his home
When the hill is breasted –
This his answer and I vow
Nothing could be fitter –
Give me Peace, a dog, a friend
And a glass of bitter!

Captain Smith, who was twenty-seven years old when he was killed, lies today in Caterpillar Valley Cemetery, Longueval.

Captain Charles Wilson was among the medical officers who went forward with their battalions on August 18. The objective of his battalion, the 1st Battalion, Royal Fusiliers, was Guillemont Station. After the British artillery bombardment of the German trenches, they were to assault in the second wave. 'We sat listening to the din as if we would miss nothing of it,' Wilson wrote. 'All at once the men ran out, in spite of the stuff that was falling all around; Boche prisoners were passing. The moral effect on our fellows was astonishing. I looked at my watch, it was exactly fifteen minutes after zero time. At the head of the prisoners was a German officer who halted and saluted whenever he met one of our officers moving up Longueval Alley. Then the string of Huns behind him, going along in their bandages with heads down, jolted into each other like trucks when the engine pulls up sharply and there was a lot of guttural murmuring.'

One or two wounded British soldiers also came: 'They told how the Huns offered them money, wrist watches, cigarettes, all that they had; how they came out of their trenches with hands up immediately the barrage lifted; our men talked on and did not notice me dressing their wounds.'

Captain Wilson then went back to headquarters for news, 'but they knew very little. We had succeeded in taking Guillemont Station. The day they thought had gone well, but Milner, who had just got his commission and was still wearing a sergeant's coat, had been shot through the head at short range, and Rowe, who had gone back to duty from the stretcher bearers to try for a commission, had come down shot through the chest, and Babs was badly smashed up going over with "A" Company, and Barnes and Steele had been killed, and the best of the men seemed to have gone out. Somewhere up there out of reach, the battalion was slipping away and I could do nothing.'

Among those killed in the struggle for Guillemont Station, while attacking a German machine-gun post that was holding up his men, was Second Lieutenant George Marsden-Smedley, 3rd Battalion, Rifle Brigade. In a letter to his parents a day before he died he thanked them for the new identity disc they had sent him. 'It makes such a difference,' he wrote, 'having a nice chain around one's neck instead of a dirty old bit of string.' Neither his body nor his new identity disc was ever found. His name is on the Thiepval Memorial. But immediately after the war his parents put up a private memorial as close as possible to where they believed he must have been killed, on the German parapet. On the memorial stone are the words 'Lively and pleasant in life. In death serene and unafraid. Most blessed in remembrance.' He was just nineteen years old, having gone straight into the army from school. Thirty members of his family were at the rededication of his memorial in 1997.

On August 18, the 6th Battalion, Somerset Light Infantry, returned to Delville Wood, where, in preparation for a new attack, they spent the night in the British front-line trenches that wended their way through the pulverized woodland. The supporting artillery bombardment began at 6 a.m. on the following morning. During the bombardment, twenty-two-year-old Second Lieutenant William Berridge, an Oxford University graduate, sent a poem home. 'I am writing this in the midst of a din which you can and probably do hear on the Leas . . . I enclose my most recent spasm,' he wrote – it 'was only half an hour old' – 'which you had better revise and set to music!' The poem reflected a deep, widespread religious faith that there was a meaning and a plan even to the worst of slaughters:

> God, wheresoe'er Thou may'st be found
>   And Whosoe'er Thou art,
> Grant in the Scheme of Things that we
>   May play a worthy part;
> And give, to help us on the way,
>   An all-enduring heart.

We know Thou watchest from above
  This fantasy of woe;
And, whatsoever pain or loss
  We here may undergo,
Let us in this be comforted –
  None from Thy sight can go.

Sometimes in folly we upon
  Thy Name profanely call,
And grumble at our destiny
  Because our minds are small,
And so we cannot understand
  The Mind that ruleth all.

Grant us to see and learn and know
  The Greatness of Thy Will,
That each one his allotted task
  May grapple with, until
We hear at last Thy Perfect Voice
  Bidding us 'Peace, be still.'

The Somerset Light Infantry, with Second Lieutenant Berridge leading his platoon, attacked in Delville Wood at 2.45 p.m. As the infantrymen entered the German trenches they bayoneted or shot those who refused to surrender. An attack was then made on two German machine-gun posts that continued to harass the attackers from one end of the German trench, and were defended by a heavy trench-mortar barrage. The machine-gun posts were overrun and the trench secured. Ninety Germans were taken prisoner, but Berridge, the first man to enter the trench, was mortally wounded by a sniper. He died the next day. His body lies today in Heilly Station Cemetery.

In London, the War Committee met on August 18. The minutes record a reference to a 'temporary standstill' on the Somme. When Balfour asked Robertson about the German losses – 'wastage' in the terminology of the time – the Chief of the Imperial General Staff replied that he 'did not really know what it was', but added that it was his 'impression' that the Germans 'were losing as many and more than we were'. Robertson then explained that the British losses 'amounted to about 6,000 or 7,000 a week'. This was the figure for dead and wounded; the number of British dead was about 2,000 a week. Balfour, after noting how many German divisions were facing the British on the Somme, 'suggested the possibility of our striking else-where at a thinner line'. Robertson replied that 'it could not be done'. The British did not have enough extra heavy guns for a second assault elsewhere on the Western Front.

The Somme offensive would go on. Balfour's hesitations were not enough to curb it. At this meeting, the Foreign Secretary, Sir Edward Grey, made another point in favour of continuing. 'The French', he said, 'would not like the idea of another winter without a definite advance to our credit.' For Robertson, it was not even necessary to have a military success. 'We should be doing very well', he told the War Committee on August 18, 'if we only held the Germans there' – and let the Russian armies in the East 'get on' against the Germans.

Holding the Germans on the Somme, as opposed to pushing them eastward, was a substantial reduction of aim. But it did not mean a reduction of effort, or of suffering. On August 20, during an attack west of High Wood, Private Reginald Giles, of the Gloucestershire Regiment, was among those killed. He was fourteen years old. His body was never identified; he is the youngest soldier recorded on the Thiepval Memorial.

In the third week of August, the Australians were in action beyond Pozières. 'When you get this, I'll be dead; don't worry,' a former bank clerk, Sergeant David Badger, wrote to his parents before the attack. He was killed on August 21. His name is on the Australian Memorial to the Missing at Villers-Bretonneux. Lieutenant Neil Shaw Stewart, Rifle Brigade, was killed that day leading his company in an attack on Guillemont. He is buried in Delville Wood Cemetery. After the war a plaque was put up in his memory in Rancourt Chapel with the inscription: 'I thank my God always on thy behalf.'

Among the Australians in action on August 23 was thirty-three-year-old Second Lieutenant John Raws. A few days earlier he had written to his brother in Australia, 'The men who say they believe in war should be hung. And the men who won't come out and help us, now we're in it, are not fit for words. Had we more reinforcements up there many brave men now dead, men who stuck it and stuck it and stuck it till they died, would be alive today. Do you know that I saw with my own eyes a score of men go raving mad! I met three in No-Man's Land one night. Of course, we had a bad patch. But it is sad to think that one has to go back to it, and back to it, and back to it, until one is hit.'

Raws was killed on August 23. His body was never identified, and his name is on the Australian Memorial to the Missing.

On August 24, Second Lieutenant Herbert Crowle, Australian Infantry, was wounded in action. The next day he wrote to his wife and son from the casualty clearing station at Puchevillers, two miles from Haig's headquarters chateau at Val Vion, 'Just a line, you must be prepared for the worst to happen any day. It is no use trying to hide things. I am in terrible agony. Had I been brought in at once I had a hope. Now gas gangrene has set in and it is so bad that the doctor could not save it by taking it off as it had gone too far and the only hope is that the salts they have put on may drain the gangrene other-wise there is no hope.'

The journey to the casualty clearing station had started across open ground in front of the German trenches. One stretcher-bearer walked in front, waving a Red Cross flag. The Germans did not open fire. After explaining this to his wife, Crowle continued, 'The pain is getting worse. I am very sorry dear, but still you will be well provided for I am easy on that score. So cheer up dear I could write a lot but I am nearly unconscious. Give my love to dear Bill and yourself, do take care of yourself and him. Your loving husband Bert.'

A few hours later Lieutenant Crowle was dead. He is buried next to the casualty clearing station where he died, in Puchevillers British Cemetery.

The exhaustion of battle could not be assuaged. 'All around me are faces which sleep might not have visited for a week,' Captain Charles Wilson, Royal Army Medical Corps, wrote in his diary on August 22. 'They have dark shadows under eyes that are older, more serious. Some that are lined before look ill, and boys have lost their freshness in the mouth. Voices too are tired and the very gait of men has lost its spring. The sap has gone out of them, they are dried up. During breakfast two officers of the 20th Division came into the dugout to take over. They looked so fresh and sleek and young they might have stepped out of a hot bath after hunting. They seemed to listen for shells though it was peaceful enough.'

The arrival of the new officers was welcome news. 'So it was true that we were to be relieved immediately,' Wilson wrote, and 'that very afternoon we should go out to a camp in Happy Valley. We were to march by platoons assembling at Carnoy where the cookers with tea, the officers' horses, and buses for the men would meet us. On the road we passed a Kitchener Battalion going up, they were resting by the roadside.' There was to be no pause and respite in the feeding of men into the front line.

New casualty clearing stations were also needed. In late August Casualty Clearing Station No. 49 was established at Contay, joined within a month by Casualty Clearing Station No. 9. More than a thousand men who could not be saved, despite devoted medical attention, were buried in the nearby Contay British Cemetery. Outside the village of Varennes, near Acheux-en-Amenois, Casualty Clearing Station No. 39 cemetery, established in August, was first used by mobile divisional field ambulances. Within two months it was also being used by Casualty Clearing Stations Nos. 4 and 11. The flow of wounded men was unabated.

A report by Haig's Intelligence Branch gave him cause for satisfaction on August 22. It revealed that, whereas a German division was worn out in four and a half days when it was opposite the British lines, opposite the French it lasted as long as three weeks. 'This clearly shows', Haig noted in his diary, 'how regular and persistent is the pressure by the British.' Haig had no illusions, however, about the desperate nature of the fighting or the advantages that the Germans could command. After lunching with Rawlinson at Querrieu on August 22, and hearing of Rawlinson's plan for an attack against the Ginchy–Guillemont road and into the north edge of Guillemont village, which was overlooked by the German machine-gun posts on Guillemont Ridge, Haig noted critically, 'Numerous shellholes afforded excellent cover for his machine guns. In fact I thought the scheme doomed to failure.'

From General Trenchard came news in mid-August of a setback in the air. Owing to clouds over the battlefield, German aircraft were able to carry out their observations relatively unmolested. But on

August 23 the weather changed, and the number of German aircraft engaged by their British aerial adversaries was then considerable. 'Fighting was continuous to dark,' Haig noted in his diary that day. 'We suffered no casualties, though Enemy in several cases was pursued back to his aerodrome.'

Air power helped the British more than the Germans. A German officer, Friedrich Steinbrecher, a veteran of the fighting on the Eastern Front, wrote that what he had been through on the Somme 'surpassed in horror all my previous experiences during the second year of the war'. He explained that 'the English, with the aid of their airmen, who are often 1,500 feet above the position, and their observation balloons, have exactly located every one of our batteries and have so smashed them up with long-distance guns of every calibre that the artillery here has had unusually heavy losses both of men and material. Our dugouts, in which we shelter day and night, are not even adequate, for though they are cut out of the chalk they are not so strong but that a "heavy" was able a few days ago to blow one in and bury the whole lot of men inside.'

Steinbrecher did not survive the Battle of the Somme. Nor, in a political sense, did General Grünert, Chief of Staff of the German Second Army, who was replaced by a relatively junior officer, Colonel Friedrich von Lossberg, with a reputation as a 'defence specialist'. But the most serious doubts were being cast against the capabilities of the German Commander-in-Chief, General Falkenhayn, the mastermind of the Verdun strategy that had turned – from the German perspective – into both the failure of Verdun and the bloodbath of the Somme.

At the end of August, Falkenhayn was replaced as Commander-in-Chief by the soldier who had directed the successful German offensives on the Russian Front, Field Marshal Paul von Hindenburg, who brought with him from the Eastern Front, as his Chief of Staff and close adviser, General Erich von Ludendorff. Henceforth this duo would direct German war policy until the end of the war.

In the last week of August, from the Russian capital, Petrograd, came appeals by the Russian High Command for a renewed Anglo-French offensive on the Somme as early as possible in September, to take the pressure off the struggling Russian forces. Haig was convinced, however, that no further attack 'on a large scale' could be launched until September 15. Meanwhile, sufficient tanks had reached the Western Front to enable a demonstration to be carried out for the benefit of the Staffs.

For twenty-four hours without a break, the tank officers worked to prepare the demonstration. It took place on August 26. A battalion of infantry and five tanks, operating together, assaulted three lines of specially prepared trenches. 'The Tanks crossed the several lines with the greatest ease,' Haig noted in his diary, 'and one entered a wood, which represented a "strong point" and easily walked over fair sized trees of 6 inches through!'

Peacemaking was much in the air in the autumn of 1916. At the end of August, the Pope, Benedict XV, told the French President, Raymond Poincaré, that the Germans would be forced to ask for an armistice by October. At a conference on August 27, held on Poincaré's train, at which Haig was present, Poincaré had no doubt what the Anglo-French answer should be. Haig noted it down: 'No talk of peace so long as one enemy remained on the soil of the Republic.'

German troops were then in occupation of most of north-eastern France, including the country's most productive coal-mining region.

The war would go on. Haig explained to Poincaré that he would launch a ten-division attack – some 120,000 men – in co-operation with Foch, on August 30. He would then make preparations for a fourteen-division attack – 168,000 men – two weeks later. For this he had 'every hope of success', but he was 'anxious that ample French reserves should be available to exploit our success'.

Poincaré, whose mind was much on the Russian appeal for help, pointed out that September 15 must be the latest date for the second major attack, 'as the weather breaks on September 25 and is usually bad for some weeks after that'. Haig said he would do his best to arrange for the attack no later than September 15. Poincaré was relieved. He had been worried by reports that the Germans were trying to get the Russian government to make a separate peace, offering Russia territorial gains greater than those that Britain and France could offer, and leaving Germany free to transfer its large eastern armies to the Western Front.

On August 27, as Haig and Poincaré were talking on the French President's train, the 1/5th Battalion, Gloucestershire Regiment – a

Territorial battalion – attacked a German trench near Ovillers that had been one of the first objectives on July 1. After a fierce struggle the trench was overrun. Two hundred Germans were killed and wounded, and fifty taken prisoner. Four British officers and fourteen other ranks were killed, among them Lieutenant Cyril Winterbotham, a twenty-nine-year-old Oxford University graduate and prospective parliamentary candidate for East Gloucestershire, who, a month before he was killed, had written a poem which he entitled 'The Cross of Wood':

> God be with you and us who go our way
> And leave you dead upon the ground you won;
> For you at last the long fatigue is done,
> The hard march ended, you have rest to-day.
>
> You were our friends, with you we watched the dawn
> Gleam through the rain of the long winter night,
> With you we laboured till the morning light
> Broke on the village, shell-destroyed and torn.
>
> Not now for you the glorious return
> To steep Strand valleys, to the Severn leas
> By Tewkesbury and Gloucester, or the trees
> Of Cheltenham under high Cotswold stern.
>
> For you no medals such as others wear –
> A cross of bronze for those approved brave –
> To you is given, above a shallow grave,
> The wooden Cross that marks you resting there.
>
> Rest you content, more honourable far
> Than all the Orders is the Cross of Wood
> The Symbol of self-sacrifice that stood
> Bearing the God whose brethren you are.

Because the battlefield continued to be pounded by artillery and mortar fire after the August 27 attack on the trench near Ovillers, Winterbotham's body was never identified. He therefore has no cross or grave. Like the other 73,335 men with no known resting place, his name is inscribed on the Thiepval Memorial.

Above the battlefield on the following day, August 28, Captain Basil Radford – the inventor of Gilbert the Filbert – was in a tethered observation balloon with his fellow observer, Second Lieutenant Moxon, watching the German lines along the River Ancre, and registering artillery targets for V Corps. Then one of the two balloon cables broke and the balloon began to drift away. The two men immediately signalled to be hauled down. As the balloon was about to reach the ground, however, the winch overran and damaged the metallic 'vee' running from the nose to the tail of the balloon, which provided the attachment point for the tethering cable from the winch. When the cable broke, the balloon shot up into the air and drifted towards No-Man's Land and the German lines, seen by thousands of British troops.

Before the balloon reached No-Man's Land, Moxon was seen to jump with his parachute and land safely. Radford was then seen to fall without a parachute. There was much speculation about what had gone wrong. It seemed most likely that, in preparation for a rapid departure from their basket as soon as it was to have reached the ground, both observers had undone their parachute harness. When their balloon subsequently broke away and flew off, Moxon managed to reattach his harness and was therefore able to jump to safety. Radford, not having refitted his harness, or having refitted it incorrectly, fell to his death. He is buried in Couin British Cemetery. He was twenty-eight years old

On August 31 the Germans launched an attack north and east of Delville Wood, to try to pinch out the British salient there. Reserve Lieutenant Trobitz, 7th Company, 88th Infantry Regiment, who was among the German attackers that day, later recalled, 'When the green flares went up we rose as one out of the trenches and, no sooner had we set off, than the enemy artillery opened up, which wiped the smile off the faces of the succeeding waves.'

'We ran and ran,' Lieutenant Trobitz continued, 'but you have to bear in mind: first, the ground, which was completely covered with shellholes; second, the clay, which sucked at our boots; and third, the load we poor soldiers were carrying: assault order, rifles with bayonets fixed, bandoliers of rifle ammunition hung around the neck, revolvers, signal pistols, with flares carried in sandbags, ration pouches, filled water bottles and, finally, digging equipment.'

After what seemed like about fifteen minutes, Lieutenant Trobitz felt that he and his men 'had possibly advanced about 300 metres without enemy interference. Then the British placed a machine gun in position and opened a slow rate of fire, but still we were not really close enough. With each step we drew nearer, until, silhouetted against the horizon, we must have presented a perfect target and they began to pick us off, one by one. There we lay; dead, wounded and unwounded, in shellholes, in the bright sunshine between the lines. Above us, enemy aircraft, some as low as one hundred metres, filled the sky and swooped down to machine gun us.' The British aircraft were learning how to participate in the land battle.

Lieutenant Trobitz's account continued, 'Those who have not lain out wounded between the trench lines can barely imagine the situation. All sorts of thoughts run through your mind: tetanus, stomach wounds, wife and family. There is plenty of time for this, until you are enfolded by blissful unconsciousness. To awake is exquisite, you are still alive! The will to resist grows. One hand clasps the revolver, while the other clutches the wound. If they come, you will not make it easy for them.'

Then the British artillery opened up. 'A comrade in the same shell-hole, so far unwounded, is suddenly hit on the collarbone by a shrapnel bullet,' Trobitz recalled. 'It is a blow like a box on the ears. Our spirits sink as he goes down. Once it goes dark, he will have to try to crawl off to get aid. The sun burns down unmercifully, torturing us with thirst. Minutes become hours. We exchange addresses. If one of us escapes, he will inform the relatives of the other. All too slowly the sun sinks. It is just 7 p.m. Suddenly the comrade who was hit on the collarbone awakes from a deep sleep, feels his shoulder and discovers that the shoulder strap of his equipment has stopped the shrapnel ball. Apart from severe bruising to the shoulder, nothing has happened to him. He offers to go and get help. Another hour passes and the shadows are lengthening across the battlefield.' That help, when it comes, will be British, not German. 'It will soon be on the way,' Lieutenant Trobitz reflected, and he added, 'The British are a noble lot. They will not shoot at stretcher-bearers working under the Red Cross flag. I have witnessed this myself.'

But no help came, either German or British. 'The waiting becomes agonising,' Lieutenant Trobitz recalled. 'We have been lying here for six hours. Many, those who can still walk, have already made it back. Why should we not try it too? Initially it is very hard, but the emergency brings forth an iron will and the waiting has become unbearable. Supporting one another, or crawling on all fours, we move carefully from shellhole to shellhole and so towards safety. The first aid men have their hands full. Tirelessly they gather in the wounded, without being interfered with by the British. Sadly there were a great many victims.'

The British line was pushed back that day – back a hundred yards into the north and eastern edges of Delville Wood. But the Germans had failed to make the advance they had hoped for, and the wood remained to all intents and purposes under British control.

Towards the end of August, the American volunteer Second Lieutenant Harvey Augustus Butters, Royal Field Artillery – who at the Battle of Loos had suffered a nervous breakdown from shell shock, but had insisted on returning to the front within a week – wrote to the chaplain of his brigade, on a personal note: 'You know how much my heart is in this great cause, and how more than willing I am to give my life for it.' Butters was killed on the night of August 31. A few days earlier a volunteer had been called for to replace a casualty, and he had volunteered, just as, a year earlier, he had done the same in order to serve with the British Army.

Second Lieutenant Butters was buried the next day in Méaulte Military Cemetery, just south of Albert. In his letter of condolence, his section commander, Captain Zambra, wrote to Butters's sister, 5,000 miles away in California, 'Harry and another officer were in the dugout at the gun position. The Germans were putting over a heavy barrage of gas shells and the air became very poisonous and oppressive. Harry said, "It's time we moved out of this," and went out. Immediately he was outside, a gas shell hit him direct. Death must have been instantaneous, and the officer with him removed his gas helmet to make sure. So some little consolation remains to us that he was spared all pain.'

Captain Zambra continued, 'A Roman Catholic Chaplain buried him beneath the Union Jack (we tried to get an American flag, but one was not procurable or he should have been honoured by both countries) in a military cemetery just outside of Méaulte, a village a mile south of Albert. The graveyard is under the care of the Graves Registration Commission, and his grave will be well tended. His body was in a coffin. There were many officers at the funeral, as many as could be spared from duty, including the Staff Captain, representing the General, and Colonel Talbot, a detachment from his battery and my section. A trumpeter sounded the Last Post.'

Six months before his death, Butters had befriended Winston Churchill, then the colonel commanding a battalion at Ploegsteert, in Flanders. Ten days after Butters's death, Churchill wrote an obituary in the *Observer*, in which he explained that he was writing about Butters 'not because his sacrifice and story differ from those of so many others in these hard days, but because, coming of his own free will, with no national call or obligation, a stranger from across the ocean, to fight and die in our ranks, he had it in his power to pay a tribute to our cause of exceptional value. He did not come all the way from San Francisco only out of affection for the ancient home of his forbears or in a spirit of mere adventure. He was in sentiment a thorough American. All his ordinary loyalties rested with his own country. But he had a very firm and clear conception of the issues which are at stake in this struggle. He had minutely studied the official documents bearing upon the origin of the war, and he conceived that not merely national causes but international causes of the highest importance were involved, and must now be decided by arms. And to these he thought it his duty to testify "till a right peace was signed". Such testimony cannot be impeached.'

On the evening of August 31, Captain Charles Wilson noted in his diary, as he and his medical orderlies and stretcher-bearers went off in search of Carlton Trench, where they were expected as reinforcements, 'The rain and the traffic had played havoc with the road near Mametz and the wheels of the Maltese cart that was carrying spare stretchers stuck fast in the mud; we pushed and heaved and attempted with the stretcher poles to lever out the wheels, but nothing happened. We left it in the mud and pushed on.'

Darkness had fallen, and Wilson 'wondered vaguely if it was the cold night air that made my teeth chatter'. Then the Germans began firing shells 'in great numbers. They detonated almost silently and without the burst of an ordinary shell. We had run into a gas shell barrage. I wanted to ask my servant if his chest felt as if it were being pressed in by an iron band that was gradually getting smaller. I wondered what gas they were using. I remembered we were told that many of the men had heart failure after the last attack.'

At that moment, Wilson recalled, a gunner came by, 'spitting and rubbing his eyes. He said there was a sunken road a little further on which led to the quarry. He thought there was an aid post there; this was the landmark we had been told to look out for. We stumbled on and met an officer, hatless and supported under each armpit by two stretcher-bearers. They said he was gassed and it may be that he was. Two winters he had been out here as a sergeant, a bold and efficient NCO. All last winter he felt the damp more and more and began to carry a flask. The damned stuff had done its work. "I wish to God I could get hit," he had once confided in me, "I am not the man I was." Now he was done.'

Captain Wilson, his battalion commander Lieutenant Colonel M. V. B. Hill and his men reached some rising ground that was fairly clear of gas. It was after three o'clock in the morning, 'and we decided to wait for the light. The night lifted reluctantly as if it were loath to let us escape and the cold dawn had passed slowly into the promise of a summer day before we found Carlton Trench. The last two companies had just arrived after eight hours' pilgrimage in the gas to find that no one expected them or knew why they had come. The Colonels of five battalions were collected in one dugout and the men were packed in the trench like herrings. It was clear we were not wanted, why were we there? Hill answered tersely "Wind." '

Fear was an integral part of the battlefield.

Three weeks later Captain Wilson's 'conspicuous gallantry and devotion to duty' on August 31 were to win him the Military Cross, the citation for which read: 'He worked for over an hour digging out wounded men at great personal risk. He then returned to his aid post and attended to the wounded. Later, hearing that an officer had been wounded, he passed through a hundred yards of the enemy's artillery barrage, dressed his wounds, and finally got him to safety as soon as the barrage permitted.'

The battalion, with 52 men killed and 345 wounded, was pulled out of the line. In Wilson's laconic words: 'It seems that a division is dipped twice into the Somme, with perhaps a week's rest in between. The second time it is kept in until it has no further fighting value.'

11

The continuing struggle: 'I am in God's keeping'

R OMANIA HAVING DECLARED war on Germany in late August 1916, on September 3 the troops of Germany, Austria–Hungary and Bulgaria attacked the newest recruit to the Allied ranks. As German troops – among them the twenty-five-year-old Captain Erwin Rommel – advanced deep into the Romanian province of Transylvania, Bulgarian aircraft bombed the Romanian capital, Bucharest. The Romanians appealed to Britain and France for help. In London, the War Committee supported the view of the Chief of the Imperial General Staff, Sir William Robertson, that the best way to help Romania was for Haig to continue the attacks on the Somme.

This was already being done. In an attempt to take the pressure off the Romanian Front, France and Britain launched a new offensive on the Somme on the very day of the Central Powers' attack. So severely did the French maul the German 1st Guards Division at Cléry on September 3 that it had to be relieved, and sent to a quiet sector of the front. The division had itself come into the line only nineteen days earlier, its history notes, to relieve 'what was left' of the 1st Bavarian Division.

Also on September 3, the Germans were finally driven out of their positions on the northern and eastern edges of Delville Wood, and also from their trenches inside the village of Guillemont. Three Victoria Crosses were won in what became known as the Battle of Guillemont: by Lieutenant John Holland, Private Thomas Hughes and Sergeant David Jones. Holland and Hughes survived the war. Jones was killed a month later in the battle for the Transloy Ridges. He is buried in Bancourt British Cemetery, east of Bapaume, his remains taken there after the war. On his gravestone are inscribed the words 'He fought for God and right and liberty and such a death is immortality.'

Also killed on September 3 was Corporal Edward Dwyer, who had won the Victoria Cross a year and a half earlier near Ypres. After his award, he had been sent back to England to help spearhead a recruiting drive, speaking of his military experiences starting with the retreat from Mons, and castigating all 'shirkers'. Then he had returned to the front. He is buried in Flatiron Copse Cemetery at the edge of Mametz Wood.

Despite the ferocity of the British attack on September 3, and its successes at Guillemont and Delville Wood, two other much-fought-over features of the increasingly desolate battlefield – High Wood and the Schwaben Redoubt – remained in German hands. At the start of the attack, High Wood had been captured, but the Germans counter-attacked and, Haig noted in his diary, 'our guns could not turn on Enemy in open as they and our men were mingled together. So our troops were forced back to their original trenches near the wood.'

On the afternoon of September 3 the Canadian Corps began replacing the Australians in the line north of Contalmaison. In the words of the official historian Captain Miles, Haig wanted the Canadians 'to have a chance to settle in before undertaking any offensive operations'. Nevertheless, the toll from mortar and artillery fire was continuous. In the 2nd Canadian Sunken Road Cemetery is a row of thirteen graves: the remains of thirteen Canadian soldiers killed on the day of the changeover. On the following day Private R. F. H. Dobson, 3rd Battalion, Canadian Infantry, was killed. Born in Bridgeport, Connecticut, he was one of many American volunteers fighting on the Somme. He was twenty-two years old when he was killed in action.

To the south of the British lines, on the banks of the River Somme, the villages of Cléry and Omiécourt fell to the French. At Verdun, however, where the French had succeeded in holding the inner ring of forts, more than five hundred French soldiers were killed that evening when the Tavannes railway tunnel, being used for the accommodation of troops, blew up. The disaster was an accident, caused by fire breaking out in an ammunition store.

One of the few eyewitnesses at the Tavannes Tunnel later described how, after the explosions, 'a shattered body flew into me, or rather poured over me. I saw, three metres away, men twisting in the flames without being able to render them any help. Legs, arms, flew in the air amid the explosion of the grenades which went off without cease.' Those men who managed to reach the exit of the tunnel were caught in a German bombardment, and several were killed. Among the dead inside the tunnel were a brigade commander and his staff, and almost the whole of two companies of Territorial troops. The fire burned for three days. When finally men could enter it, they found only the dead.

The French were preparing to counter-attack at Verdun. The disaster in the Tavannes Tunnel could not deter them.

The failure to take the Schwaben Redoubt on September 3 by frontal assault led to an acrimonious inquest at II Corps headquarters. General Jacob, commander of the corps, blamed the lack of 'martial qualities' in the troops under his command. General Gough blamed lack of 'discipline and motivation', as well as 'ignorance' on the part of the commanding officers and 'poor spirit' in the men.

North of the Schwaben Redoubt, the British had been forced to cede ground along the River Ancre. This, too, was within the sphere of operations of Gough's Reserve Army. On September 4, Haig drove to see Gough at his headquarters at Toutencourt. After their discussion, Haig noted in his diary that the failure to hold the positions gained the previous day on the Ancre, or to take the Schwaben Redoubt, was due to the 49th Division, commanded by General Perceval. Haig commented, 'The units did not really attack, and some men did not follow their officers. The total losses of this division were under a thousand! It is a Territorial division from the West Riding of Yorkshire. I had occasion a fortnight ago to call the attention of the Army and Corps Commanders (Gough and Jacob) to the slackness of one of its battalions in the matter of saluting when I was motoring through the village where it was billeted. I expressed my opinion that such men were too sleepy to fight well, etc.! It was due to the failure of the 49th Division that the 39th (which did well, and got all their objectives) had to fall back.'

Fighting had continued throughout September 4. Among the British officers in action that day was a leading Irish nationalist, thirty-six-year-old Tom Kettle, a Professor of National Economics in Dublin, and former Member of the British parliament, who had enlisted in the Royal Dublin Fusiliers on the outbreak of war. He had done so, he wrote, to fight 'not for England, but for small nations': that is, for Belgium. In a letter to his brother on September 4 he wrote, 'I am calm and happy, but desperately anxious to live. If I live I mean to spend the rest of my life working for perpetual peace. I have seen war, and faced modern artillery, and know what an outrage it is against simple men.' A few weeks earlier Kettle had written to his wife, 'I want to live, too, to use all my powers of thinking and working, to drive out this foul thing called War and to put in its place understanding and comradeship.'

On September 5 an attack was made on Leuze Wood, which had been three miles behind the German front line on July 1. The stench of the dead in the communication trenches going up to the wood was so strong that some of the men going to the front line used foot powder on their faces. Before the attack the officers of the Royal Dublin Fusiliers were given pieces of green cloth to be stitched on the back of their uniforms, a symbol of Irish patriotism. Touching his patch, Tom Kettle told his soldier servant, 'Boy, I am proud to die for it!' Leading his men into action that day, Kettle was killed. His batman wrote in a letter of condolence to Kettle's wife, 'He carried his pack for Ireland and Europe. Now pack-carrying is over. He has held the line.'

One of those near Kettle when he was killed later wrote, 'I was just behind Tom when we went over the top. He was in a bent position and a bullet got over a steel waistcoat that he wore and entered his heart. Well, he only lasted about one minute, and he had my crucifix in his hand. Then Boyd took all the papers and things out of Tom's pockets in order to keep them for Mrs Kettle, but poor Boyd was blown to atoms in a few minutes.'

Boyd was twenty-nine-year-old Second Lieutenant William Hatchell Boyd, Royal Dublin Fusiliers. His body was never found. His name is on the Thiepval Memorial.

Four days before his death, Kettle – whose body was also never found, and whose name is likewise on the Thiepval Memorial – had written a poem to his baby daughter, for that future time when she might ask why her father had 'abandoned' her to go to 'dice with death':

> And oh! they'll give you rhyme
> And reason: some will call the thing sublime,
> And some decry it in a knowing tone.
> So here, while the mad guns curse overhead,

And tired men sigh with mud for couch and floor,
Know that we fools, now with the foolish dead,
Died not for flag, nor King, nor Emperor,
But for a dream, born in a herdsman's shed,
And for the secret Scripture of the poor.

Had Kettle survived the attack of September 5, he would have taken up the post of base censor, away from the daily dangers of the front line, and the assault. In his last letter to his brother he had written, 'Somewhere the Choosers of the Slain are touching, as in our Norse story they used to touch, with invisible wands those who are to die.'

Also killed on September 5 were a father and son, Sergeant George Lee, aged forty-four, and nineteen-year-old Corporal Robert Frederick Lee. Both were serving in the 156th Brigade, Royal Field Artillery. They are buried next to each other in Dartmoor Cemetery, near Albert.

On September 6, Leuze Wood was captured by men of the London Scottish Regiment – a Territorial regiment – the Royal Irish Fusiliers and the Devonshire Regiment.

Among the Canadian soldiers killed north of Contalmaison on September 7 were forty-eight-year-old Private T. Tattersall, one of the oldest private soldiers serving in the front line, and also one of the youngest, sixteen-year-old Private W. E. Dailey. On Dailey's tombstone in the Sunken Road Cemetery are the words 'Mother's darling'.

There were those who thought that the worst of the battle might be over. 'It is nice to think that our heavy fighting is coming to an end,' Noel Chavasse wrote home on the day of Private Dailey's death. 'The Huns are beaten to a frazzle in front of us. We are feeling top dogs. There is nothing like the losses we had at first.' Unknown to Chavasse, a new offensive was in prospect. Two days earlier, at Contay, Haig had seen General Byng, commanding the Canadian Corps, whose men had become known as the Bing Boys – after a revue then playing in London's West End. Haig told Byng of the plan to launch a new attack towards Flers and Lesboeufs: 'I wished him to economise his men so as to be fresh when an opportunity offered to exploit this success.'

In early September the British Prime Minister, Asquith, visited the Somme, and dined twice with Haig at Val Vion. In his diary Haig noted on September 6, 'He said he and the government are well pleased with the way the operations have been conducted here, and he is anxious to help me in every way.'

On September 8, after suffering heavy losses between Mouquet Farm and Martinpuich, the German 1st Guards Reserve Division was forced to leave the Somme for a 'calm sector' of the front north of Ypres.

That same day there was a potential setback to Haig's plan to attack Ginchy on the following day when, at Querrieu, Foch told him that the strength of the German third line was such that 'it was necessary to prepare the attack on it most thoroughly'. Foch wanted a postponement of two or three days, but finally agreed that, while the French would postpone their advance, they would lend artillery support to the British on September 9, especially against the German artillery batteries that so often caused heavy losses.

The renewed battle for Ginchy began on September 9. At heavy cost on both sides, and particularly heavy German losses, the pulverized ruins of the village were finally secured. Captain Ewald Weismann-Remscheid, of the 1st Company, 19th Bavarian Infantry Regiment, was in the German trenches a hundred yards behind Ginchy as the British artillery began its pre-attack bombardment. Earlier, the British had fought over this same ground. 'Heavy enemy fire poured down on us, sending pillars of mud, as high as houses, up into the air and showering our steel helmets with hard clods of earth,' Weismann-Remscheid later wrote. 'The drumfire grew and grew in intensity. It seemed as though the trench, which could hardly be described as such anyway, was going to be buried totally. We dug down, but we found it difficult to go deep, because as we dug we kept finding newly buried British corpses, whose stench of decomposition poisoned the air.'

There was nothing that the captain and his men could do to ease the situation. 'No chloride of lime was available,' he wrote. 'A feeling of nausea rose in our gullets! The sun climbed higher and higher. We heaved the corpses of the Tommies up in front of the trench. To have attempted to move to the rear would have meant certain death, so the medical orderlies threw our fallen comrades into the shellholes behind the position. There they lay with distorted faces and glazed eyes staring up at the sky.'

It was the British 16th Division that attacked the German trenches in front of Ginchy. The village was captured, two hundred Germans were taken prisoner, and a German counter-attack at night failed because the German troops lost their way in the dark. But it had been a fierce twenty-four-hour struggle, during which two commanding officers were killed: fifty-year-old Lieutenant Colonel Hubert Dalzell-Walton, 8th Battalion, Royal Inniskilling Fusiliers, who is buried in the Bronfay Farm Military Cemetery at Bray-sur-Somme, and Lieutenant Colonel FitzRoy Curzon, 6th Battalion Royal Irish Fusiliers, who is buried in the Carnoy Military Cemetery.

So heavy were the British losses in the capture of Ginchy – 240 officers and 4,090 other ranks out of 435 officers and 10,410 other ranks – that the division was withdrawn. Even holding a static line was never free of risk.

Among those Britons killed in the capture of Ginchy was twenty-seven-year-old Major Cedric Charles Dickens, 13th Battalion, London Regiment (the Kensington Battalion). Major Dickens was a grandson of the author Charles Dickens. He was hit by machine-gun fire from a German strongpoint near Bouleaux Wood. His men buried him in the shellhole where he fell. After the war, when the war cemeteries were being established, his body could not be found. He is named on the Thiepval Memorial. Down a track near Bouleaux Wood is one of the few private memorials on the Somme; it was set up by his parents, who also put up a plaque to him in Ginchy Church.

Also killed on September 9 was one of the American volunteers who were fighting on the Somme: Private Burton J. Wellington, of Troy, New York, who had enlisted in the 1st Canadian Infantry. He was nineteen years old. His grave is in the Sunken Road Cemetery near where he fell.

Haig was in confident mood. On September 9, as the battle for Ginchy was under way, he was visited at Val Vion by General Kavanagh, commander of the Cavalry Corps. Haig explained to Kavanagh, 'I thought that after the next attack' – the one planned for September 15 – 'the crisis of the battle is likely to be reached, and the moment might possibly be favourable for cavalry action.' Haig then went into details about how the cavalry should operate, starting with three 'main groups' and being prepared to 'put forth the greatest effort and be ready to suffer privation for several days in order to reap the fruits of victory'.

Here once more was the hope of a cavalry breakthrough beyond the German third line that would penetrate deeply into German-held territory. Haig also spoke that day to his Quartermaster General, General Maxwell, about 'the supply of troops in the event of a pursuit'. The difficulty, Haig noted in his diary, of infantry exploiting the cavalry's success would be 'due to the broken state of the ground and roads from shell fire'.

The suffering of the German troops was becoming acute. On September 10 the German 4th Guards Division, which had already been forced to withdraw from the battlefield three weeks earlier because of heavy casualties, and had then returned to the Thiepval sector, was forced to withdraw again, after what its history describes as 'some severe local battles'. Also in action on the Thiepval sector, and later near Pozières, the 2nd Guards Reserve Division was to lose 51 per cent of its men in dead and wounded during its five months on the Somme. The 17th Reserve Division experienced the same scale of loss between September 21 and October 10.

During September 10, three members of the London Regiment (Royal Fusiliers) were killed by a German shell at Falfemont Farm, near Combles: they were twenty-nine-year-old Captain Richard Heumann, thirty-six-year-old Company Sergeant Major B. Mills, and twenty-four-year-old Sergeant A. W. Torrance. They were buried where they were killed, in what is today the smallest war cemetery on the Somme: theirs are the only graves there.

On September 11 the 10th Canadian Infantry Battalion was holding the line opposite Mouquet Farm. 'Nothing out of the ordinary occurred,' writes the battalion historian. Forty men were wounded, and six were killed. One of the dead was Private Gibson Skelton, whose brother had been killed in action three months earlier. Four days before he was killed, Skelton had written to his mother, 'One never knows what the next morning may bring forth, especially here where the "Huns" use such means of taking life. Should anything happen to me do not weep too much or be heartbroken. Remember that I am in God's keeping.' Wounded in the stomach by shrapnel, Private Skelton was taken back to a dressing station, where he died later that day. He is buried in the Albert Communal Cemetery Extension.

September 12 saw the capture of the village of Bouchavesnes by the French Light Infantry Brigade, commanded by General Messimy, a former Minister of War. This was the furthest French advance on the Somme, and, according to Foch, the most significant French gain. What Foch could not reveal was that, following the capture of Bouchavesnes, a French Army radio intelligence unit, intercepting and decrypting German radio signals, learned sufficient details of the counter-attack – the size of the troop concentration and the precise timing – to forestall it. Péronne, the town that had been the French objective on July 1, remained firmly under German control.

Also on September 12, the British Secretary of State for War, David Lloyd George, visited the British sector of the front. As he emerged from a captured German dugout near Fricourt, the troops watching gave him a rousing cheer. Within three months he was to be their Prime Minister. That same day, Lloyd George met Haig, Joffre and the French Minister of Munitions, Albert Thomas, at 14th Army headquarters at Méaulte.

Haig was growing dissatisfied with French support, writing in his diary on September 14, 'It is interesting to see how the French have kept on delaying their attacks! Their big attack south of the Somme which was to have gone in on the 3rd has not yet been launched, and will probably not go in till the 15th. While the attacks of the 6th Army which were to have gone in with such vigour at the beginning of the month have not yet materialised!'

Haig added, critically, 'The fact is that the French infantry is very poor now and lacks the offensive spirit. On the other hand such progress as the French have made has been achieved against a much smaller concentration of artillery than the Enemy has collected against the British, and judging by a comparison of the German prisoners working on the roads, those taken by the French are very much inferior in physique.'

Asquith, during his visit to the Somme, had been able to see his son Raymond, then with the Guards Division, and to gain some impression of the battlefield. On September 12 he reported on his visit to the War Committee. At Fricourt, he told the committee, he had found the generals, officers and men 'all in highest spirits'. The men of the 7th Division, who were getting ready to attack Ginchy at the time of his visit, were 'full of confidence'. Although their assault had not been 'entirely successful', two days later the Irish had turned it into a 'successful operation'.

These were bland words with regard to a fierce fight, but Asquith did not shy away from the problems the operations faced. 'The advances were a question of push, push and must necessarily be slow work,' he told his colleagues. He had seen many German prisoners, and found that 'they were fine men and looked well fed.' When he had asked General Allenby, commanding the Third Army, what the prospects were of employing the cavalry – as Haig continued to hope, to exploit the breakthrough – Allenby warned that it was 'no use sending Cavalry through a small opening', and that it would be 'a great mistake to send Cavalry forward unless they can take a whole length of front'.

Asked by a Conservative member of the committee, Lord Curzon – a former Viceroy of India – whether it was expected to push through the German line by Christmas, Asquith said he 'did not think so'. Sir Edward Grey, the Foreign Secretary, agreed that 'we must keep going', but wanted to know 'what it leads to'. General Robertson gave the committee the benefit of his expert military advice that there was 'nothing else to be done'.

There was, however, one glimmer of hope, a new weapon which, the War Committee was told, would be going into action in three days' time. This was the 'caterpillar machine-gun destroyer', soon to be better known as the tank. Asquith told the War Committee that he was worried that these experimental vehicles 'could be knocked out with ease by an artillery barrage'. On becoming Commander-in-Chief at the end of 1915, Haig had ordered a thousand of them, but, Asquith told the War Committee, only sixty-two would be available for the attack on September 15.

In answer to questions about whether the tanks should be kept out of the battle until there were more of them, Asquith told the committee that the timing of the use of the new weapon 'could be safely left to Sir Douglas Haig'.

★

On the Somme, awaiting the new offensive, Captain Harold Macmillan wrote to his mother on September 13, 'The flies are again a terrible plague, and the stench from the dead bodies which lie in heaps around us is awful.' Macmillan added, 'The act of death in battle is noble and glorious. But the physical appearance and actual symptoms of death are, in these terrible circumstances, revolting only and horrid.'

In the early hours of September 15, Captain Oliver Lyttelton, 3rd Battalion, Grenadier Guards, moved forward with his men. 'It was pitch dark, and we marched slowly in our heavy equipment,' he wrote later. 'There was a sensation that this slowness was prolonging our last night on earth and drawing out our last living hours.' When German artillery fired a few salvos of gas shells, the battalion 'was ordered to halt and put on gas masks: we moved off again down the far slope. Pitch dark: a Verey light or two: a little shelling: silence: curses.'

One of the climactic confrontations of the Battle of the Somme was about to begin.

12

The arrival of the tanks:
'We are feeling top dogs'

A POTENTIALLY DRAMATIC turn in the British and Allied fortunes took place on September 15, when tanks were used for the first time in battle. Sixty-two had been promised by the War Office in July. Forty-nine had been sent over to France at the end of August. Thirty-two had been assembled near Trones Wood and then dispersed along the front on the eve of the attack. Eighteen were in action. The attack began at daylight. Private Thomas Littler, 5th Battalion, Cheshire Regiment, noted in his diary, 'We made a big attack at Leuze Wood and advanced 1 mile in depth taking four lines of trenches, we had 12 large caterpillars to help in this attack, which began at 4.30 a.m. Our losses were slight in comparison with the Germans.'

At 8.40 that morning, three of the new war-making devices were seen entering Flers. Flying over the village, an Allied airman reported, 'A Tank is walking up the High Street of Flers with the British Army cheering behind.' The village of Flers, the first objective, soon fell to New Zealand troops, supported by the new armoured monster.

During the fighting on September 15, the 11th Battalion, Queen's Own Royal West Kent Regiment, advancing towards Flers, came to a trench – named Flers Trench – that, in the words of the regiment's historian, C. T. Atkinson, 'was full of Germans, but very few put up a stiff fight; many surrendered, others bolted towards the village under heavy fire from machine guns of the tanks which had by now overtaken the infantry.' Casualties were, however, heavy, and on the following day the commander of the 11th Battalion, Lieutenant Colonel Arthur Fitzhenry Townsend, who had been hit by shrapnel during the advance, died of his wounds. Taken back from the front to a casualty clearing station south-west of Albert, he is buried at Heilly Station Cemetery, near where he died.

Lieutenant Colonel the Earl of Feversham, commanding officer of the 21st Battalion, King's Royal Rifle Corps, and the highest ranking British aristocrat in action on the Somme, was killed on September 15, having taken two hundred men forward in the struggle for the Flers Trench. After the battle his body was one of 4,000 brought in from the battlefield to the Australian Imperial Force (AIF) Burial Ground at Flers. Of these 4,000, 2,263 were unidentified.

Progress on the right flank of the attack on September 15 was 'not satisfactory', Haig noted in his diary. Having driven from Val Vion to Querrieu early that afternoon, he 'impressed upon General Rawlinson the necessity for getting forward to Lesboeufs and Gueudecourt tonight if possible'. Haig was told that the Guards were within five hundred yards of Lesboeufs, but that 'there was a strong line in their front with good wire.'

While at Querrieu, Haig pressed for greater action on the battlefield, urging that Lord Cavan, commanding XIV Corps, attack Martinpuich 'as soon as possible', so that Gough's Reserve Army could capture Courcelette. After driving from Querrieu to Gough's headquarters at Toutencourt, Haig learned that the Canadian Corps was about to attack Courcelette.

The Canadian attack began at three o'clock in the afternoon, when Private John Chipman Kerr, of the 49th (Edmonton) Battalion, led a charge that was to enter the annals of Canadian military history. As Lieutenant Colonel G. R. Stevens, chronicler of the military service of soldiers from Edmonton, Alberta, wrote, 'Although his finger had been blown off he sprang from shelter and raced along the top of the trench, shooting down the enemy bombers from traverse to traverse. His astonishing onslaught proved the last straw for the badly shaken Germans and sixty-two unwounded prisoners surrendered. Having delivered his captives at a support trench, Kerr returned to action without troubling to have his wound dressed.'

Kerr was awarded the Victoria Cross. He was one of fourteen volunteers from a single family. In order to enlist, he and his brother had walked fifty miles in midwinter from their remote farmstead to the nearest railhead. He survived the war, returning to British Columbia, where he died in 1963 at the age of seventy-six.

The Princess Patricia's Canadian Light Infantry were also in action on September 15. Among their officers was Lieutenant Harold

Gitz-Rice, whose song 'Keep Your Head Down, Fritzie Boy' ended with the chorus:

> We beat them on the Marne,
> We beat them on the Aisne,
> We gave them hell
> At Neuve Chapelle
> And here we are again!

As they advanced, the Princess Pat's – of whom it was said that they were 'scared of nought except rats' – found it difficult to make out anything in the shell-shattered landscape, and suffered heavy casualties from German machine-gunners hidden in the shellholes. But they pushed ahead, and took more than seventy prisoners.

High Wood saw the most effective German resistance on September 15. The 47th (London) Division was beaten off in the morning, but in the afternoon it mounted a second attack, which drove out the defending 4th Bavarian Division. Within forty-eight hours, the Bavarians were forced to withdraw from the battle. In three weeks of fighting between Martinpuich and Longueval, in what its history calls the 'violent battles' for High Wood, their division lost 5,361 men dead and wounded – 60 per cent of its strength.

There was also success in the air for the attackers on September 15. During the day, three Royal Flying Corps aeroplanes hit and blew up a German troop and munitions train as it steamed into Gouzeaucourt Station. Five bombing planes hit Bapaume Station, flying low to drop their bombs on a train, stationary wagons and the station itself. Other planes attacked troops and munitions trains at Ribécourt and Epéhy, and a supply dump at Bantouzelle. Lieutenant Albert Ball – later a Victoria Cross winner – was among the fighter pilots who, with his machine gun, shot down one of the many German aeroplanes that tried to intercept the bombers. At the end of the day, six British and fourteen German aeroplanes had been shot down. In all, twelve British airmen were killed.

Among the troops taking advantage of the tanks during the advance on September 15 was the 3rd Battalion of the Guards Division. At four in the morning, sandwiches and an issue of rum were served to the men, who then had to try to get some sleep. At six o'clock the British artillery began to fire on the German trenches. A German barrage followed in almost immediate retaliation. At 6.20 a.m. the whistles were blown and the assault began.

The 3rd Battalion's objective was German-held Lesboeufs. Hardly had the soldiers left their trenches than Lieutenant Raymond Asquith, the Prime Minister's son, and the prospective Liberal candidate for Derby, was shot through the chest leading his men forward. In order that they should not know that he was mortally wounded, he lit a cigarette as he lay on the ground. He died on the stretcher while being taken to a dressing station.

Raymond Asquith's grave is in Guillemont Road Cemetery. He was thirty-seven years old. Three days before he was killed he had written to his wife, Katherine, his 'Fawnia', 'I am getting terribly tired of not being at home, and not seeing my sweetest Fawnia. But I must see out the fighting season. Tomorrow we shall move forward again, probably into the line.'

Three months later, Winston Churchill, a friend of the Asquith family for more than a decade, wrote to Katherine Asquith – whose younger son was born five months after his father was killed – 'I always had an intense admiration for Raymond, and also a warm affection for him; and both were old established ties . . . I remember so vividly the last time I saw him – at Montreuil in early May. We sat or strolled for two hours on the old ramparts in bright sunshine, and talked about the war, about the coming offensive, about his son, about all sorts of things.' Churchill added, 'I like to dwell on these wartime memories. These gallant charming figures that flash and gleam amid the carnage – always so superior to it, masters of their souls, disdainful of death and suffering – are an inspiration and an example to all. And he was one of the very best. He did everything easily – I never remember anyone who seemed so independent of worldly or physical things: and yet he enjoyed everything and had an appreciation of life and letters and men and women, and manners and customs refined and subtle to the last degree.'

In the battle for the outskirts of Lesboeufs on September 15, Captain Harold Alexander – later Commander-in-Chief of the Allied forces in Italy in 1944 – was in action with the 2nd Battalion, Irish Guards.

Of the thousand men in the battalion, only 166 were alive and unin-jured when the roll was called at the end of the day.

Another Guards officer in action on September 15 was Captain Oliver Lyttelton, 3rd Battalion, Grenadier Guards. 'A few yards after leaving our trenches', he later wrote, 'we were met by a withering fire. Our friends on the right were soon brought to a stop, and the rattle of machine-gun fire from the flank showed that our fears of being enfiladed had been well founded. At this moment, the commanding officer was hit through the thigh, a very severe wound, and the drill sergeant killed. Although they could not have been more than a yard from me, I was unaware that either of them had fallen.'

The Germans, who had been 'severely hammered by shellfire in their trenches on the top of the ridge, had pushed forward a company or two to the foot of the slope in front of us, and were firing at us from a group of shellholes. Suddenly the men saw them and, with a hoarse blood cry which I can still hear in my dreams, rushed this line and before we could stop them had bayoneted or shot most of the defenders. I say before we could stop them, because my confused impression is that the enemy shot at us till we were less than ten yards away, and then put their hands up.'

After that, Lyttelton wrote, 'nothing would have stopped the Grenadiers – nothing.' Ahead of them was a glacis – a gentle upward slope. 'We stumbled forward, under increased fire, up the glacis. I was myself in a great state of excitement and for a few minutes fighting mad. We took the trench at the summit, and some prisoners, got our breath, and looked around. I found the units much mixed up: some Coldstreamers, Grenadiers and Irish Guardsmen were on either side of me. I could not find an officer at the moment, so I organized about a hundred men and put myself in command.'

Lyttelton went in search of a machine gun. As he did so, 'I stumbled into Lieutenant Colonel Guy Baring of the Coldstream Guards. He said, "Where's my battalion?" "I've just been trying to give them some covering fire, Sir: there is one company trying to get forward now." "I must join them at once," he said, and started to climb the trench. "Not that way, Sir, go round a little, you will get hit here. No, please, Sir," I said. "Please." He paid no attention and clambered up the trench. I heard a bullet strike him, and he fell back dead into my arms.'

Baring is buried in Citadel New Military Cemetery, Fricourt.

A minute or two after Baring was killed, Lyttelton remembered seeing his colonel, John Campbell, 'with his headquarters in a shell-hole a few yards behind our line. He had a hunting horn, which he was blowing from time to time, though for what reason I could not guess. He was full of fight and enthusiasm. He saw me, and shouted, "Come here, Oliver." I joined him in the shellhole. We argued about exactly where we were, and I convinced him that it was not where he thought. "Those bastards in that redoubt are holding us up: go and get a few men and bomb them out." This was not far from a sentence of death, but needs must when you get an order. Back I went, collected a dozen men and a few boxes of bombs, and started bombing down the trench. The method I employed was the conventional one of rushing to the place where the last bomb had exploded, with a couple of men overground on either side of the trench.'

After moving forward in this way about forty yards, Lyttelton 'heard the drum of feet making towards us down the trench. I pulled the sides of the trench down and rapped out an order to one of the men to mount our Lewis gun. The first German to appear was shot dead at about five yards' range: he had his hands up, but it was impossible to see this in time to stop. "Cease fire!" I shouted, and then appeared eighty or ninety others, all with their hands up. I passed them quickly down the trench, rather in fear that they might knock us on the head when they saw that we were only twelve. Of course forty yards away there were quite enough men to deal with them.'

Proudly, Lyttelton reported back to Colonel Campbell in his shell-hole: 'The redoubt is cleared, Sir, and I've captured a hundred prisoners.'

Another Guards officer in action that day, with the 4th Battalion, Grenadier Guards, was Captain Harold Macmillan, the future Prime Minister, who in 1944 was Field Marshal Alexander's political colleague as British Minister Resident in Italy. From 1951 to 1955 Macmillan, Lyttelton and Alexander served together as Cabinet colleagues in Churchill's post-war government: three veterans of the Somme in a single administration.

Macmillan was badly wounded in the attack. He survived throughout the morning in No-Man's Land, lying in a shellhole. Twice the shellhole was blown in on top of him by German shells exploding a few yards away. While lying there, in pain, he read his pocket edition of Aeschylus's *Prometheus Bound*, in the original Greek. Then, as he later wrote to his mother, as afternoon drew on 'I took ½ grain morphia and succeeded in sleeping till 3.30 p.m.,' when the company sergeant major, reaching him in the bottom of the shellhole, requested, as if on the parade ground, 'Thank you, sir, for leave to carry you away.'

Macmillan later tried to reconstruct what happened to him next. He was first, as he recalled, taken into the captured German trench, where the battalion doctor gave him first aid for his wounds and the commanding officer, Brigadier General 'Crawley' de Crespigny, told him, 'Well, I think you'd better be off.' So Macmillan and another officer, Captain 'Dog' Ritchie, who had been wounded in the arm, were taken away on two stretchers under cover of darkness. The field ambulance to which they were being taken was said to be in Ginchy, but the stretcher-bearers did not know the way, and when they eventually reached Ginchy the village was being heavily shelled and they could not find the ambulance.

After talking together, the two wounded officers decided not to risk the lives of four able bodied guardsmen any further. They therefore told the stretcher-bearers to return to the battalion, saying that they themselves would make what progress they could. In the darkness and confusion of the shelling, Macmillan and Ritchie became separated. Then, Macmillan later told his biographer, Alistair Horne, for the first time that 'grim day fear set in'. He went on to explain that 'bravery is not really vanity, but a kind of concealed pride, because everybody is watching you. Then I was safe, but alone, and absolutely terrified because there was no need to show off any more, no need to pretend . . . there was nobody for whom you were responsible, not even the stretcher-bearers. Then I was very frightened . . . I do remember the sudden feeling – you went through a whole battle for two days . . . suddenly there was nobody there . . . you could cry if you wanted to.'

Macmillan was fortunate. Somehow, and he never quite knew how he made it, as his right knee 'was stiff and unusable – and painful' – he managed to drag himself in the dark out of Ginchy and the enemy shelling, and rolled into a ditch. Later – he was unable to remember just how many hours passed – he was picked up by a transport officer of the Sherwood Foresters, who had him put in a horse-ambulance cart and took him further down the line to the proper dressing station.

After that, Macmillan recalled nothing more until he regained consciousness in a French hospital in Abbeville. From there he was sent back to hospital in England, where the surgeons decided it would be too risky to try to remove the bullet fragments in his pelvis. This gave him, for the rest of his life, a shuffling walk. He remained on crutches, with a tube in the wound, in pain and discomfort, for four years.

During the day on which he was wounded, Macmillan recalled seeing a tank – one of 'these strange objects' – bogged down in a shellhole.

Ten of the eighteen British tanks in action on September 15 had been hit by German shellfire. Nine broke down with mechanical difficulties. Five failed to advance. But those that did manage to go forward were able to advance more than 2,000 yards – by far the deepest penetration of the German lines since the battle had begun on July 1.

The attack on September 15 was in marked contrast to that of July 1. Three heavily fortified villages, Flers, Martinpuich and Courcelette, were captured, together with 4,000 German prisoners, and an advance was made of almost a mile, along a six-mile front. Only in the French sector were the attacks unsuccessful, with neither of the day's objectives, Rancourt or Frégicourt, being captured. 'I don't think there was much vigour in them' was Haig's comment about his ally.

Reading about the first appearance of the tanks in action, Winston Churchill, who had urged their development almost two years earlier, and put Admiralty money behind their construction, wrote to his former First Sea Lord, Admiral Fisher, 'My poor "land battleships" have been let off prematurely and on a petty scale. In that idea resided one real victory.' Recognizing the potential of the new weapon, Haig asked the War Office for a thousand of an improved pattern, with heavier defensive armour. He was told that he could have forty more of the existing type by October 14, and, starting on November 12, about twenty a week of the improved version.

The military successes on September 15 encouraged Haig to renew the offensive on the following day. But, as he wrote in his diary, 'Owing to the disorder and mixing up of units which is inseparable from every fight, and in the case of an inexperienced Army is more difficult to

straighten out, the attacks proposed for 9 a.m. today did not take place.'
The 'disorder' was easy to account for. Captain Miles, in his official
history, described the scene that evening, when showers of rain 'made
the muddy, shell-shattered ground still more difficult to negotiate'. At
the same time, in bringing down the wounded, 'stretcherbearers
laboured to the point of exhaustion, despite the assistance they
received from the combatant troops and from parties of prisoners'.

There would have to be at least a four-day postponement. 'Time is
required to relieve troops and prepare,' Haig wrote in his diary that
night. As for his ally to the south, Haig was scathing: 'How different
the French talk today, to last week! Then they were making such dispositions in depth that there would be no delay – once the attack
started, it would be continuous until the line was pierced. Now the
experience of the reality has shown the folly of their previous ideas!
A delay of four days is wanted to prepare for the next attack.'

13

The struggle intensifies: 'Death and decomposition strew the ground'

HAVING VISITED THE Western Front for the first time on 6 September 1916, Field Marshal Hindenburg and General Ludendorff, who hitherto had entirely focused on Germany's war with Russia, came to the conclusion that it was in the West that the war must be won; that a victorious peace could be secured for Germany only by the defeat of the Anglo-French armies in France and Flanders. But already, the Romanian entry into the war on the side of the Allies had raised the spectre of Germany's vulnerability in the East.

Hindenburg reacted swiftly. On September 15, the very day of Britain's greatest success thus far on the Somme, he declared, 'The main task of the Armies is now to hold fast all positions on the Western, Eastern, Italian and Macedonian Fronts, and to employ all other available forces against Romania.'

Not only military manpower, but civilian labour was to be conscripted into the German war effort. A newly devised 'Hindenburg Industrial Programme' involved the recruitment of German labourers and the forcible deportation to Germany of 700,000 Belgian workers. These forced labourers were to be put to work immediately. On September 16, while visiting Cambrai, Hindenburg gave orders for a 'semi-permanent' defence line to be constructed behind the Western Front, ten to thirty-five miles east of the front-line trenches. This was to be known as the Hindenburg Line, a deep fortified zone that was intended to halt any Allied military breakthrough before it could approach the Belgian or German frontier.

The struggle on the Somme continued. Among those killed on September 16 was Dillwyn Parrish Starr, a thirty-two-year-old American, serving as a lieutenant in the Coldstream Guards. Born in

Philadelphia and educated at Harvard, Starr had volunteered in 1914 as an ambulance driver with the French, served with the British armoured cars at Gallipoli, and then transferred to the Guards, with whom he went to the Somme. He is buried in the Guards' Cemetery at Lesboeufs.

Among the thousands of soldiers ordered into action on September 16 was one who was soon to face a firing squad of his fellow soldiers. When the order came to move forward to the front line, Private Henry Farr refused. 'I cannot stand it,' he said. He was then dragged forward, screaming and struggling, but broke away and ran back. He had only recently been released from hospital after treatment for shell shock, having been at the front since the outbreak of war more than two years earlier. Court-martialled for cowardice, Farr was executed.

Seventy-seven years after Farr's execution, his granddaughter, Janet Booth, hoped that a Private Member's Bill, introduced by Andrew Mackinlay into the House of Commons on 19 October 1993 on behalf of all those executed for cowardice and desertion in the First World War, would lead to a posthumous pardon. The bill was unsuccessful. Fifteen year later, on 9 January 2006, a former child refugee to Britain, Lord Dubs, raised the issue in the House of Lords. Andrew Mackinlay plans an amendment to a future Armed Forces Disciplinary Bill. The search for pardons goes on.

As September 16 came to an end there was yet more action. Private Thomas Littler noted in his diary how, that night, 'we had reinforcements sent to us, and went forward and dug an advanced fire trench, but the guide took us the wrong way, and led us into the enemy lines, the Germans opened a heavy fire on us, and we retired hastily but with casualties.'

Also during the night of September 16, the 6th Battalion, Oxfordshire and Buckinghamshire Light Infantry – the Oxs and Bucks – moved forward into the line from its billets in Corbie and Méaulte. Leaving its billets at 8.30 p.m., the battalion reached the front line a gruelling six hours later, at 2.20 a.m. Among those going forward was Captain Arthur Graeme West. A student at Balliol College, Oxford, when war broke out, he had been rejected for an officer's commission because of poor eyesight. He therefore enlisted as a private, becoming an officer in 1916.

From his forward trench on September 17, Captain Graeme West wrote to a friend, 'The men were dog-tired when they got here, and though ordered to dig, complied very unwillingly, and were allowed to sit about or lean on their spades, or even to stand up and fall asleep against the side of the trench. It was a smelly trench. A dead German – a big man – lay on his stomach as if he were crawling over the parados down into the trench; he had lain there some days, and that corner of trench reeked even when someone took him by the legs and pulled him away out of sight, though not out of smell, into a shell-hole. We sat down and fell into a comatose state, so tired we were. On our right lay a large man covered with a waterproof, his face hidden by a sandbag, whom we took to be a dead Prussian guardsman, but the light of dawn showed him to be an Englishman by his uniform.'

Three days later, Captain West described the arrival of a German shell on the Oxs and Bucks trenches. 'It exploded, and a cloud of black reek went up – in the communication trench again. You went down it; two men were buried, perhaps more you were told, certainly two. The trench was a mere undulation of newly turned earth, under it somewhere lay two men or more. You dug furiously. No sign. Perhaps you were standing on a couple of men now, pressing the life out of them, on their faces or chests. A boot, a steel helmet – and you dig and scratch and uncover a grey, dirty face, pitifully drab and ugly, the eyes closed, the whole thing limp and mean-looking . . . Perhaps the man is alive and kicks feebly or frantically as you unbury him: anyhow, here is the first, and God knows how many are not beneath him. At last you get them out, three dead, grey muddy masses, and one more jibbering live one. Then another shell falls and more are buried.'

In aerial combat on September 17, against British pilots who had flown from the Somme to Cambrai on a bombing mission, the future German air ace Manfred von Richthofen had his first 'kill', qualifying him for the award of a silver drinking goblet with the inscription 'To the Victor in Air Battle'. He quickly ordered a miniature version from a Berlin jeweller. A year and a half later, with as many as eighty downed British and French aircraft to his credit, Richthofen – the Red Baron – was shot down and killed over the very area that had been the Somme battlefield.

During that aerial combat on September 17, led by the then top German air ace, Oswald Boelcke, the British planes met their match in a new German aeroplane, the Albatross, that was both faster and better armed than its British and French counterparts. This German superiority would soon become clear to the British commanders, and to the infantrymen watching the fierce and often fatal struggles in the sky above them.

Among those killed on September 17 in an attack on a German trench near Mouquet Farm was Private Herbert Rice of the Lincolnshire Regiment. His name is on the Thiepval Memorial. Eighty-nine years after his death his niece Irene Palfrey and her husband, George, left a message at one of the cemeteries on the battlefield: 'Lost forever on the Somme, never found, never forgotten'.

Private Herbert Rice's brother Arthur was killed almost a year later; his name is on another memorial to the missing, at Arras, on which are inscribed the names of 34,739 soldiers with no known grave. A third Rice brother, Ernest, who had emigrated to Canada before the war, fought on the Somme with the 4th Canadian Division, and survived. Irene Palfrey's grandfather on her mother's side, Gerard Miles, a skipper in the Royal Naval Reserve, was killed at sea on Christmas Day 1916. His name is inscribed on the Chatham Memorial; he is one of 8,500 First World War British sailors with no known grave.

George Palfrey's side of the family also fought in the First World War. His grandfather Harry, who was wounded during the retreat from Mons in 1914, was killed in Palestine in 1917. His name is one of 3,298 on the Jerusalem Memorial to the Missing.

Encouraging news reached Haig on September 18, when General Trenchard reported, in what turned out to be one of his last encouraging reports that year, that the Royal Flying Corps aeroplanes were 'taking the offensive and carrying the war in the air beyond the Enemy's lines', with the result that they were 'free to carry on their important duties of observation and photography unmolested'. The most important result of this was that those who were planning the coming battles were able to examine detailed photographs of the German trenches and fortifications.

The prospect of success was ever-present in Haig's mind, and in the minds of many of the commanders. On September 18 there was a large cavalry march near Hardecourt Wood, watched by the infantrymen, who were still the main arm of the offensive. But there was, even so, no sector of the front where the cavalry could exploit an infantry success.

Although the British and French offensives had been delayed, the daily hazards of trench warfare continued without respite, for both sides. On September 19, after only a week in action against the French forces south of the River Somme, the German 13th Division suffered such heavy losses that it was forced to pull out of the battle altogether. New troops on both sides were always ready to be sent into the line. On September 22 a Canadian officer, Major William Ashplant, from London, Ontario, who three weeks earlier had been wounded in the head by a shellburst, returned to action with his battalion, in an attack on the German trenches east of Courcelette. His military file records that he was last seen that day 'in a shellhole with Machine Gun wounds in stomach and leg'. A search party on the following morning 'failed to locate him'. His name is inscribed on the Vimy Memorial to the Missing; he is one of 11,167 Canadians killed in France in the First World War who have no known graves.

On September 22 there was another British attack on Lesboeufs. Among those who took part was nineteen-year-old Lieutenant Edward Wyndham Tennant. Having left his school, Winchester, at the age of seventeen in order to enlist, he had been in the trenches since shortly after his eighteenth birthday. His poem 'The Mad Soldier' opened with the lines:

> I dropp'd here three weeks ago, yes – I know,
> And it's bitter cold at night, since the fight –
> I could tell you if I chose – no one knows
> Excep' me and four or five, what ain't alive.
> I can see them all asleep, three men deep,
> And they're nowhere near a fire – but our wire
> Has 'em fast as can be. Can't you see
> When the flare goes up? Ssh! boys; what's that noise?
> Do you know what these rats eat? Body-meat!

The rats were a never-forgotten feature of the battlefield. In 2004, eighty-six years after he was on the Somme in 1918, Private Cecil Withers, 17th Battalion, Royal Fusiliers, then aged 106, told the historian Max Arthur, for his book *Last Post*, 'I remember once, on the Somme, seeing half a dozen of our English boys, all in pieces in a big shellhole. They were half buried, stinking. It was hot and there was a terrible stench and they were covered in bluebottles and cockroaches. It was a terrible sight. These poor boys. It made me sick. We had to smoke strong Turkish cigarettes to hide the smell. On the firestep in the trenches during the night, you could hear the groaning of the dying – but you couldn't go out to help them. There were rats feeding on their flesh. They were dying there, dying in misery and pain, and the rats were nibbling away at their flesh.'

Two days before going into action, Lieutenant Tennant wrote to his mother, 'I am full of hope and trust and pray that I may be worthy of my fighting ancestors. The one I know best is Sir Henry Wyndham, whose bust is in the hall of 44 Belgrave Square, and there is a picture of him on the stairs at 34 Queen Anne's Gate': their two London homes. As to the coming action, 'We shall probably attack over about 1,200 yards, but we shall have such artillery support as will properly smash the Boche line we are going for, and even (which is unlikely) if the artillery doesn't come up to our hopes, the spirit of the Brigade of Guards will carry all resistance before it. The pride of being in such a great regiment! The thought that all the old men "late Grenadier Guards", who sit in the London clubs, are thinking and hoping about what we are doing here!'

Tennant added, 'I have never been prouder of anything, except your love for me, than I am of being a Grenadier. Today is a great day for me.' A line of General Sir Henry Wyndham, who as a young officer had served at the Battle of Waterloo, rang through his mind: 'High heart, high speech, high deeds, 'mid honouring eyes.' Tennant told his mother, 'I went to a service on the side of a hill this morning and took the Holy Communion afterwards, which always seems to help one along, doesn't it? I slept like a top last night, and dreamed that someone I know very well (but I can't remember who it was) came to me and told me how much I had grown. Three or four of my brother officers read my poems yesterday, and they all liked them very much which pleased me enormously.'

On September 22, Lieutenant Tennant was sniping, in a sap – a covered trench dug to a point near or within an enemy position – that was occupied by both British and German soldiers, separated only by a small barrier. He was killed by a German sniper. His grave, like that of his family friend Raymond Asquith, who had been killed a week earlier, is in Guillemont Road Cemetery. The two graves were deliberately put near each other by their commanding officer. On hearing of Raymond Asquith's death, and the deaths of several others whom he knew, Tennant had written home, 'It is a terrible list . . . Death and decomposition strew the ground.'

Still in the forward trenches with the Oxfordshire and Buckinghamshire Light Infantry, on September 24 Captain Arthur Graeme West was spurred to a reflection on war-making. 'Most men', he wrote, 'fight if not happily, at any rate patiently, sure of the necessity and usefulness of their work. So did I – once! Now it all looks to me so absurd and brutal that I can only force myself to continue in a kind of dream-state; I hypnotise myself to undergo it. What good, what happiness can be produced by some of the scenes I have had to witness in the last few days? Even granting it was necessary to resist Germany by arms at the beginning – and this I have yet most carefully to examine – why go on? Is it not known to both armies that each is utterly weary and heartsick? Of course it is. Then why, in God's name, go on?'

Captain West survived the fighting on the Somme, including a shell that killed seven men at the moment his battalion reached Trones Wood on September 29. Then, six months later, in a trench outpost far to the east of the Somme battlefield, he was killed by a stray bullet. His grave is in Ecoust-Saint-Mein Cemetery, five miles north-east of Bapaume.

On September 25 a substantial and sustained British attack was launched along a six-mile front, when Lord Cavan's XIV Corps moved against Morval and Lesboeufs. As the battle began, Royal Flying Corps airmen bombed German troops in their trenches, and British counter-battery work silenced 24 of the 124 German heavy-artillery batteries, one of the highest success rates in the Somme battle.

The strongly fortified Morval, which was on high ground, fell to the 5th and 6th Divisions. Unusually for a commanding officer,

Lieutenant Colonel P. V. P. Stone of the 1st Battalion, Norfolk Regiment, received permission to lead his battalion forward in person, on the grounds that the many newcomers from three other regiments had not yet settled down. Stone was said at the time to have 'treated the attack as a pheasant shoot, with his servant as loader'. He and the men he led forward took the first objective in a single rush, killing many Germans and capturing more than a hundred.

Lesboeufs – in earlier attacks on which Raymond Asquith and Edward Tennant had been killed and Harold Macmillan wounded – was attacked by the Guards Division, including the 2nd Battalion, Grenadier Guards, who, when they found the German wire uncut by the British artillery, braved intense German machine-gun fire to cut it by hand.

By late afternoon on September 25, some of XIV Corps had penetrated 500 yards beyond Morval and Lesboeufs. When Haig visited Cavan that afternoon at his headquarters at Méaulte, Cavan told him 'that the Enemy only put up a good fight on the first line which was attacked. After that was taken they held up their hands and surrendered on the advance of our troops to the succeeding lines. The losses were comparatively small in consequence. The Guards had only 800 to 900 losses.'

During the battle on September 25, forty British soldiers, mostly men of the 2nd Battalion, Grenadier Guards, who were killed near Lesboeufs, were buried near where they fell. That site became the Guards' Lesboeufs Cemetery. More than three thousand soldiers are buried there now, many brought to the cemetery after the war from other parts of the battlefield. Among those buried there on September 25 was Captain Harry Verelst, commanding the 2nd Battalion, Coldstream Guards, killed by the same shell as his adjutant as they went forward in support of the Grenadiers.

As part of the Battle of Morval, General Horne's XV Corps advanced towards Gueudecourt, which was entered by the 21st Division, against heavy opposition, as darkness was falling. The 55th Division and the New Zealand Division were in action west of Gueudecourt, reaching Factory Corner. To the left of the New Zealanders, the 1st and 50th Divisions advanced to within 700 yards of Le Sars. But the 23rd Division, attacking north of Martinpuich, was beaten back.

Encouraged by the Fourth Army successes of September 25, on the following day General Gough launched his Reserve Army in a sustained five-day frontal assault on the village of Thiepval, which had held out since the first day of the Somme offensive. As a result of the repeated shelling since July 1, not one house in the village was intact, but more than a hundred cellars – the official British estimate was 144 – had been prepared by the German machine-gunners to serve as their strongpoints.

Of the four assault divisions, two were Canadian.

The battle on September 26 saw tanks in action once more, to good effect. Thirteen took part in the attack on Thiepval, which, Haig noted in his diary, 'was defended with desperation'. During the assault, Second Lieutenant Tom Adlam, acting as a bomb-thrower, and his men 'came under heavy machine-gun and rifle fire'. Nevertheless, as his Victoria Cross citation noted, 'Adlam ran from shellhole to shellhole under fire, collecting grenades and gathering men for a sudden rush on an enemy village. Despite receiving a leg wound, he led the rush, captured the village and killed its occupants.' Forty dead Germans were brought out of the trenches.

Thiepval was taken that day; its capture removed a serious German vantage point in the centre of the British line. Also on September 26, Lord Cavan's XIV Corps took part in an advance on Combles, which fell to an infantry assault, supported by two tanks. At Gueudecourt, where the tanks went forward assisted by air reconnaissance, 500 Germans were taken prisoner for only 5 British casualties.

South-east of Gueudecourt the Germans counter-attacked in force. More than a hundred British artillery pieces were turned against them. The 'Enemy', Haig noted, 'literally ran away, throwing down his arms'. Haig added, 'We now have the observation which makes so much difference to the success of our operations.' Success was also measured by the low casualties compared with earlier attacks. 'The casualties for the last two days' heavy fighting', Haig noted on September 27, 'are just 8,000. This is very remarkable, and seems to bear out the idea that the Enemy is not fighting so well, and has suffered in morale.'

In the attack on the Schwaben Redoubt on September 27 the British infantrymen were driven back after much hand-to-hand fighting, bayonet against bayonet. Not until October 2 did they secure a strong-point on the southern edge of the redoubt, but the fortified mass remained in German hands.

Organizing the communications back from the Schwaben Redoubt through Thiepval Wood was Second Lieutenant Tolkien, who had reached the wood with his eight runners on September 27. On the following day, when the 11th Battalion, Lancashire Fusiliers – Tolkien's battalion – raided the German trenches from which machine-gun fire was impeding the main attack, more than thirty German prisoners were taken. When Tolkien, speaking German, offered a drink of water to a wounded German officer, the German corrected him on his pronunciation.

On the following morning the captain who had led the trench raid was killed by a sniper's bullet as he was returning to the British trenches with yet more prisoners. Later that day the senior lieutenant, Rowson, was talking to his commanding officer when a shell burst between them. When the dust and debris settled, Rowson had disap-peared. Second Lieutenant Stanley Rowson's body was never found. He is commemorated today on the Thiepval Memorial.

It was at this time that Tolkien received a letter from the wife of one of his signallers, Private Sydney Sumner, who had not been seen for more than two months. 'I have not heard from him for this long time', wrote Sumner's wife, 'but we have had news from the army chaplain that he has been missing since July the 9th. Dear Sir I would not care if I only knew how he went. I know that they cannot all be saved to come home.' Sumner had left a one-year-old daughter in England. His name is inscribed on the Thiepval Memorial.

The fears and destruction of trench warfare were unremitting. So too was the routine of shellfire, death and injury. On the last day of September, Lieutenant Arthur Preston White, of the 1st Battalion, Northamptonshire Regiment, wrote to his father, 'Our last three days up were fairly uneventful, though we had two officers killed and two wounded. Most of our work consisted of digging a new communica-tion trench, and carrying up supplies to a regiment which had taken a bit of the German line. The digging was conducted part of the time under shell fire, but as we had orders to carry on regardless of that sort of thing, we had to stick it out. Three of my party were buried, but they were a lot more scared than hurt. I got one bit on the top of my steel helmet, but no damage was done.'

The carrying parties, White added, 'were rather a sweat for the men, as we had to go a couple of miles over country we did not know at night. There were no distinctive landmarks, so I had to rely mainly on the compass. We had guides, of the usual stamp. The fellow we had on Tuesday night informed us at the start that he wasn't quite sure of the way, which was about the truest thing he ever said in his life. He then proceeded to lead us into a barrage, after which we took charge of affairs ourselves. We got into a trench just in time to escape machine-gun fire at uncomfortably close range. Finally I picked up a wandering machine-gunner who led us to our destination.'

As he and his men were sent far to the rear, to Acheux-en-Vimeux, for a complete rest, White confided to his sister, 'Those who have been right through the show in this part want a rest pretty badly.'

The fighting between September 15 and 30 captured as much ground from the Germans as all the attacks between July 1 and September 14. The tanks had shown that they could be effective against German defenders in the ruins of villages. Encouraged by the successes of the last two weeks of September, Haig devised, in his words, a 'Grand Design' for October: the breakthrough in which he had always believed. The French were supportive. At Val Vion on September 28, Foch was insistent that he would continue the battle into November, 'or until the bad weather stops all chance of attacking'.

Under Haig's plan, the Reserve Army and the Fourth Army, in a concerted attack, would advance to Bapaume and beyond, followed by an advance to Cambrai, more than twenty-four miles from the Fourth Army front. One encouraging fact with regard to this plan was that the first, second and third lines of the German trenches – the original German defence lines on July 1 – had all been captured by the end of September. But a fourth line had already been built, in depth, along the Le Transloy ridge four miles south of Bapaume, and a fifth and sixth line were under construction, the work being done on them clearly visible to British aerial reconnaissance.

To reach the fifth and sixth lines would require – once the Transloy Line had been overcome – an advance across five miles of German-held ground, the same distance that it had taken the previous three months to achieve.

On September 29, Haig went to Querrieu to explain his plan to Rawlinson. 'He is a bold fighter', Rawlinson noted in his diary, 'and I greatly admire his scheme . . . I am sure he is right to widen the battle front, and I pray that Gough's army may succeed.'

Under Haig's plan, what had proved impossible in July would be achieved in October. It would be accompanied and assisted by an attack fifteen miles to the north, from Arras, under General Allenby, driving eastward more than ten miles, as far as the Canal du Nord, to a point six miles north of where Gough and the Reserve Army would cross the canal. Encouraged by Haig, Rawlinson called for detailed maps of Beaumetz, Marcoing and Cambrai, the latter fifteen miles beyond Bapaume.

This was the bold vision that had impelled Haig's thinking on the eve of the Battle of the Somme. Late, but not too late, this two-pronged attack would constitute the final phase of that battle. But Haig understood the problem confronting the British artillery. 'Our position is difficult from artillery point of view,' he wrote on the last day of September, 'as our troops are on the forward ridge of the slope, time is required to bring guns forward to new positions from which to deal with hostile artillery, and further, concealed positions for guns are difficult to find on forward slope! When Le Sars is taken, situation will become better.'

That day Haig lunched at Val Vion with General Kavanagh, commanding the Cavalry Corps, and Kavanagh's Chief Staff Officer, General Home. After their talk, Haig discussed with his own Chief of Staff, General Kiggell, his ambitious plan for a cavalry breakthrough. 'I pointed out that the attack on north side of Ancre might take Enemy by surprise,' Haig wrote in his diary, 'and at any rate it turns the lines of trenches which he is now making to envelop our left on the Ancre.' As regards the direction of the pursuit, Haig told Kiggell that, 'if the Enemy breaks', he would 'aim at getting the Enemy into a trap with the marshes to the east of Arras (about Hamel) on his north side and the Canal du Nord on the east of him. The latter is a broad new canal running in deep cuttings in places 150 feet deep. With the object of carrying out this manoeuvre, I hope to arrange for Allenby to attack on the south side of Arras and capture Monchy-le-Preux ridge. On the south side Rawlinson (if the Enemy breaks) would press on and occupy the ridge near Beaumetz. Kavanagh must think over the best dispositions for his Cavalry Corps.'

Haig's next visitor at Val Vion was General Allenby, commanding the Third Army, whose task was the ten-mile advance to the Canal du Nord. 'Bombardment should commence now', Haig told Allenby, 'and be carried out methodically at different hours by day and night, cut wire, keep gaps open etc. Attack will then come as a surprise and will be preceded by a line of tanks; only a barrage at zero hour, no preliminary bombardment.'

After three months of fighting, many severe setbacks and several dramatic successes, yet another struggle on the Somme was imminent, even more ambitious in its scope than that of July 1. It was the successes since July 1, small though they were on the map, that made such a plan possible, for the German Army had suffered losses as high, if not higher, than those of the British and French combined.

14

October 1916: The Grand Design begins

THE RENEWED OFFENSIVE began on 1 October 1916 – 'a fine autumn day', wrote Captain Miles in the official history. From the start, the attackers met with tenacious German machine-gun fire and made almost no progress. The Canadians, attacking a thousand yards north-west of Courcelette, captured the first German trench, but were driven out of it the following day. They also failed to occupy another section of German trench that they had attacked. Haig was indignant, noting in his diary on October 2, after driving to see General Byng at Canadian headquarters at Contay, 'I think the cause was that in the hope of saving lives they attacked in too weak numbers. They encountered a brigade of the German Marine Corps recently arrived from Ostend, and had not the numbers to overcome them in a hand-to-hand struggle. They (the Canadians) have been very extravagant in expending ammunition! This points rather to nervousness and low moral in those companies which are frequently calling for a "barrage" without good cause.'

On the morning of October 2, President Poincaré visited Haig at Val Vion. He apologized for the fact that the French troops south of the British lines were so far behind the British right flank, but explained that they were unable to make full use of the large reserves at their disposal because the German artillery commanded the defile north of Combles through which they would have to pass to be able to join the battle.

The French President then asked Haig his views about continuing the fighting on the Somme. 'I pointed out', Haig answered, 'that we had already broken through all the Enemy's prepared lines and that now only extemporised defences stood between us and the Bapaume ridge; moreover the Enemy had suffered much in men, in material, and in moral. If we rested even for a month, the Enemy would be able to strengthen his defences, to recover his equilibrium, to make good deficiencies, and, worse still, would regain the initiative! The longer we rested, the more difficult would our problem again become, so in my opinion we must continue to press the Enemy to the utmost of our power. The President quite agreed, and assured me that the French Army would continue to act with energy.'

Heavy rain fell on the Somme front on October 2. The mud of Picardy was sticky and deep, so that prolonged rainfall made it difficult for artillery ammunition to be brought forward. This forced a reduction in the scale of the artillery barrages that were an essential preliminary to any infantry advance. However, on October 3, two companies of the 10th Battalion, Duke of Wellington's Regiment, attacked that portion of Flers still held by the Germans. The historian of the 23rd Division wrote, 'To gain their objective the Duke of Wellington's had but one hundred yards to cross. But their advance lay across mud and mire of the most appalling description, and was met by a withering fire of rifles and machine guns. Nevertheless they reached the German wire, but could get no further. The distance from their assembly trenches to the wire had been too narrow to allow the British artillery to destroy it.'

Of the three officers who led the attack, two, Second Lieutenant Henry Stafford and Second Lieutenant Henry Harris, were killed. Stafford's body was never identified: his name is on the Thiepval Memorial. Harris lies in the predominantly Canadian Adanac Military Cemetery. ('Adanac' is 'Canada' backwards.) The third officer leading the attack, Second Lieutenant Henry Kelly, survived, leading the only three available men into the German trench, and fighting alongside them until they were wounded and German reinforcements came up. He then carried them, and another wounded soldier, back, under German fire. He was awarded the Victoria Cross. Twenty years later he went to Spain to fight with the Republicans in the Spanish Civil War. In the Second World War, while serving as a lieutenant in the Cheshire Regiment, stationed in London, he was court-martialled and severely reprimanded for making two false claims for travel expenses to the value of two pounds, ten shillings. He resigned his commission, dying in 1960 at the age of seventy-three.

French forces were in action on October 4 just east of Cléry. That day twenty-year-old Gustave Fuméry and 150 of his comrades-in-arms were killed. After the war, a memorial cross was erected in their memory.

Rain fell again on October 5, 6 and 7, preventing the Royal Flying Corps observers from acting as spotters for the British artillery. The ground became so wet as to be impassable for any sustained infantry assault. Gough and Rawlinson were therefore forced to postpone their second attacks, planned for October 5 and October 7, which gave the Germans time to repair and strengthen their defences. At the same time, the German artillery wreaked havoc on the British front-line trenches, and on the men waiting to go forward.

Another problem in the air was that German aviators had begun to outfight their British opponents, while photographing the British lines and occasionally machine-gunning British troops on the ground. Trenchard had warned Haig on the last day of August, 'Within the last few days the enemy has brought into action on the Somme front a considerable number of fighting aeroplanes which are faster, handier and capable of attaining greater height than any at my disposal' with the exception of three squadrons. Other than these three, all the 'fighting machines at my disposal are decidedly inferior'.

Haig remained confident, writing to the King on October 5, 'I venture to think that the results are highly satisfactory, and I believe the Army in France feels the same as I do in this matter. The troops see that they are slowly but surely destroying the German Armies in their front, and that their Enemy is much less capable of defence than he was even a few weeks ago. Indeed there have been instances in which the Enemy on a fairly wide front (1,400 yards) has abandoned his trench the moment our infantry appeared! On the other hand our divisions seem to have become almost twice as efficient as they were before going into the battle, notwithstanding the drafts which they have received.'

Once a division had been engaged, Haig told the King, 'all ranks quickly get to know what fighting really means, the necessity for keeping close to our barrage to escape loss and ensure success, and many other important details which can only be really appreciated by troops under fire! The men too having beaten the Germans once gain confidence in themselves and feel no shadow of doubt that they can go on beating him.'

★

Among the German regiments brought as reinforcements to the Somme for the fighting in October was the List Regiment. A German corporal, Adolf Hitler, who was a dispatch runner with the regiment, was later to recall this fierce conflict in his memoirs. 'At the end of September, 1916,' he wrote nine years later, 'my division moved into the Battle of the Somme. For us it was the first of the tremendous battles of materiel which now followed, and the impression was hard to describe – it was more like hell than war.'

Hitler's account in his book *Mein Kampf* ('My Struggle') continued, 'Under a whirlwind of drumfire that lasted for weeks, the German front held fast, sometimes forced back a little, then again pushing forward, but never wavering.' On October 7, a British shell penetrated his dispatch runners' dugout and exploded. Several of his fellow runners were killed. Hitler was wounded in the left thigh. After treatment in a field hospital he was sent to hospital in Germany, at Beelitz, near Berlin. Later he was assigned to light duty in Munich, but after five months asked to go back to the front. Permission was granted.

To help bring a vast quantity of supplies up to the front – weapons, ammunition, barbed wire, food and clothing – across the areas that had been captured from the Germans, a series of light railways was being constructed. By the first week of October several of these railways were in operation. One ran from Albert to the British military cemetery that had been established near Pozières. Another ran from the River Ancre up Nab Valley to Mouquet Farm. A third railway – broad gauge, and thus capable of taking heavier loads – ran from Dernancourt to Trones Wood, serving both British and French needs. Its last section was completed on October 4.

Each week soldiers were taken out of the line and back to rest areas. In the first week of October the 1st Battalion, Northamptonshire Regiment, was at Acheux-en-Vimeux, thirty miles from Albert and less than eight miles from the English Channel – 'in some lousy old stables of a farm', grumbled Private Bernard Whayman. A few dozen of those at rest were sent to attend a bombing school at nearby Frières. Whayman later commented, 'as we had all thrown plenty of live bombs this seemed superfluous.'

There was another hazard. 'Unfortunately,' Whayman explained, 'we had two men killed here by an instantaneous burst when throwing, caused by a flaw in the casting. They were buried in the churchyard at Acheux.' Also buried there is Private Alexander Scott, killed in action nearby in May 1940.

On October 5, the 11th Battalion, West Yorkshire Regiment, was ordered to take up its position in the front line that night, facing the German-held village of Le Sars. In the battalion was Second Lieutenant Eric Poole, who had earlier been knocked unconscious by a shell explosion, hospitalized for a month with shell shock, and declared unfit for further front-line service. That decision was later overturned, and he was sent back to his battalion. Instead of going up the line on October 5, Poole disappeared for two days. His battalion attacked north of Le Sars, losing 8 officers and 217 other ranks in an attack that achieved its objective.

When Poole was court-martialled, the arresting officer told the court that he had found him 'in a confused state of mind'. The battalion medical officer spoke sympathetically about his previous shell shock, suggesting that the battle conditions on October 5 might have caused him to 'succumb to such a condition'. Poole was sentenced to death, with no recommendation for mercy. Despite an appeal for the commutation of his sentence from his brigadier general, he was executed. His army death certificate states, 'Shot for desertion'. His father was told that he had died of wounds. He was buried far from the Somme, in the Poperinghe New Military Cemetery, Ypres.

In the early afternoon of October 7, the Fourth Army attacked the Transloy Ridge. One French and six British divisions took part. The French under General Fayolle, using the British artillery-barrage system, advanced almost to Sailly-Saillisel. The Fourth Army took the village of Le Sars, straddling the Albert–Bapaume road. But the Transloy Line was unbroken. One reason for the failure was noted by the commander of XV Corps, General du Cane, who wrote in his corps war diary, 'Perhaps all concerned were too optimistic owing to previous successes.'

General Gough had another criticism of one sector of the line – that from which the Canadian 3rd Division was to advance. 'In some parts', he told Haig the next day, 'they had not left their trenches for the attack.' The Canadian 1st Division, which had attacked north-west of Le Sars, had gained some trenches but 'been driven out again'. In many sectors of the Canadian advance the preliminary British artillery had failed to cut the German wire. In some places the Germans had filled the gaps in the wire by pushing new barbed wire into No-Man's Land just as the Canadians were going over the top. Almost all the Canadians who reached the German wire were shot by German machine-gun fire before they could try to cross it.

The 12th Battalion, London Regiment – The Rangers, a Territorial battalion – also took part in the attack of October 7. The Rangers' war history described the scene: 'October 7th 1916 was a disastrous day for the Rangers and for many others. The attack of the Brigade on our left failed as also did that of the troops on our right. The weather was appalling – the ground was greasy and slippery with recent rain and there was more than one subsequent abortive attack after we were relieved before the position was finally won.'

Among those fatally wounded during this attack was twenty-seven-year-old Sergeant Frederick Coulson, in peacetime a Reuters news-agency correspondent, who had refused an officer's commission on the grounds that he preferred to 'do the thing fairly. I will take my place in the ranks.' He is buried in Grove Town Cemetery, Méaulte, just south of Albert. A week before his death he had written to his father, 'If I should fall do not grieve for me. I shall be one with the wind and the sun and the flowers.' After his death a poem entitled 'Who made the Law?' was found among his possessions, and sent back to his family. The first two stanzas read:

> Who made the Law that men should die in meadows?
> Who spake the word that blood should splash in lanes?
> Who gave it forth that gardens should be bone-yards?
> Who spread the hills with flesh, and blood, and brains?
> Who made the Law?
>
> Who made the Law that Death should stalk the village?
> Who spake the word to kill among the sheaves,
> Who gave it forth that death should lurk in hedgerows,
> Who flung the dead among the fallen leaves?
> *Who* made the Law?

★

In the 56th Division's attack on the Transloy Ridges on October 7, heavy rain had turned the fields into liquid mud. Reading the reports of the fighting, Lord Cavan, whose XIV Corps included the 56th Division, questioned whether the continuous effort was worth the loss in men.

Inexorably, the losses of battle were mounting. At their talk on October 8, Haig advised Gough that he should 'hold back from the fight the best drill sergeants in a battalion because they cannot be replaced now'. Senior officers were also at risk. On October 7, Brigadier General Philip Howell, the General Staff Officer of V Corps, had been killed instantly by a shell fragment that struck him in the back while he was walking through Authuille village, more than three miles behind the front line. He was thirty-seven years old. His grave is in the Varennes Military Cemetery, just south of the Doullens–Albert road.

The heroism of war was inextricably bound up with its horrors. On October 8 a Scottish-born Canadian soldier, Piper John Richardson, having played his company over the top near Morval, saw that the men were being held up by the strong German wire and intense machine-gun fire. Determined to help maintain the fighting spirit of the men, he reached the German wire and, in the words of his Victoria Cross citation, 'strode up and down' in front of it, 'coolly playing his pipes'. The citation continues, 'Inspired by his music and his bravery, the company rushed the wire with such ferocity that the position was captured.'

On the following day, October 9, while carrying a wounded man 200 yards back from the front line, Richardson realized that he had left his pipes behind. Returning to get them, he was killed. His grave, marked with the insignia of the Victoria Cross, is in the Adanac Military Cemetery.

On October 9, in London, the War Committee noted a communication from Haig urging the continuation of the Somme offensive 'without intermission'. The committee made no comment. On the Somme, the Canadian effort continued for four days, with small gains made but no breakthrough until October 11. That day a Canadian soldier, Private Earl Hembroff, who was serving with the Canadian

Field Ambulance, described in his diary a captured German trench being used as part of an advance dressing station to which the wounded were being brought. It had earlier been the scene of a desperate struggle. 'Dead lying all over, especially in pieces as shells persist in bringing them to the surface. Bodies in chamber all blackened from smoke bomb. One Tommy with arms around Boche as in a deadly struggle.' Chaplains buried the dead at night. The troops were exhausted, 'and some of the biggest cried like babies'.

That day, a British visitor, Viscountess D'Abernon, reached the town of Albert, seven miles behind the front lines. 'I left Paris full of eagerness and excitement to see the British Front, where, up to the present, no women visitors had been allowed,' she wrote in her diary. Looking over the battlefield with her military escort, General Davidson, 'we saw the whole Pozières–Thiepval horizon come under a barrage of German fire.' For more than an hour she watched the bombardment. 'Several of our aeroplanes came over, making for hangars, many miles behind, and tales were told of gallant deeds and especially of the prowess of a young fellow, named Albert Ball, who has just brought down his thirtieth Boche aeroplane, is aged nineteen, and lives to tell the tale'.

Ball was killed in action on 7 May 1917. He was awarded a posthumous Victoria Cross for his conspicuous bravery during the eleven days before his death. He was buried in Annoeullin Communal Cemetery, behind German lines: one of twenty-three Britons among 1,600 Germans.

Lady D'Abernon's visit on October 11 was remarkable. 'We stood for a long while riveted by the strange Satanic scene,' she wrote, 'but, at last, it was a relief to turn away. The ground which we were treading, the shellholes we avoided, are broken patches of the battlefield of only a short month ago. It was here and then that Raymond Asquith's brilliant promise was extinguished and my dear nephew, Charles Feversham, was killed, and on the grey horizon beyond Albert there are, at this moment, thousands of fellow-countrymen, their trenches the playground for shells bursting so thickly and continuously that General Davidson thought they must herald an impending attack. The scene had a Lucifer, Prince of Darkness kind of splendour, but uppermost in my mind was a sense of the wickedness and waste of life, the lack of any definite objective commensurate with all this destruction, desolation and human suffering.'

Lady D'Abernon was taken to a casualty clearing station. 'The beds are very small,' she wrote, 'and have only one regulation blanket on the top of the coarsest of unbleached sheets. In the officers' tent the only difference made (but religiously observed) is that a coloured cotton quilt instead of a white one covers the regulation blanket. Except for this mark of somewhat chilly, comfortless distinction, everything is identical. In the officers' tent the faces were, almost without exception, the faces of mere boys. Special tents are set apart for the abdominal wounds, for chest wounds, for eyes, for gas-gangrene, etc., and of course separate tents for the Boches. Amongst these, one lonely figure, still on a forgotten stretcher, was lying with his face turned to the wall. Unlike others he did not speak nor even look round as we passed through, and remains in memory a lonely pathetic figure.'

The soldiers in their rest billets had a brief respite from the battle. As it had been before the Big Push, Amiens was a favourite watering hole for officers. Among them was Captain Theodore Percival Cameron Wilson, who wrote:

> Lord! How we laughed in Amiens!
> For there were useless things to buy.
> .   .   .   .
>
> And still we laughed in Amiens
> As dead men laughed a week ago.
>
> What cared we if in Delville Wood
> The splintered trees saw hell below?
> We cared. We cared. But laughter runs
> The cleanest stream a man may know
> To rinse him from the taint of guns.

Wilson survived the Somme, but not the war. Killed in March 1918, his name is on the Arras Memorial to the Missing.

15

The soldiers' sacrifice: 'What else had they been born for?'

ON 12 OCTOBER 1916, in a renewed attempt to break through the German lines, Lord Cavan launched an attack on the XIV Corps front towards the Transloy Ridges beyond Gueudecourt. In Haig's words, it 'was not altogether a success'. One reason was that the Germans had sited their machine guns not in the front line – where they could have been vulnerable to the British artillery barrage as it moved forward in front of the attacking troops – but 500 to 800 yards in the rear. When the attacking troops reached the German trenches, the machine guns opened fire, intact in their rearward positions. Cavan suggested to Haig, when they met two days later at Méaulte, that the British use smoke shells to mask the advancing troops from these well-sited machine-gunners. But the artillery on the Somme had not been issued with smoke shells.

There were other problems making things difficult for the attackers. The British battalions, which at the beginning of the battle had consisted of a thousand men each, had been so depleted by the losses since July 1 that few of them could muster more than four hundred men for an attack. Many of those who could be mustered were not fully trained. In addition, the essential aeroplane support that enabled the British counter-artillery batteries to locate German artillery in the rear was severely limited by poor visibility.

For the first time since their costly struggle on July 1, the 1st Battalion, Newfoundland Regiment, was among those in action on October 12 in the attack on the German front line just north of Gueudecourt. The British were experimenting with a creeping barrage, whereby the men moved forward behind a steadily advancing curtain of explosions designed to pulverize the German wire and to stun the German soldiers. The barrage was timed to go forward in lifts of fifty yards each minute. But, in the words of the Newfoundlanders' official historian, 'in their eagerness to get to the grips of the enemy many pressed ahead through the curtain of fire; and platoons of the supporting companies, treading impatiently on the heels of those in front, became mixed with the leading waves, the result being partial loss of control.'

More than one in ten of the attackers were killed by this barrage, as they moved forward too quickly, or as shells fell short. Among the advancing Newfoundlanders was eighteen-year-old Lance Corporal Raymond Goodyear. It was his first battle. As he ran forward, he seemed to stumble and fall; his captain turned to help him up, then saw that Goodyear had been hit by a shellburst just below the waist. The historian of the Goodyear family, David Macfarlane, writes: 'For a moment his round blackened face looked puzzled beneath his over-sized tin hat. He didn't seem to realize what had happened. He'd been ripped open as if he'd run into the full swing of an axe.' Goodyear is buried in the Bancourt British Cemetery beyond Bapaume.

Despite running into their own artillery barrage, and also being hit by shells falling short, the Newfoundlanders advanced 600 yards, halfway to their objective, and then drove back a German counter attack with sustained Lewis- and Vickers-gun fire. But they could advance no further. The German High Command had made special efforts to strengthen what it called 'the apparently insatiable Somme front'. Among the German troops defending the Transloy Ridges was the 6th Brandenburg Division, known as the Iron Division.

Despite failing to reach their objective, the Newfoundlanders had made a greater advance into the German lines than any other unit advancing that day. They had killed an estimated 250 Germans, taken some 75 prisoners, and captured 3 German machine guns. The historian of the Newfoundland Regiment points out that 'there was keen satisfaction' in the regiment that 'in some measure the losses of Beaumont Hamel had been avenged.' Their losses in the Transloy battle had been 120 dead and 119 wounded. It was their second and last battle on the Somme; following this second encounter with the Germans they were relieved by an Australian division and sent back to billets at Ville-sur-Ancre, a mile and a half south of Albert.

Another of those killed on October 12 in the unsuccessful attack on the Transloy Ridges was a New Zealand artilleryman, Gunner Ernest

Piner, aged twenty-nine, who, like many of the Newfoundlanders, had fought at Gallipoli. He is buried in the Dartmoor Cemetery, near Albert. Also killed that day was Second Lieutenant Donald Hankey, 1st Battalion, Royal Warwickshire Regiment. Hankey's body was never identified; his name is inscribed on the Thiepval Memorial. His father, later Lord Hankey, a former Royal Marine, was the Secretary to the British Cabinet, and to the War Committee.

Since the autumn of 1915, Second Lieutenant Hankey had written articles in the *Spectator* magazine, signed 'A Student in Arms', that had made him, in the words of his *Spectator* obituary, a 'liaison officer between the nation and its Army'. In his last letter he had written of the pleasure he felt in going back to the trenches, and the opportunity he would have 'of testing once more in practice' the theories he had about 'the fear of death'. That letter was printed in the *Spectator* after Hankey's death. In it he wrote of those who were killed, 'They did not value life! They had not been able to make much of a fist of it. But if they lived amiss they died gloriously, with a smile for the pain and the dread of it. What else had they been born for? It was their chance. With a gay heart they gave their greatest gift, and with a smile to think that after all they had anything to give that was of value. One by one Death challenged them. One by one they smiled in his grim visage, and refused to be dismayed. They had been lost, but they had found the path that led them home; and when at last they laid their lives at the feet of the good shepherd, what could they do but smile?'

Haig's plan for a breakthrough to the Canal du Nord and Cambrai had failed. As winter approached, the generals tried to find a balance between what could be done and what they felt ought to be done. 'The bad weather which has forced us to slow down', General Rawlinson wrote in his diary on October 14, 'has given the Boche a breather. His artillery is better organised, and his infantry is fighting with greater tenacity, but deserters continue to come in; and, the more we bombard, the more prisoners and deserters we shall get. I should like therefore to be more or less aggressive all the winter, but we must not take the edge off next year.'

In his official history of the Battle of the Somme, Captain Wilfrid Miles wrote of how, by the middle of October, 'conditions on and behind the battle-front were so bad as to make mere existence a severe trial of body and spirit. Little could be seen from the air through the rain and mist, so counter-battery work suffered and it was often impossible to locate with accuracy the new German trenches and shellhole positions.' Objectives could not always be identified from ground level, 'so that it is no matter for surprise or censure that the British artillery sometimes fired short or placed its barrages too far ahead'.

Bursts of high explosive, Captain Miles wrote, 'were smothered in the ooze; many guns had been continuously in action for over two months and were too worn for accurate fire; and in some partially flooded battery positions sinking platforms had to be restored with any battle debris which came to hand.' The mud was so deep that in order to move a single eighteen–pounder gun 'ten or twelve horses were often needed, and, to supplement the supplies brought by light-railway and pack-horse, ammunition had to be dragged up on sledges improvised of sheets of corrugated iron. The infantry, sometimes wet to the skin and almost exhausted before zero hour, were often condemned to struggle painfully forward through the mud under heavy fire against objectives vaguely defined and difficult of recognition.'

On October 18, Rawlinson's Fourth Army launched a second major attack on the Transloy Ridge. Continuing bad weather made British artillery support difficult, but during the advance a thousand German soldiers were captured – a boost to the morale of the attackers. Later that day Haig wrote to the King, 'The Fourth Army attacked in places this morning at 3.45 a.m. to straighten up their line with a view to getting into a more suitable position for a more serious effort later on . . . The ground was very slippery and unfavourable for the advance of infantry. However, the majority of objectives for this morning's attack were at no great distance, and about 60 per cent of them were taken. In many places the enemy is reported as running away as soon as our infantry were seen advancing!'

On the French sector of the attack of October 18, the French forces entered Sailly-Saillisel village, but failed to take that part of the village from which there was a view of the next line of German trenches. Haig told the King, 'There is no doubt that the French have not really exerted themselves on the north of the Somme: but then they rather meant to save their troops and avoid casualties in view of their losses at Verdun, and previously.'

A new British force was being made ready for the Somme: the Royal Naval Division, soldiers who had fought at Antwerp in October 1914, keeping the Germans from a sweep to the Channel ports, and then at Gallipoli. On October 18 they were put into the line facing Beaumont-Hamel, with their right flank on the River Ancre, in preparation for a major attack. A new commanding officer was sent to lead them, Major General Cameron Shute. His reiterated complaints about the state of their trenches, their weapons and their equipment grated on these battle-hardened men, one of whom, Sub-Lieutenant A. P. Herbert – later a distinguished humorist, writer and parliamentarian – wrote a poem that the men sang with glee, albeit only when Shute was not around:

> The general inspecting the trenches
> Exclaimed with a horrified shout,
> 'I refuse to command a division
> Which leaves its excreta about.'
>
> But nobody took any notice,
> No one was prepared to refute,
> That the presence of shit was congenial
> Compared with the presence of Shute.
>
> And certain responsible critics
> Made haste to reply to his words,
> Observing that his staff advisors
> Consisted entirely of turds.
>
> For shit may be shot at odd corners
> And paper supplied there to suit,
> But a shit would be shot without mourners
> If somebody shot that shit Shute.

As the rain continued to churn up the clay and mud of the Somme into glutinous slurry, efforts were made to hold the trenches that had been gained and make it possible to bring supplies forward. To supply the troops in the captured areas, more than 120 miles of water pipes were laid, and a hundred water-pumping plants were erected. Road surfaces were prepared to enable motor cars, motor lorries, motor ambulances and motor cycles, as well as horse-drawn vehicles, to traverse the battle-battered zone. By the end of October, the 7th Field Company, Royal Engineers, had completed eight more miles of prefabricated tramway tracks in two lines across the former battlefields: one from Contalmaison to beyond Martinpuich, and the other from Mametz Wood to High Wood. The officer in charge of this endeavour was Lieutenant John Glubb, who thirty years later was to be the commander of the Arab Legion.

On October 21, Edmund Blunden took part in a massive four-division, 48,000-man assault on the German-held Regina Trench and Stuff Trench. It was the coldest day since the battle had begun on July 1: the first day on which the temperature fell below zero degrees Centigrade. Even the ubiquitous mud was frozen. Six minutes after midday, the British artillery bombardment began. Then the infantrymen went forward. The action against Stuff Trench, the objective of Blunden's battalion, was successful – 'the first in which our battalion had seized and held any of the German area,' he later wrote, 'and the cost had been enormous; a not intemperate pride glowed among the survivors, but that natural vanity was held in check by the fact that we were not yet off the battlefield.'

Blunden's battalion then went into a quieter section of the line, the trenches around Thiepval Wood. 'The land in front was full of the dead of July 1,' he recalled.

During the assault on Regina Trench and Stuff Trench on October 21, Second Lieutenant Tolkien was with his communications equipment and runners in the British front-line Hessian Trench. After the first two waves of infantrymen went over the top, Tolkien's signallers followed in the third. Following them was the chaplain, Evers, and the stretcher-bearers. Within half an hour, the first German prisoners had been brought back to Hessian Trench.

Tolkien's signallers had done their work well. At 1.12 p.m., when the Lancashire Fusiliers raised their red flags in Regina Trench, Tolkien knew that they had achieved their objective. But a heavy German artillery bombardment from far behind the lines caused a high toll of the wounded British soldiers in No-Man's Land. At one point the signaller carrying the battalion's pigeon basket was hit.

Another man rescued the basket and its pigeons, bringing them back to Hessian Trench. A pigeon was then sent back to brigade headquarters with the message that Regina Trench had been captured.

It was on the following day that Chaplain Evers walked back into Hessian Trench, covered in blood. He had spent the night in No-Man's Land in the fierce cold, under German artillery fire, tending the wounded and comforting the dying.

Haig was confident that a final offensive could push the Germans back even further – perhaps even as far as Bapaume, just over three miles beyond the new British front line. On October 18 the writer and poet John Masefield had visited him at Val Vion to ask if he could write an account of the battle for the British public. Masefield was impressed by this 'wonderful' man: 'No enemy could stand against such a man. He took my breath away.' In the book he agreed to write, which was published in 1917 as *The Old Front Line*, Masefield noted Haig's 'fine delicate gentleness and generosity', his 'pervading power' and his 'height of resolve'.

A less favourable portrait was penned by the future crime writer Dennis Wheatley, who served in the Royal Field Artillery in the First World War, and who wrote of Haig in his memoirs, 'He was a pleasant, tactful, competent, peacetime soldier devoted to his duty, but he had a rooted dislike of the French and was not even a second-rate General. Many of the high-ups were well aware of that, but the question had always been, with whom could they replace him?'

Winston Churchill also left a portrait in words of the British Commander-in-Chief. It described the time in 1917–18 when Churchill, as Minister of Munitions, visited Haig on a number of occasions at Haig's headquarters at Saint-Omer. After describing the participation of John Churchill, Duke of Marlborough, in the heat of battle at the beginning of the eighteenth century, Churchill reflected on how 'All this was quite different from the trials of our latter-day generals. We will not belittle them, but they were the trials of mind and spirit working in calm surroundings, often beyond even the sound of the cannonade. There are no physical disturbances: there is no danger: there is no hurry.' Churchill went on to explain, 'The generalissimo of an army of two million men, already for ten days in desperate battle, has little or nothing to do except to keep himself fit and cool. His life is not different, except in its glory, from that of a pains-taking, punctual public official, and far less agitating than that of a Cabinet Minister who must face an angry Chamber on the one hand or an offended party upon the other.'

There was 'no need for the modern commander to wear boots and breeches', Churchill wrote: 'he will never ride a horse except for the purposes of health. In the height of his largest battles, when twenty thousand men are falling every day, time will hang heavy on his hands. The heads of a dozen departments will from hour to hour discreetly lay significant sheets of paper on his desk. At intervals his staff will move the flags upon his map, or perhaps one evening the Chief of the Staff himself will draw a blue line or a brown line or make a strong arrow upon it. His hardest trials are reduced to great simplicity. "Advance", "Hold", or "Retreat". "There are but ten divisions left in reserve: shall we give three today to the beseeching, clamouring battle-zone, or keep them back till to-morrow or the day after? Shall we send them in trains to the north or to the south?"'

The modern Commander-in-Chief's 'personal encounters', Churchill noted, 'are limited to an unpleasant conversation with an Army commander who must be dismissed, an awkward explanation to a harassed Cabinet, or an interview with a representative of the neutral Press. Time is measured at least by days and often by weeks. There is nearly always leisure for a conference even in the gravest crises.' It was 'not true', Churchill concluded, 'that the old battle has merely been raised to a gigantic scale. In the process of enlargement the sublime function of military genius perhaps happily – has been destroyed for ever.'

Churchill also wrote about Haig in an obituary article in *Pall Mall* magazine in November 1928, twelve years after the Battle of the Somme. It was a stern assessment. 'He does not appear to have had any original ideas,' Churchill wrote. 'No one can discern a spark of that mysterious, visionary, often sinister genius which has enabled the great captains of history to dominate the material factors, save slaugh-ter, and confront their foes with the triumph of novel apparitions. He was, we are told, quite friendly to the tanks, but the manoeuvre of making them would never have occurred to him. He appeared at all times quite unconscious of any theatre but the Western Front. There were the Germans in their trenches. Here he stood at the head of an army corps, then of an army, and finally of a group of mighty armies. Hurl them on and keep slogging at it in the best possible way – that was war. It was undoubtedly one way of making war, and in the end there was certainly overwhelming victory. But these truisms will not be accepted by history as exhaustive.'

As Churchill had written, Haig's responsibilities were not to be belittled. They included the smooth working of a massive effort behind the front line. 'The working of the railways, the upkeep of the roads, even the baking of bread and a thousand other industries go on in peace as well as in war!' he noted in his diary. In an attempt to improve the communications system behind the lines, on October 20 a leading British civil engineer, Henry Maybury, was appointed Director of Roads for the British Expeditionary Force. 'To put soldiers into such positions, merely because they are generals and colonels,' Haig noted in his diary, 'would be to ensure failure!' To give Maybury the authority he needed to deal with those 'soldiers', Haig appointed him brigadier general.

Two days after Maybury's appointment, the First Lord of the Admiralty, A. J. Balfour, a former Prime Minister, who was visiting the Western Front, called at Val Vion. Haig was relieved to learn that Balfour no longer supported the primacy of the Balkan theatre of operations, as he had done earlier because, as Balfour explained to his host, 'he then thought the German front in France could not be pierced'. 'Now', Haig noted, 'our successes proved that his opinion was wrong.'

On the following day, October 23, General Joffre was the luncheon guest at Val Vion. Haig noted in his diary, 'He did full justice to a good lunch and then we had a talk for an hour or more. He gave me his views on the general situation and agreed with me that we must *continue* to press the Enemy here on the Somme battle front throughout the winter. There must be no reduction of strength on this battle front, so that whenever the weather is fine, we can carry out an attack without any delay to concentrate troops etc.'

On October 26, with rain still falling, Haig instructed Gough to plan the next offensive as soon as possible. 'We agreed that we should watch the weather,' Haig wrote in his diary that day, 'and be able to put his plans into execution after 3 fine days.' That same day Haig rode around the billets of the 25th Division, meeting the three brigadiers and most of the battalion commanders, and shaking hands with and congratulating 'four or five NCOs and men in each battalion who were brought to my notice as having performed specially good service'.

The last billets that Haig visited that day were at Beauval, just south of Doullens. 'I was much struck', he wrote in his diary, 'by the small size and generally poor physique of the men in this division, yet no division has done better or seen more hard fighting.' Also at Beauval was Casualty Clearing Station No. 4. At the time of Haig's visit, a second casualty clearing station had just been opened there, No. 27. In the nearby Beauval Communal Cemetery are 248 First World War burials.

Among the troops whom Haig inspected and thanked on October 26 were the men of the 11th Battalion, Lancashire Fusiliers, who had taken part in the capture of Regina Trench. On the day after the inspection, the signalling officer, Second Lieutenant Tolkien, reported sick with a temperature of 103. It was 'trench fever', a bacterium that enters the bloodstream through the burrowing of the eager, ever-present lice. He was sent to the officers' hospital at Gézaincourt, his fighting days at an end.

After his meeting with Haig on October 18, John Masefield had gone forward with an army escort into the battle zone. In his book *The Old Front Line* he described the way up to the trenches. 'Here and there,' he wrote, 'in recesses in the trench, under roofs of corrugated iron covered with sandbags, they passed the offices and the stores of war, telephonists, battalion headquarters, dumps of bombs, barbed wire, rockets, lights, machine-gun ammunition, tins, jars and cases. Many men, passing these things as they went "in" for the first time, felt with a sinking of the heart, that they were leaving all ordered and arranged things, perhaps for ever.'

In some sectors men even passed rows of coffins.

During the fighting on October 26, twenty-year-old Lieutenant Roland Hett, Lincolnshire Regiment, a former pupil at St Edward's preparatory school, Oxford, was badly wounded in the leg. After his wound had been dressed and bound at an advanced dressing station, he was being carried back by stretcher when a shellburst killed him and two of his four stretcher bearers. His name is on the Thiepval Memorial to the Missing.

★

On October 28 the British 33rd Division captured several German trenches north-east of Lesboeufs, an essentially defensive operation. On the following day the German 6th Division was forced to withdraw from the Somme altogether after heavy losses near Gueudecourt, a mile north of Lesboeufs.

Slowly and steadily the British forces moved forward. Small though these advances were, they pushed the British front line three miles in front of its starting point. This created problems of its own. 'The difficulties of the long carry to this part of our front', Haig wrote in his diary on October 29, 'are such that all reserve troops have to be employed. Otherwise necessities such as water, food, ammunition, bombs of all kind etc. cannot be kept up. The carry is roughly 5,000 yards each way. Some packhorses have had to be destroyed owing to being hopelessly bogged. One man does one round journey carrying a load per 24 hours.'

Lord Cavan estimated, so Haig recorded, that a pause of 'at least four days' was needed between each offensive operation 'in order to keep up!'

Haig's concern with the conditions under which the men were fighting was shown on October 31, when he rode to Reserve Army headquarters at Toutencourt. Lieutenant Colonel Neil Malcolm, Gough's senior Staff Officer, received him. 'I wanted definite information', Haig wrote in his diary, 'as to the state of the front trenches, and whether the winter leather waistcoats had yet been issued, also whether an extra blanket per man had been sent up. Malcolm assured me that everything possible was being done for the men, but the mud in front was quite terrible. Today, being fine, things were fast improving, and where the 5th Canadians are (north of Le Sars), the ground is fit to attack over.' The Reserve Army had been given the extra services and Staff 'to place it on the same footing as the other armies'. Henceforth it would be called the Fifth Army.

Yet another Somme offensive was imminent, the fourth in four months. It awaited only the arrival of better weather. And it would begin in some places as much as five thousand yards from the starting point on July 1; but in one sector, facing Beaumont-Hamel, from the July 1 starting point itself.

16

The first two weeks of November:
'The mud of the moment'

A s THE BATTLE of the Somme ended its fourth month and moved into its fifth, and no one knew when it would end, each side made public something of the achievements and costs thus far. On 1 November 1916 the British and French governments announced that, since the start of the battle on July 1, they had taken 72,901 German prisoners and captured 303 artillery pieces, 215 mortars and nearly 1,000 machine guns.

The statistics of death were also being calculated by both sides. The British and Empire dead on the Somme in the four months since July 1 amounted to 95,675. The French death toll on the Somme was 50,729. The German death toll, 164,055, was larger than the Anglo-French toll combined. 'The Enemy seems to be feeling a shortage of men,' Haig noted on November 2. Letters found on German prisoners showed 'that a number of sailors at Cuxhaven have been medically examined with a view to being incorporated in the Army'.

The German prisoners were the fortunate ones: sent to the rear, and to prisoner-of war camps. The International Committee of the Red Cross supervised their conditions, and ensured that they were properly fed.

At Buckingham Palace on November 1, King George V received Pamela Congreve, the widow of Major William ('Billy') Congreve, who was pregnant with Billy's child. The King gave her three medals on her husband's behalf: the Victoria Cross he had been awarded on the Somme in July, and the Distinguished Service Order and Military Cross he had been awarded before the Somme. Congreve was the first officer in the British Army to win all three awards. His daughter, Gloria, was born in March 1917.

The weather on the Somme was still not suitable for a renewed

Allied offensive. Napoleon's implacable 'General Winter' had arrived. 'The weather has been very unkind to us this last week,' Rawlinson wrote to Sir William Robertson in London, 'and the state of the roads in the forward area, coupled with the immensely long carry of 4,000 yards down to the front trenches, are causing me considerable anxiety, for they are using up the vital energies of the troops much faster than I like.' Nevertheless, Rawlinson added, 'We must and will continue the offensive.'

The short-story writer Saki, forty-six-year-old Lance Sergeant Hector Munro, who in 1915 had deliberately falsified his age in order to enlist, was about to go into action. In his essay 'The Square Egg (A Badger's-Eye View of the War Mud in the Trenches)', he described the mud on the battlefield. 'Much more to be thought about than the enemy over yonder or the war all over Europe is the mud of the moment,' he wrote, 'the mud that at time engulfs you as cheese engulfs a cheesemite. In Zoological Gardens one has gazed at an elk or bison loitering at its pleasure more than knee-deep in a quagmire of greasy mud, and one has wondered what it would feel like to be soused and plastered, hour-long, in such a muck-bath. One knows now. In narrow-dug support-trenches, when thaw and heavy rain have come suddenly atop of a frost, when everything is pitch-dark around you, and you can only stumble about and feel your way against streaming mud walls, when you have to go down on hands and knees in several inches of soup-like mud to creep into a dug-out, when you stand deep in mud, lean against mud, grasp mud-slimed objects with mud-caked fingers, wink mud away from your eyes, and shake it out of your ears, bite muddy biscuits with muddy teeth, then at least you are in a position to understand thoroughly what it feels like to wallow – on the other hand the bison's idea of pleasure becomes more and more incomprehensible.'

Saki was far from alone in being astonished at the nature and power of the mud. 'The battlefield had become a quagmire,' recalled Paul Maze, a French painter, who had joined the British forces as a sergeant and was serving on the Ancre. 'Yet the war went on and every night men lined up in the mud to attack. Moving in trenches became a sore trial. One kept to the side, clutching at the face of the slippery parapet until after slipping down several times, the cold water squelching through boots and puttees, one gave up and just slushed through it.

The mud had turned everything into a liquid paste and as one sank into it equipment of every description came to the surface; one picked it up and laid it to dry on the parapet. Corpses had also sunk into the mud. Gingerly one stepped over them.'

Rudyard Kipling, in his history *The Irish Guards in the Great War*, included the reflections of a guardsman on those mud-dominated days. 'It is funny, maybe, to talk about now, that mud-larking of ours; but to sink, sink, sink in the dark and you not sure whether they saw you or could hear you, puts the wind up a man worse than anything under Heaven. Fear? Fear is not the word. 'Twas the Somme that broke our hearts. Back, knees, loins, acrost your chest – you was dragged to pieces dragging your own carcass out of the mud. 'Twas like red-hot wires afterwards – and all to begin it again.'

In the first week of November the rain, mud and fog proved too harsh a combination for battle. On November 2, Haig rode to Toutencourt, where he told General Gough 'to have patience, and not to launch the main attack until the weather was better and the ground dry'. Haig added, 'It was better to wait than to start a series of small operations which would not have the same decisive results.'

Haig was cheered that day by the arrival of the Chancellor of the Exchequer, Reginald McKenna, at Val Vion. 'He takes quite the right view of the importance of the Western Front', Haig commented, and went on to quote McKenna's words: 'Everything possible should be sent to France.' Unknown to Haig, on the following day, November 3, at a meeting of the War Committee in London, Lloyd George led the criticisms of the Somme offensive. 'We were not getting on with the war,' he said; 'the enemy had recovered the initiative . . . At no point had the Allies achieved a definite, clear success.' The 'policy of attrition' had inflicted greater losses on the Allies than on their enemies.

The minutes of the War Committee recorded the meeting's conclusion: 'It was generally agreed that the offensive on the Somme, if continued next year, was not likely to lead to decisive results, and that the losses might make too heavy a drain on our resources having regard to the results to be anticipated.' Then, reflecting a disillusionment with all that had happened since July 1, the War Committee agreed 'that we should examine whether a decision might not be reached on another theatre'.

★

On November 4 the 33rd Division attacked two German trenches in front of Le Transloy. The attack was beaten off. That day Haig received a critical letter from Lord Cavan, under whose XIV Corps the 33rd Division was serving. Cavan wrote, 'No one who has not visited the front trenches can really know the state of exhaustion to which the men are reduced. The conditions are far worse than in the First Battle of Ypres, and my General Officers and Staff Officers agree that they are the worst they have seen, owing to the enormous distance of the carry of all munitions, food, water and ammunition.'

At an emergency conference at Querrieu on the afternoon of November 4, Haig, Rawlinson and Foch discussed what was to be done the next day to take the two trenches. They agreed to a deception plan, whereby Le Transloy itself would be bombarded and the German artillery positions counter-batteried as if Le Transloy itself was the objective.

The three men and their Staff Officers then discussed the next substantial attack. During the discussion, as Haig noted, Foch 'laid great stress on the dangerously exposed position in which his troops would be north and northeast of Sailly Saillisel if we did not also press on, and asked me to give him a date when I would put in the attack with my Fifth Army. I said the attack was all ready to go in, but the wet weather had destroyed our communications. My plan was to get these into a proper state and after four fine days to dry the ground, then to put in the attack. But if by the 15th the attack, for one reason or another, had not gone in, then I proposed to commence an operation to capture the same objectives little by little.'

Gough, who was also at Querrieu, asked Haig whether he should attack on November 8 'if the military situation required him' to do so 'even if the weather made success doubtful'. Haig reiterated to Gough his earlier instructions – that the Fifth Army should not attack until the ground was dry.

The disagreement between Foch and Haig was summed up by Haig when he confided in his diary, 'Foch gave me the impression that he was not very keen to carry on fighting during the winter!' But the British Commander-in-Chief himself was proving to be the supreme pragmatist. When General Kavanagh lunched with him at Val Vion on November 5, Haig told him clearly that, as regards the Cavalry Corps, 'owing to the state of the ground, the cavalry in the Fourth Army area could not hope to break through this winter, unless a hard frost came! So they might now be withdrawn to more comfortable billets.'

Comfortable billets were not easy to come by. On November 3, Private Bernard Whayman of the 1st Battalion, Northamptonshire Regiment, recalled a night at Bresle, behind the lines, 'under canvas and in mud', followed the next evening, as the battalion moved up to Albert, by an aerial attack as 'enemy planes machine-gunned and dropped bombs, some with time fuses', that were still exploding the following morning.

On November 6, Whayman's battalion marched up the line to Flers, Eaucourt-l'Abbaye and Le Sars, which lay at the furthest limit of the British advance. 'At this time,' he wrote, 'we were carrying up water, bombs etc., often in the open, and also by night to the front line. We were under enemy observation here and had to "run the gauntlet" of severe "whiz-banging" and on one occasion both men behind me were wounded in the legs.' The whiz-bang was the shell fired from a seventy-seven-millimetre German quick-firing gun.

Whayman added, 'We had much rain at this time, and the churned-up chalky area was reduced to a bog of cement-like mud which hampered movement badly.' This problem continued to trouble the Commander-in-Chief. Despite the railways and tramways that had been laid down, the movement of men and supplies from the original front line to the new front line was problematic. 'The communications are still very bad,' Haig confided to his diary on November 8. 'In fact, we are fighting under the same conditions as in October 1914, i.e. with rifle and machine guns only, because bombs and mortar ammunition cannot be carried forward as the roads are so bad.'

In the second week of November, Haig was preparing for a conference of all Allied commanders, to be held at French headquarters at Chantilly on November 15. His intention was to present his French, Italian, Russian, Romanian and Serb colleagues with the story of the successful endeavours of the British Expeditionary Force. For this he wanted one final successful offensive on the Somme. On November 8 he sent his Chief of Staff, General Kiggell, to see General Gough at Fifth Army headquarters at Toutencourt. Gough was so astonished by what Haig required of him that he asked his senior Staff Officer, Lieutenant Colonel Malcolm, to write down Kiggell's words.

Kiggell told Gough that, with regard to the November 15 conference of the Allied commanders, 'the British position would be somewhat strengthened if it should be possible for the Fifth Army to win
some success before that date' – that is to say, within the coming seven
days. The note of Kiggell's remarks continued, 'There was no desire
to pressure Gough into an action where the prospect of success was
not sufficiently good to justify the risk, but on the other hand a tactical success would very probably have far reaching results.'

Gough and his three corps commanders discussed what to do. The
most they could contemplate was to attempt an advance of a thousand yards. The attack was set for November 13, just in time to give
Haig his victory. On the day before it was to begin, Haig visited
Gough at Fifth Army headquarters. In his diary, Haig recorded that,
while telling Gough that 'nothing was so costly as failure', he went
on to tell his Fifth Army commander that 'success at this time was
much wanted.'

Haig set out in his diary three reasons for a new British offensive.
First, the Romanians, the most recent recruits to the Allied Powers,
needed to feel that their continuing struggle against the Germans in
Transylvania had some Western Front support. Second, the Russians,
deep into a major offensive against the German forces on the Eastern
Front, also needed to feel that their western allies were active. And third,
Haig wrote, 'on account of the Chantilly conference which meets on
Wednesday', the British position 'will doubtless be much stronger (as
resources are short) if I could appear there on top of the capture of
Beaumont Hamel, for instance, and 3,000 German prisoners'.

On November 12, Gough warned Haig that the divisions under his
command in Fifth Army 'had been waiting on so long for fine weather
that we could not keep them hanging on any longer with any prospect of success'. Either they should attack on the following day, or they
should be relieved 'and a new lot prepared for the operations say in a
month's time'. Haig, with the Chantilly Conference a mere three days
away, was himself unwilling to wait any longer to launch a new attack.
It would take place on November 13. Gough's plans were ready.

17

The final battle: 'A light from our household is gone'

O N THE FIRST day of the Battle of the Somme, the British attack along the whole length of the Gommecourt–Thiepval sector had been so unsuccessful that the front line there had not moved forward. As a result, part of the assault of 13 November 1916 along both banks of the Ancre was mounted from the original British front line, and did not have to cope – as it would have had to do in any other sector of the battlefield – with 4,000 to 5,000 yards of ground torn up by months of shelling.

Forty-three battalions, belonging to seven different divisions – some forty thousand men in all – attacked on November 13. Their main objectives were three villages – Beaumont-Hamel, Beaucourt and Saint-Pierre-Division, which had eluded all attempts to reach them on July 1 – and the village of Serre, on the high ground a mile and a half north of Beaumont-Hamel, which had likewise been attacked in vain on the first day of the battle.

For fifteen minutes, starting at 5.30 a.m., there was an artillery barrage so fierce that it woke up Haig at Val Vion, sixteen miles away. The troops attacked at 5.45, with intense artillery support for another hour. The attackers were also aided in their approach to the German defences by dense fog, so that they could not be seen by the German machine-gunners. But this fog also proved to be a curse: as the British advanced, groups of Germans were left intact behind the forward line of the attackers, and continued firing at the attackers from the rear.

Lance Corporal Albert Barker, 13th Battalion, East Yorkshire Regiment – the 4th Hull Pals, known as the Hull T'Others – later recalled seeing men stuck in the mud in front of the German front line who were shot down before they could move. In that same attack, Private John Cunningham of the 12th Battalion, East Yorkshire

Regiment – the Hull Sportsmen – won the Victoria Cross opposite Hébuterne. His citation described how, after the German front line had been captured, he 'proceeded with a bombing section up a communication trench. Much opposition was encountered, and the rest of the section became casualties. Collecting all the bombs from the casualties, this gallant soldier went on alone. Having expended all his bombs, he returned for a fresh supply and again proceeded to the communication trench, where he met a party of ten of the enemy. These he killed and cleared the trench up to the enemy line.'

Some members of the 12th Battalion, York and Lancaster Regiment – the Sheffield Pals – managed briefly to enter Serre on November 13, before they were driven out. While in the village they found the bodies of members of their battalion lying where they had fallen on July 1.

The objective was no longer a breakthrough, but – in order to give Haig the more limited success that he felt he needed for the Chantilly Conference – an advance of a thousand yards and the capture of as many prisoners as possible. As the battle began, there were encouraging episodes that the British soldiers had not seen before. In the sector of German trenches attacked by the 99th Brigade, Haig was told a week later, 'the Enemy was quite surprised and many were not fully dressed, when our men entered their trenches. The Germans readily surrendered if our troops were in sufficient numbers.' The officer told Haig, 'They held up their hands, saluted once, and then readily rushed down to their dugouts to pack their kit for London.'

Officer Cadet Pukall, of the 3rd Company, 62nd German Infantry Regiment, and his eleven men were holding a section of a trench defending the line east of Auchonvillers. As the morning fog cleared, Pukall saw long lines of men in German field-grey uniform coming towards his trench. Then he saw that they were being guarded by British soldiers. They were prisoners of war. The column of prisoners then veered away in search of the British lines. Shortly afterwards British troops advanced towards the trench, opening fire. Puckall and his men had no machine gun and no hand grenades, only rifles and rifle ammunition. 'Then came a shout that Schrott was dead! . . . He had been hit in the temple by a bullet. He lay there in front of me on the floor of the trench. He had been a friend to all; tirelessly he had worked for the common good. His experience had been indispensable, as had his presence in battle. Now he was no more. I did not want to believe it. But there was no time for mourning.'

Pukall had to decide what to do. British soldiers were all around his position. Others were advancing down the road from Auchonvillers. 'We were almost out of ammunition. We each had a few rounds left, which would probably have sufficed for troops pulling back. We went on waiting then it occurred to me that there were very few men left in the trench. I called out the names of individuals. "They've had it," came the reply.' Even his friend Huismann was no longer in his place: 'He limped past me, weak from loss of blood. We spoke briefly and he headed for the aid post. He waved and I had no idea that it was the last time we should greet one another.'

The time had come for Pukall to seek reinforcements. 'With my rifle at the ready I advanced along the trench. It was deserted! There was not a trace of our right flank platoon. Suddenly I came across four British soldiers sitting in the trench. They immediately raised their hands. I called for Olbrich and the others, but there was no reply. The Tommies, who were unwounded, noticed this too, but I got back safely.'

A rapid consultation took place: 'I felt like a whipped cur; I had to throw all my ideals overboard. I now believe this dreadful decision to have been justified, because the nine men who were still with me could be of far greater use to Germany alive than would be our bleaching bones in France.' As the British troops approached, 'we laid down our arms.'

On the northern bank of the River Ancre, Sub-Lieutenant John Bentham of the Hood Battalion, Royal Naval Division, was among the men setting off at 5.45 a.m. into the German lines, machine guns 'taking a toll of those of us advancing. Where there had been hundreds on either side of me, I seemed to be alone with my runners and bodyguard; everything was smoke and hell let loose.' The first group of Germans that Bentham and his men came to 'had their hands up', he later wrote, 'except one whom I shot through the stomach. We threw phosphorus bombs down the dugouts, which forced the inmates to come up, and some of my men bayoneted them as they did so. It was not that they were that way inclined, but that they had lost all semblance to a civilised being. The inferno was enough to send any sane man berserk.'

As to the Germans who were taken prisoner, Bentham noted, they were disarmed and sent to the rear, 'and, not being able to spare any man to go with them, a lot were shot on sight by the waves coming behind'.

A few moments after sending the German prisoners to the rear, Bentham and his men were caught by a German shell. Two of his runners were killed, and he was wounded in the thigh. He gave his map to a non-commissioned officer and told him to carry on. 'He was killed just as he left me.' It was 6.15 a.m. 'We had certainly had a hectic half hour and now it was all over.'

For the rest of that day and the following night and morning, in freezing cold, and thick fog, Bentham and the wounded men with him remained in the shellhole where they had taken shelter. 'Another badly wounded boy died that morning,' he wrote, 'and others were of the opinion that we should perish there.' At 2 p.m. their iron rations were all eaten. Then a group of German prisoners came by, under guard, with stretchers. 'I saw every man depart and wished them luck, and at last it was my turn. Off I went on a stretcher and was taken to the advanced dressing station, which was under shellfire. I saw many of my brother officers, some so mutilated that it was only a question of hours before they died.'

Among those killed on the Ancre on November 13 was the twenty-one-year-old Lieutenant Vere Harmsworth, of the Hawke Battalion, Royal Naval Division, one of the three sons of the newspaper proprietor Lord Rothermere. After the war, Rothermere became a leading supporter of Hungarian claims for the restoration of territory lost by Hungary as a result of the war. At the base of his son's grave in the Ancre Cemetery is a bronze wreath put there in 1929 by Hungarian Boy Scouts 'in gratitude'. Vere Harmsworth's brother Harold, a Captain in the Irish Guards, died fifteen months later of wounds received in action. A third brother, Esmond, survived as an artillery officer.

Returning in late 1917 to the scene of the fighting on the Ancre, Lieutenant A. P. Herbert of the Hawke Battalion wrote of his feelings as, with fresh troops, he came to the scene where so many of his friends had been killed a year earlier:

I wandered up to Beaucourt;
I took the river track,
And saw the lines we lived in,
Before the Boche went back.
And here the lads went over and there was Harmsworth shot
And here was William lying – but the new men knew them not.
And I said, 'There is still the river, and still the stiff, stark trees
To treasure here our story, but there are only these;
But under the white wood crosses the dead men answered low,
'The new men knew not Beaucourt, but we who are here – we know.'

As the 51st (Highland) Division stormed the labyrinth of fortified German underground tunnels, dugouts and command headquarters at Beaumont-Hamel on the morning of November 13, Sergeant Paul Maze was sent forward to report on the situation. He later recalled, 'I wandered about a good deal before I found the old German front line, but, once I did, I followed in their wake, as I recognised their dead.' At one moment a friend passed in the other direction. 'He looked exhausted and dishevelled in contrast with the two carrier-pigeons he had in a basket, whose eyes glittered with eagerness.' At that moment, the only effective communication between the forward troops and their headquarters was by pigeon.

After lunching at Val Vion, Haig rode to Fifth Army headquarters at Toutencourt, where he thanked General Gough and his Staff 'for all their efforts'. Haig noted in his diary, 'The success has come at a most opportune moment.' By the end of the day, 5,000 German soldiers had been taken prisoner, but none of the objectives of the Fifth Army attack had been achieved.

Battle was resumed on November 14. Approaching Beaumont-Hamel, two British tanks managed to cross the German front-line trench before becoming stuck in the mud. Unable to move, they fired their guns at everything in front of them, until the officer of the leading tank noticed that the trench in front of them was covered with 'some flickering white substance'. Opening his protective flap, he saw that all the German troops in the trench were frantically waving white handkerchiefs, paper, pieces of cloth – anything white that they could find – in sign of surrender.

There were 16 men in the two immobilized tanks, and 400 armed Germans in the trench. Urgently, the tanks signalled to some infantrymen to come up and take the Germans prisoner. The Germans were astonished to discover, as they were being led away into captivity, that both tanks were unable to move. The giants had – literally – feet of clay. Their power was an illusion.

Lance Sergeant Hector Munro – the writer Saki – was among those in action at Beaucourt on November 14. He was killed that day by a German sniper. Just before he was shot he called out to the man next to him, 'Put that bloody cigarette out!' – but it was too late. His body, pounded into the mud he had earlier described so vividly, was never found. His name is on the Thiepval Memorial.

Led by a much-wounded veteran of Gallipoli, Lieutenant Colonel Bernard Freyberg, the attacking Royal Naval Division troops entered Beaucourt, one of the four objectives of the Ancre assault, on November 14. One of the company commanders, Captain 'Cardy' Montague, also a veteran of Gallipoli, recalled a week later how, in the ruins of Beaucourt, 'the Germans could not face our men and were surrendering in hundreds. It was an amazing sight, they came out of their holes, tearing off their equipment.' Six hundred Germans were taken prisoner that day.

Freyberg led the attack on the German trenches in person. Knocked over by a bullet that hit his helmet, he picked himself up and continued to advance. After both his adjutant and his signals officer had been killed on either side of him he carried on. For having 'inspired all with his own contempt of danger', he was awarded the Victoria Cross. The official history of his division, the Royal Naval Division, stated, eight years later, 'By his initiative, fine leading and bravery, Lieutenant Colonel Freyberg won the battle of Ancre. Probably this was the most distinguished personal act in the war.'

Freyberg's leadership came to an abrupt end. 'There was a bang, a curious ringing note in my ear, and I lost consciousness,' he later recalled. 'When I came to, my head gave me a great deal of pain, and as I lay face downwards hot blood was dropping from my nose and chin. I thought at first my head had been smashed, but I located the wound in my neck with two dirty fingers. I looked at the man on my left; he was curled up. I moved his head, and found he was grey and dead.'

On being taken back to the casualty clearing station with his head and eyes covered in blood-soaked bandages, and his colour gone through loss of blood, Freyberg was put in the tent with those who were expected to die, and who were given no treatment except pain-killing drugs. Later he heard a quiet voice giving orders for him to be moved to the tent for those expected to live, where treatment was given. He could not find out who his saviour was.

A quarter of a century later, and in another war, Freyberg was General Officer Commanding the New Zealand forces in the Western Desert. While in a hotel foyer in Cairo, he heard that same voice. Asking the man if he had been on the Ancre in November 1916, he learned that he was the medical officer who had saved his life, Captain S. S. Greaves, who was then commanding a hospital ship.

An account of the battle for Beaumont-Hamel appeared in both the *Daily Mirror* and the *Paris Daily Mail*. It was by W. Beach Thomas, who wrote of the dead British soldier, 'Even as he lies on the field he looks more quietly faithful, more simply steadfast than others.' Commenting on Thomas's account of the battle, one officer wrote home, 'He has drawn well on his imagination, as half of it is not true, but just what he thought it would be like.'

The reality was not described in the newspapers, and only glimpsed in letters home. Lieutenant Guy Chapman described that reality in his curt diary entry on November 16: 'No. 1 Company is badly knocked out. Lauder and Young both badly wounded, Sergeant-Major Dell wounded. Farrington killed. Sgt Brown not expected to live. Sgt Baker wounded. Westle, poor fellow, killed. Foley – the last of his family – killed, a lot of other good men, too many to speak of.' Farrington, Westle and Foley are named on the Thiepval Memorial.

Near Beaucourt Station, Chapman wrote in his diary, lay 'the skeleton of five wagons and their team, the grisly evidence of the tragedy of a Bosche ration convoy. There is a sickly stench, the mixed smell of exploded picric acid, gas, blood, putrefying corpses and broken bricks. Here and there lie the bodies of the fallen.' Burial parties were working without ceasing: '800 Englishmen and forty Germans were buried yesterday – evidence of what price the assaulting parties must pay for some few yards of ground. Damn Germany!'

Guy Chapman was awarded the Military Cross in 1918. He was later a distinguished historian of France, and subsequently Professor of Modern History at the University of Leeds.

On November 15, at the inter-Allied conference at Chantilly, Haig was able to report the capture of Beaucourt and Beaumont-Hamel. He also agreed with his fellow commanders that the Western Front was 'the main one', and that the resources employed in other theatres 'should be reduced to the smallest possible'.

That day, as for the past ten days, an intense struggle was taking place in the German trenches five miles west of the Ancre for control of the Butte-de-Warlencourt, a low hill just beyond Le Sars that was the last natural obstacle before Bapaume.

The Butte was a German stronghold, a mass of tunnels and barbed-wire entanglements, with a plethora of well-hidden mortar and machine-gun nests. Again and again British and South African troops overran the hill, but were driven off. It was the closest the Allies were to get to Bapaume after four and a half months of fighting. The Butte is said to have been taken and retaken seventeen times during the five-day struggle. A bronze sign on the hill today states, 'This site is sacred, respect it. Passers by, you are entering this site at your own responsibility. British soldiers fell in 1916 in the Battle of the Somme and still lie here.'

On the night of November 17 the first snow fell on the battlefield. The combination of snow and mud was formidable. Private John Jackson, 6th Battalion, Cameron Highlanders, later recalled how, while taking hot tea and rum that night to a front-line trench facing the Butte-de-Warlencourt, he and three other soldiers came across two men in a trench who had been stuck 'hard and fast' in the mud for several hours, and could not get out. 'They were members of a party who had been relieved about midnight,' Jackson wrote, 'and now, they had given up hopes of being rescued alive. Their strength was done, and our efforts to haul them out were of no use, until we leaned over the edge of the trench and unbuckled their equipments, and loosened the greatcoats they wore. After that, our united efforts managed to drag them free, but we left the coats and equipment sticking in the mire.'

★

The final assault on the Ancre, towards Serre, began at 6.10 a.m. on November 18. It was carried out, the official British war historian Captain Miles recorded, 'in whirling sleet which afterwards changed to rain'. His account continued, 'More abominable conditions for active warfare are hardly to be imagined: the infantry, dark figures only visible for a short distance against the white ground, groped their way forward as best they could through half-frozen mud that was soon to dissolve into chalky slime.' Miles added, 'Little wonder that direction was often lost and with it the precious barrage, whilst the objectives, mantled in snow, were hard indeed to identify. Observation from the air was impossible; ground observers could see little or nothing, so that the batteries, in almost as bad a plight as the infantry, were, for the most part, reduced to firing their prearranged programme, regardless of the fortunes of the advance. To the sheer determination, self-sacrifice and physical endurance of the troops must be attributed such measure of success as was won.'

That morning, in an attempt to capture the village of Serre, the British attacked the fortified German trenches of the Soden Redoubt. Among the German defenders was Reserve Captain Achilles, 3rd Battalion, 77th Reserve Infantry Regiment, who recalled, 'Suddenly British soldiers appeared right in front of our command post. By the time the first attempt was made to reach the exit, hand grenades had been thrown in. The grenades silenced the machine gun and wounded, on the left, Reserve Lieutenant Lüders and, on the right, Lance Corporal Blume. Two men from the 65th Infantry Regiment fell dead into the entrance. An attempt was made to contact the nearby machine-gun officer, to request assistance, but this link was broken as well.'

There was, Captain Achilles added, 'no escape. The telephonists destroyed the telephone at the very last minute. We had to lay down our arms and, under the direction of the British Lieutenant Davidson of the Manchester Regiment of the 32nd Division, we were led across country through our own and the enemy's artillery fire, in the direction of Beaumont.'

That day, November 18, the war diary of the 11th Battalion, Lancashire Fusiliers, recorded that Second Lieutenant J. R. R. Tolkien was struck off the battalion's fighting strength and evacuated to Britain

– to a hospital in Birmingham. His trench fever, which continued to flare up, forced him to stay in Britain for the rest of the war. Many years later, commenting on *The Lord of the Rings*, Tolkien reflected, 'The Dead Marshes and the approaches to the Morannon owe something to Northern France after the Battle of the Somme.' So too, he said, did his fictional character Sam Gangee, 'a reflection of the English soldier, of the privates and batmen I knew in the 1914 war, and recognised as so far superior to myself'.

In one of the passages in *The Lord of the Rings* in which Sam Gangee appears, Tolkien writes, 'Hurrying forward again, Sam tripped, catching his foot in some old root or tussock. He fell and came heavily on his hands, which sank deep into sticky ooze, so that his face was brought close to the surface of the dark mere. There was a faint hiss, a noisome smell went up, the lights flickered and danced and swirled. For a moment the water below him looked like some window, glazed with grimy glass, through which he was peering. Wrenching his hands out of the bog, he sprang back with a cry. "There are dead things, dead faces in the water," he said with horror. "Dead faces!" Gollum laughed. "The Dead Marshes, yes, yes: that is their name," he cackled.'

Many soldiers on the Somme had been confronted by corpses, often decaying in the mud, that had lain undisturbed, except by the bombardment, for days, weeks and even months.

On the night of November 18/19 the final assault of the campaign took place: an advance of a thousand yards along the River Ancre. It was much hampered by thick mist and falling snow. Among those killed that night was Sergeant Alexander Macdonald, a British sniper. In his memory, his friend Ewart Macintosh wrote a parody of the soldiers' favourite tongue-twister, 'Sister Susie's sewing shirts for soldiers'. The chorus went:

> Sniper Sandy's slaying Saxon soldiers,
> And Saxon soldiers seldom show but Sandy slays a few,
> And every day the Bosches put up little wooden crosses
> In the cemetery for Saxon soldiers Sniper Sandy slew.

Canadian troops were in action on November 18 south of the Ancre, reaching their objective, the second German trench line north of Courcelette. Among the Canadians killed that day was Private

Bertram Pasmore, of the 75th Battalion, Canadian Infantry Brigade. He was thirty-two years old, from Edmonton, Alberta, and had served with the Canadian forces in the Boer War fifteen years earlier. For the base of his tombstone in the Adanac Military Cemetery his wife, Kate, chose the words 'A light from our household has gone. One we can never replace.'

To the left of the Canadians, II Corps failed to link up with them or to reach its own objective, the western outskirts of the village of Grandcourt. Conditions for all the attacking troops were appalling. L. W. Kentish, an officer who took part in the II Corps attack, wrote twenty years later to General Edmonds, 'This was the only occasion in which I saw men dead from exhaustion from their efforts to get out of the mud.' In the following year, in the notorious struggle for the village of Passchendaele in the Ypres Salient, Kentish was to see men 'mudbound', but they 'could be dragged out, but at the Ancre at this time, we were pitchforked into a quagmire in the dark and there was no possibility of a man helping the one next to him'.

Kentish added, 'It was the worst instance I came across of what appeared to be a cruel useless sacrifice of life.' The climatic conditions alone were such, Kentish wrote, that they made it clear 'to the very stupidest brain that no success could possibly result'. One divisional history recorded that two companies that had taken part in the assault on November 18 had disappeared 'entirely, being overwhelmed by machine-gun fire'.

The final line on the River Ancre when the battle came to an end on November 19 included the three villages that had been among the original British objectives on July 1: Beaumont-Hamel, Beaucourt and Saint-Pierre-Division. But the fourth objective of this final battle, the village of Serre, remained behind the German lines.

There were to be no more British offensives on the Somme. The weather had proved the ultimate decision-maker. Haig did not take the ending of his grand design too tragically. 'The Enemy's power has not yet been broken,' he wrote in his final dispatch on December 23, 'nor is it yet possible to form an estimate of the time the war may last before the objects for which the Allies are fighting are to be attained. But the Somme battle has placed beyond doubt the ability of the Allies to gain those objects.'

Sergeant Paul Maze, who had been with the British troops in the final push beyond Beaumont-Hamel, later wrote, 'Since July we had gained a great deal of ground and taken many guns, but the flower of British manhood lay beneath the sodden earth.'

18

Aftermath on the Somme:
November 1916 to November 1918

THE SOMME HAD failed in its expectations for the British, as
Verdun had failed for the Germans. 'In 1916 English, French and
Germans alike saw victory within their grasp, and expected it after
every local advantage,' wrote Charles Edmonds, a young officer
during the Battle of the Somme; 'in 1917 the war seemed likely to go
on for ever.'

Despite the British hopes of a breakthrough, between the first day
of the Battle of the Somme on 1 July 1916 and the last day, November
21, the deepest Anglo-French penetration of the German lines was
less than six miles. At the end of the battle the British front line was
still three miles short of Bapaume, which it had been hoped to capture
within a few days of the first attack. No permanent gap through
which the cavalry could advance had been driven in the German
defences. No German lines of communication and supply had been
disrupted. No French town had been liberated. No fatal demoraliza-
tion had affected the tenacious German defenders, despite their losses
of more than 170,000 dead.

Robin Prior and Trevor Wilson, the biographers of the commander of the British Fourth Army, comment, 'So it transpired that
at the close of the battle, after all, Rawlinson had not needed those
larger maps detailing the whereabouts of Beaumetz, Marcoing, and
Cambrai. Not even his preliminary objective of 1 October, the
Transloy Ridge, had been vouchsafed to him.'

Nevertheless, the balance sheet of the Battle of the Somme was not
entirely negative from the British point of view. Brigadier General Sir
James Edmonds, the British military historian, reflected in 1932, in his
volume on the first day of the battle, that on German evidence 'the
24th June 1916 saw the German Army at its zenith, still possessing large
numbers of officers and NCOs of the Old Army, and well-trained

men. These troops sacrificed their lives to obey the order not to give up an inch of ground; and after this loss', Edmonds writes, the German Army 'never fought so well again. Its morale for the first time was shaken, never quite to recover.'

There was another positive result for Britain that Edmonds points to: that Hindenburg and Ludendorff, who replaced General Falkenhayn in mid-battle as a result of the heavy losses, 'decided that the German Army could not continue such a battle on equal terms, and immediately set about organizing a chosen line in rear'. On a February night in 1917 'the divisions of the German Army on the Somme and adjacent front slipped away to man the Hindenburg Line.' This, commented General Edmonds, 'signified more than the giving up of a little territory; it was a sacrifice of ground of immense military importance.' One of those who recognized this was General Hunter-Liggett, the commander of the American First Army, who later pointed out that 'had the German attack that was to come in March 1918 been launched from the old position rather than from the Hindenburg Line to which the enemy retreated in March 1917, the Germans would have been in Amiens.' Hunter-Liggett added, 'That retreat, caused by the British success on the Somme in 1916, may well have saved the Allies from defeat in 1918 before we could aid them in force.'

Wherever fighting took place on the Somme, the towns and villages that were in the zone of conflict suffered enormous destruction, and in many cases total annihilation. In *The Old Front Line*, John Masefield wrote, 'It is as though the place had been smitten by the plague.'

At Verdun, similar destruction had soured the final phase of the French endeavour, the recapture of Fort Vaux on 3 November 1916. In five months, the contending armies at Verdun fired more than twenty-three million shells. This was on average more than a hundred shells a minute. Verdun remained in French hands throughout, but 650,000 French and German soldiers were killed. When added to the death toll on the Somme, this made a five-month total – in the precise figure of the clerks whose task it was to add them up – of 960,459 men: almost a million men, in two areas each of which can be crossed by car today in less than an hour.

The Somme and Verdun together saw an average of more than 6,600 men killed every day: more than 277 every hour, nearly 5 men every minute. The two battles over, 127 German divisions faced 169 Allied divisions. The Allied force consisted of 106 French, 56 British, 6 Belgian and 1 Russian division. Despite the high death rate on the Somme, the British Expeditionary Force, which in August 1914 had consisted of 160,000 men, had multiplied tenfold in just over two years. By the end of 1916 it was 1,591,745 strong. This included 125,517 Australian and New Zealand (Anzac) troops and 104,538 Canadians.

General Gough, the commander of the Reserve (later Fifth) Army, had particular cause for satisfaction, noting in his memoirs that Rawlinson's Fourth Army had suffered 278,125 men dead and wounded and captured 15,650 German prisoners, while his army had suffered 'only' 125,531 casualties and captured 17,723 prisoners.

The deaths that can be attributed to the Battle of the Somme include several that took place after the battle ended. On December 1, Private A. Ingham of the Manchester Regiment was executed for desertion. On his Commonwealth War Graves headstone is the inscription 'Shot at dawn. One of the first to enlist. A worthy son of his father.' That same day, twenty-three-year old Private William Simmonds of the Middlesex Regiment was executed for having 'absented himself' during the battle. Three days later Private John Cameron, Northumberland Fusiliers, who had gone absent after taking part in several attacks, was also executed. On December 7, Rifleman Samuel McBride, Royal Irish Rifles, was shot for having absented himself from the battlefield. He had previously received a two-year hardlabour sentence for the same offence, but that sentence had been suspended so he could go back into action. Also on December 7 a Canadian infantryman, Private John Higgins, Western Ontario Regiment, aged twenty-four, who had left his home on Prince Edward Island in order to enlist, was executed for desertion. His next of kin were told that he had died of wounds.

Did these deserters develop a 'wrong attitude' to the fighting – a phrase used by Charles Wilson (later Lord Moran) in his book *The Anatomy of Courage*, based on letters he had written shortly after the Armistice. Wilson had served on the Somme as a doctor. How was courage spent in war? he asked, and he went on to give his answer: 'Courage is will-power, whereof no man has an unlimited stock; and when in war it is used up, he is finished. A man's courage is his capital and he is always spending. The call on the bank may be only the daily drain of the front line or it may be a sudden draft which threatens to close the account. His will is perhaps almost destroyed by intensive shelling, by heavy bombing, or by a bloody battle, or it is gradually used up by monotony, by exposure, by the loss of the support of stauncher spirits on whom he has come to depend, by physical exhaustion, by a wrong attitude to danger, to casualties, to war, to death itself.'

A German soldier wrote in the immediate aftermath of the war, 'The tragedy of the Somme battle was that the best soldiers, the stoutest-hearted men were lost; their numbers were replaceable, their spiritual worth never could be.' Lord Moran commented on this, 'Our own forces were in no better plight. Most of those who were meant by nature to lead men had been struck down by two years of war.'

The Battle of the Somme had many political repercussions. On 5 December 1916 King Albert of the Belgians, whose small army was holding the northernmost part of the line, Belgium's only free soil, by the North Sea coast, wrote in his diary, 'The general conduct of the war has been entrusted to incompetent men – there the trouble lies.'

In Britain, on December 7, David Lloyd George, who had emerged as a critic of the Somme, replaced Asquith as Prime Minister. He had no intention of renewing the Somme offensive, though he was to become a strong advocate of an attempted British breakthrough elsewhere. On December 12 the French Commander-in-Chief, General Joffre, was replaced by the younger and more energetic General Nivelle. No change was made in the British High Command. On the Western Front, Sir Douglas Haig, for whom the Battle of the Somme had been his first test as Commander-in-Chief, looked forward with confidence to new battles and greater successes in the coming year, as did General Nivelle.

The statistics of confrontation reflect the intention, and determination, of all the opposing armies to continue to fight. As 1916 came to an end, the German Army possessed 16,000 machine guns on the Western Front, the Russian Army had 16,000 machine guns on the Eastern Front. Three years earlier this weapon, with its rapid, uninterrupted, stuttering fire, had been a symbol of European dominance over distant, alien and despised peoples in Africa and Asia. In the words of the popular British imperial jingle:

> Whatever happens, we have got
> The Maxim gun, and they have not.

By the second decade of the twentieth century, Hiram Maxim's invention had become a means whereby those societies that felt they shared the highest values of civilization, religion, philosophy, science, culture, literature, art, music and a love of nature, were able to continue to bleed each other barbarically year after year. On the Somme, it had been the German machine-gunners who had wreaked the most immediate havoc on the advancing British and French forces. It was the artillery, however, that had accounted for by far the largest number of dead and wounded on both sides.

Artillery fire – both shell and trench mortar – accounted for just over 58 per cent of all wounds; rifle and machine-gun bullets accounted for just under 39 per cent; bombs and grenades just over 2 per cent; and bayonets less than one third of 1 per cent. As 1917 began, artillery production was accelerated in every warring nation.

The leaders of Britain, France and Germany were confident and determined. But the savage impact of the Somme was felt in many homes, and in many forms. A British writer, Israel Zangwill, a pre-war novelist of wit and charm, summed up the year 1916 with a bitter tone:

> The world bloodily-minded,
> The church dead or polluted,
> The blind leading the blinded,
> And the deaf dragging the muted.

On Boxing Day 1916 an execution took place in the French village of Yvrench, ten miles north-east of Abbeville. The victim was Private Charles Skilton, who in the attack on Delville Wood on July 27 had been suspected of 'shirking his duty', and who had gone absent before the mid-November offensive. At his court martial he was described as lazy, avoiding his share of work in the trenches, 'unreliable' and 'useless'. Although his body must have been buried in a known grave, his name appears on the Thiepval Memorial to the Missing. He was twenty years old.

Another execution took place two days later. Private Peter Cairnie, 1st Battalion, Royal Scots Fusiliers, had refused to go forward in the attack on Serre on November 13. At the time of his execution, his battalion was at Courcelles; it is possible that his grave was destroyed in the subsequent fighting. He too is listed on the Thiepval Memorial.

Another court martial, held on Boxing Day, also related to the attacks on November 13. In the attack on the River Ancre against Beaucourt that day, when it became known that the casualties in his battalion were high, twenty-one-year-old Sub-Lieutenant Edwin Dyett, Nelson Battalion, Royal Naval Division, had gone forward with a group of reinforcements. In a letter to a friend a few weeks later he described the scene: 'There was considerable hostile artillery, gas shells and tear shells falling all around us, and snipers were all over the place; we had very narrow shaves more than once.'

When night fell, Dyett returned through the mud and fog towards the British lines. Ordered by an officer of the same rank to return to the front as an escort for a group of stragglers who had been rounded up, Dyett chose to go back to brigade headquarters for fresh orders. He was accused of 'refusing a lawful order'. Instead of going back to brigade headquarters, he had taken refuge in a dugout with a group of men who were lost in the darkness. At his trial, the court-martial panel was told that he was 'a bundle of nerves quite unfit for soldiering'. When questions were asked about the case in the House of Commons, it was said that he had been missing for two days, although Dyett claimed he had reported to headquarters the next day. None of the men with whom he had taken refuge in the dugout were called to testify.

Dyett was tried on Boxing Day 1916 and condemned to death, but with a recommendation for mercy – by a panel whose members all had first-hand experience of battle – on the grounds that the prevailing conditions on November 13 'were likely to have a detrimental effect on any but the strongest of young men'. The recommendation for mercy was overruled, first by the commander of V Corps, General Fanshawe, and then by the Fifth Army commander, General Gough. Dyett was executed ten days after being sentenced. His grave is in the communal cemetery at Le Crotoy, at the mouth of the River Somme. On 8 January 1917, the day after Dyett's execution, Private James Tongue, 1st Battalion, King's Liverpool Regiment, was executed for desertion during the same battle on the River Ancre. In all, more than sixty soldiers were executed for desertion or cowardice during the Battle of the Somme.

The immediate aftermath of the battle also saw many hundreds of soldiers die of the wounds they had sustained during the offensive. One of these was nineteen-year-old William Warren, who had been severely wounded that September and died on December 28. On 1 July 2005, almost eighty-nine years after his death, flowers were laid at the Lochnagar Crater with the message 'For Peace and Reconciliation, in memory of Pte Billy Warren, Gloucester Regiment, talented artist . . .'

On what had been the Somme battlefield, the shelling and sniping continued without respite. On December 28, twenty-five-year-old Captain John Lauder, of the Argyll and Sutherland Highlanders, was killed by a sniper. His father, the Scottish singer and comedian Harry Lauder, was distraught, making a journey to his son's grave in Ovillers Military Cemetery six months after his son's death. A father's grief led to one of the most popular morale-boosting songs of its time, 'Keep Right on to the End of the Road':

> Ev'ry road thro' life is a long, long road,
> Fill'd with joys and sorrows too,
> As you journey on how your heart will yearn,
> For the things most dear to you.
> With wealth and love 'tis so,
> But onward we must go –
>
> (*chorus, after each verse*)
> Keep right on to the end of the road, keep right on to the end,
> Tho' the way be long, let your heart be strong, keep right on round
>   the bend.
> Tho' you're tired and weary still journey on, till you come to your
>   happy abode,
> Where all you love you've been dreaming of will be there at the end
>   of the road.
>
> With a big stout heart to a long steep hill,
> We may get there with a smile,
> With a good kind thought and an end in view,
> We may cut short many a mile.
> So let courage ev'ry day,
> Be your guiding star alway –

Following his son's death, Harry Lauder tried to enlist, but at the age of forty-six he was judged too old. He then asked if he could sing to the soldiers, a proposal not at first favoured by the War Office. Eventually he was allowed to entertain Scottish troops wherever they were, even at the front. He had a small five-octave piano specially made for him. He also formed his own recruiting band that travelled at his expense, playing to attract a crowd and, when enough men gathered to listen, marching with them to the recruiting office. Lauder also spoke on the stage, encouraging men to join up; more than twelve thousand were recruited through his efforts. A year after his son's death he established the Harry Lauder Million Pound Fund for maimed Scottish soldiers and sailors. He was knighted for his efforts.

At the beginning of 1917 the German Kaiser made a fateful decision: to embark on unrestricted submarine warfare against both Allied and neutral shipping. One of the strongest supporters of this widening of the war was General Ludendorff, who told a high-level conference on January 9, 'The U-boat war will also bring our armies into a different and better situation. Through the lack of wood needed for mining purposes and for lack of coal, the production of ammunition is hard-pressed. It means that there will be some relief for the Western Front. We must spare the troops a second battle of the Somme.'

Unrestricted submarine warfare meant that German U-boats would attack all merchant ships, including those flying the colours of the United States. Inevitably, this decision would lead to the drawing in of the United States on the side of the Allies, and provide the Allies with a fresh, powerful, and in due course decisive partner.

To prepare for the fighting in the summer of 1917, on February 4 that year the Germans began to withdraw from their hard-fought final line on the Somme – as well as territory they were holding both to the north and south – and pulled back between ten and thirty-five miles. On February 25, without a fight, the British 151st Brigade took the Butte-de-Warlencourt, scene of such fierce fighting the previous November, and moved on to their objective of 1 July 1916, Bapaume, which the Germans had evacuated, leaving its facilities in ruins. Gommecourt, which had resisted all British attacks on July 1, was evacuated by the Germans on February 27.

Following the German withdrawal, one of the grimmer aftermaths of the Battle of the Somme began: the search of the evacuated terrain for the bodies of those who had been posted as missing since July 1. Thousands of bodies were found. More than half were decayed beyond possibility of identification. They were brought back into the former British lines and buried, some in the existing war cemeteries, others in cemeteries made specially for them. One of these was Railway Hollow Cemetery, west of Serre. It was set up by V Corps, originally as V Corps Cemetery No. 3, and contains the graves of more than a hundred soldiers of the 3rd, 19th and 31st Divisions, fifty-three of whom were killed on July 1 and fourteen on 13 November 1916. Forty-four of the bodies brought in were unidentifiable. Another cemetery made after the German withdrawal was Grandcourt Road Cemetery, established when the Ancre battlefield was cleared. It now contains 391 burials, of which 108 are unidentified.

The new German front was the fortified Hindenburg Line. Hindenburg and Ludendorff did not wish to face another offensive on the Somme. But they had a determined enemy, and only two months after the German withdrawal to the Hindenburg Line the commander of the Canadian Corps, General Byng, won a major British and Empire success at Vimy Ridge, twenty miles north of the Somme.

Allied hopes of victory rose. In November 1917, General Byng was General Officer Commanding the Third Army in a combined tank and infantry attack towards Cambrai. In the words of Gary Sheffield and John Bourne, the editors of Haig's diary, Byng and the forces under his command 'pioneered important artillery techniques that restored surprise to the battlefield and used tanks en masse for the first time in war'. On a six-mile front, the Allied troops advanced five miles, breaching the Hindenburg Line.

November 1917 saw British tanks drive the Germans back to Cambrai. It also saw the culmination of Haig's main strategy for that year, the Third Battle of Ypres, and the desperate struggle, as that battle came to an end, for the village of Passchendaele. For those who fought at Passchendaele, the greatest horror was the mud. Those who had fought a year earlier on the Somme knew how horrendous mud could be.

★

In the third week of March 1918, a year after they had abandoned their trenches on the Somme for the greater safety of the Hindenburg Line, the Germans launched Operation Michael, their first sustained offensive action for three years, and a determined attempt to win the war in the West. It was a favourable time for them. The United States, having declared war on Germany, did not yet have sufficient trained troops in Europe to constitute an independent army. Russia, in the grip of revolution, had pulled out of the war altogether, ceding vast tracts of territory to Germany and Austria–Hungary under the Treaty of Brest-Litovsk.

The omens were good for a German victory against the British and French lines. Within a few days those lines were broken and the Anglo-French forces fell back. On March 22 the 51st (Highland) Division, the victors of Beaumont-Hamel in November 1916, were driven out of Beaumetz-les-Cambrai, on the road from Cambrai to Bapaume. On what had been the Somme battlefield, seventy specially trained German 'assault divisions' attacked thirty-five British divisions, and in a few weeks the woods and villages reached at such heavy cost between July and November 1916 were quickly abandoned.

Bapaume, which had been within the British lines since the German withdrawal to the Hindenburg Line, was retaken by the Germans on March 24. On the following day the 6th (Scottish) Division was driven out of Bernafay Wood, which it had seized in the first week of the July battle. That same day, High Wood, Mametz Wood and Delville Wood, all captured at such heavy cost in 1916, were swept into the German net. So too was Beaumont-Hamel. One of those killed in this ferocious single-day assault was Captain Cameron Wilson, a veteran both of the fighting in Delville Wood and the pleasures of Amiens. He was thirty years old. In one of his war poems he had written:

> Still though chaos
> Works on the ancient plan;
> Two things have changed not
> Since first the world began.
> The beauty of the wild green earth
> And the bravery of man.

That bravery was seen throughout the German advance. South of the Somme, on the River Avre, British troops put up a determined defence at the town of Roye, but were driven back on March 26. On the following day, at Rosières, the 8th Division and the 16th Brigade, Royal Horse Artillery, had to beat a hasty retreat.

In an effort to co-ordinate the Allied armies and halt the German advance, General Foch was made Supreme Commander of all the Allied armies in the West, with the rank of Generalissimo. In terms of strategy, Haig became Foch's subordinate, but he retained a firm grip on the British and Empire forces under his command, whom he exhorted on April 11, 'There is no other course open to us but to fight it out. Every position must be held to the last man. There must be no retirement. With our backs to the wall and believing in the justness of our cause, each one of us must fight on to the end.'

As in the same 'just cause' on the Somme in July 1916, the battle in March and April 1918 was fierce. For the first time in war, the tanks of one side were in combat with those of the other. On April 24, seven British tanks met six German tanks in combat at Cachy, near Villers-Bretonneux. A roadside memorial commemorates that historic encounter. On the following day – a day already known as Anzac Day in memory of the Gallipoli landings three years earlier – the 5th Australian and 6th Australian Divisions, in what Haig called 'an enterprise of great daring', drove the Germans out of Villers-Bretonneux. The thirty-mile German thrust from Cambrai was halted, and the city of Amiens was saved.

Today the Australian National Memorial at Villers-Bretonneux commemorates 10,797 Australians who were killed on the Somme and other sectors of the Western Front and have no known grave. A French Canadian is also buried there, the Victoria Cross winner Lieutenant Jean Brillant, killed during the later fighting in August. On his gravestone is the inscription 'Fell gloriously on the soil of his ancestors. Good blood never lies.'

Having been halted twelve miles short of Amiens, the Germans subjected the city to an artillery bombardment in which more than two thousand houses were destroyed. At Albert, the statue of the Madonna and Child still lurched crazily at the top of the basilica, a sign to the troops that the war was not about to end. Nor was it: on April 26 the German Army entered Albert. But they were halted a mile beyond the western outskirts of the city by a determined British defence, and could advance no further. Three miles behind Albert, at

Senlis-le-Sec, the 12th (Eastern) and 38th (Welsh) Divisions established a casualty clearing station for the defenders. Ninety-seven men are buried in the war cemetery there.

By the end of April, both Val Vion and Querrieu, twin havens of repose and command for Haig and Rawlinson, came within the range of German artillery. At the war cemetery in Querrieu the 3rd Australian Division buried almost two hundred of the defenders of Amiens. There are also twelve German soldiers buried there. Four miles to the west, just south of Corbie, across the River Somme, ninety-four soldiers were buried at Aubigny and thirty-eight at Fouilloy Military Cemeteries. Bavelincourt, a mile from the former Casualty Clearing Station No. 49 at Contay, became the base for the field ambulances of the 47th (London) and 58th (London) Divisions, and, inevitably, the location of yet another war cemetery, adding to the proliferation of headstones and human sorrow on the Somme.

The Somme battlefield of two years was under German control. For five months there was stalemate, but no end to the continual attrition of trench warfare. The war cemetery at Bagneux attests to that: it has 1,374 burials, mostly men from the 2nd Canadian Division who died at the 3rd Canadian Stationary Hospital, located less than two miles away, in the citadel at Doullens. Several graves are the result of a German bombing raid over Doullens on 30 May 1918.

Then, on 8 August 1918, four years and four days after Britain had declared war on Germany, British and Dominion troops under Haig's command, and a French Army inspired by the patriotic zeal of Georges Clemenceau – who at the age of seventy-five had become Prime Minister of France for the second time – and by Generalissimo Foch, launched a massive assault on the Western Front. The Anglo-French forces had a new and effective ally: the powerful new American Army under General Pershing. The combined Allied forces had far greater artillery at their disposal than in 1916 or 1917.

In the British bombardment of Albert on the first day of the August battle, the Madonna and Child were hit, and came crashing to the ground. The prophecy that the war would end once they had fallen was coming true. Entering Albert, British troops pushed swiftly on towards Bapaume. For the fourth time in four years the battlefield of the Somme was the scene of hard fighting, with the Germans in full retreat.

A memorial at Pozières commemorates more than 14,000 British and 300 South African soldiers who died in France either during the British retreat across the former Somme battlefield on March 21 or during the return on August 8, and who have no known grave. The corps and regiments represented include the Rifle Brigade, with more than 600 names; the Durham Light Infantry, with 600 names; the Machine Gun Corps with more than 500; the Manchester Regiment, with approximately 500; and the Royal Horse Artillery and Royal Field Artillery, with more than 400 names.

Among those in action on August 8 was a Newfoundlander, Lieutenant Hedley Goodyear, whose brother Raymond had been killed on the Somme in 1916 and whose brother Stanley had been killed near Ypres in 1917. 'This is the evening before the attack and my thoughts are with you all at home,' Hedley Goodyear wrote to his mother. 'But my backward glance is wistful only because of memories, and because of the sorrow which would further darken your lives should anything befall me in tomorrow's fray.' The attack was to be the first of what Foch called his 'liberating attacks' against the new German line, aimed at driving its defenders back along a fifteen-mile front. Goodyear understood the importance of the attack, telling his mother, 'A blow will be struck tomorrow which will definitely mark the turn of the tide . . . I shall strike a blow for freedom, along with thousands of others who count personal safety as nothing when freedom is at stake.'

Goodyear was right: the battle was a turning point. He and his fellow Newfoundlanders, fighting alongside their neighbouring Dominion force, the Canadians, advanced six miles, taking 12 villages, 5,000 prisoners and 161 guns. Goodyear was killed on August 22. He is buried in Hillside Military Cemetery, Le Quesnel.

After capturing Rifle Wood outside Hourges, Canadian troops advanced nine miles to the east. Ten miles south of Albert, Australian troops drove the Germans out of Harbonnières and crossed the Amiens–Saint-Quentin road; among the 1,860 soldiers buried at the Heath Cemetery just north of the village are men of the Australian Trench Mortar Battery, Machine Gun Corps, Army Medical Corps, Pioneers, Engineers and Field Artillery.

Australian troops drove the Germans from seven villages east of Harbonnières on August 8, taking nearly 8,000 prisoners and 173 guns. 'We have reached the limits of capacity,' the Kaiser told Ludendorff that day. 'The war must be ended.' In the Kaiser's view, however, it had to end at a time when Germany was making progress on the battlefield, so that it could obtain at least a minimum of its 'war aims'.

With increasing momentum, the Allied armies drove the Germans back along the whole Western Front. The Germany victory on the Somme in March and April 1918 was swiftly reversed. On August 9, Canadian troops entered Le Quesnel and Vrély, in the former French sector of the Somme battlefield, while the Tank Corps, assisted by the 2nd Canadian Division, captured Rosières. On August 10, the 10th Canadian Infantry Brigade entered Fouquescourt.

For the August battles, new cemeteries had to be opened. On August 15 the burial officer of the 18th Division established Beacon Cemetery, south-west of Albert, when the 12th (Eastern) and 18th and 58th (London) Divisions advanced from the Ancre to the Somme, across what had been the rear and rest areas in the July to November battles. More than five hundred men are buried there. At Bouzincourt Ridge Cemetery, north-west of Albert, which had been opened before the start of the Big Push in July 1916, and then fought over in March 1918, extra plots were made by the V Corps burial officer, who cleared the new battlefields after the village was finally reoccupied in late August 1918.

On August 27 the 18th Division regained Bernafay Wood, which the 9th (Scottish) Division had captured in July 1916 and lost in March 1918. At every village and wood on the Somme it was the same story: once more the Germans were driven out. It was to be twenty-two years before they would return.

The German forces were unable to hold the line anywhere along the Somme. On September 5 the 32nd Division crossed the Somme and entered the village of Brie. As it moved forward again, it established Casualty Clearing Stations Nos. 5, 47 and 48, in whose cemetery are more than four hundred burials. North-east of the Somme, on September 3, at Buissy, the Third Army had broken through the last major German defence system between Drocourt and Quéant. Two more casualty clearing stations were established, the 2nd and the 57th: today their cemetery holds 2,377 burials.

The Allied troops moved forward on all fronts, but the Germans were a tenacious adversary. North and east of the Somme the war cemeteries are a mute testimony to the continuing struggle. Near Cambrai, Canada Cemetery holds 265 graves, the first from October 13.

On 11 November 1918, three months after the start of the August offensive, the German government signed an armistice and the guns fell silent. On the Somme, that first Armistice Day saw much cause for sadness as well as rejoicing. Villages had to be rebuilt; fields and woods had to be cleared of the human and metallic detritus of war; land had to be set aside for the burial places of those who had been killed there; war memorials had to be put up for the many thousands of French soldiers who had died on battlefields far from their homes.

The Big Push had failed to achieve its initial and most ambitious aim: a breakthrough that could be exploited by cavalry, driving the Germans back to the cities of Cambrai and Douai. It did succeed in its crucial secondary aim: to break the intensity of the German attack on Verdun, and give the French forces embattled there a breathing space to recover their strength. It also prevented the Germans from transferring troops to where they were badly needed on the Russian and Romanian Fronts.

The four-and-a-half-month battle had forced the Germans out of their strongly fortified first and second line of trenches, and out of much of their third line, inflicting enormous casualties upon them. While not breaking the German determination to continue the fight, the Allies had weakened the Germans' military capacity, forcing them to pull back in February 1917 as much as thirty miles in search of a more defensible line, fearful that the battle on the Somme would be renewed. The Allied losses were so heavy that they might have sapped the British and Commonwealth will to fight, but they did not do so.

Epilogue: 'We feel proud to be able to cry'

THE FIRST WORLD War was over. Sir Douglas Haig, who had commanded the British Expeditionary Force in its final, victorious advance, was awarded an earldom and was voted £100,000 by the British Parliament, the equivalent of £3 million pounds today. General Rawlinson, whose Fourth Army, the main British force on the Somme, had participated in the final push to victory in 1918, was also elevated to the House of Lords and received £30,000 and the thanks of both Houses of Parliament for his wartime services. But, in the immediate aftermath of victory, there were many who could not drive the horrors of the Somme from their minds. In March 1919 Siegfried Sassoon wrote, in his poem 'Aftermath':

> Do you remember the dark months you held the sector at Mametz –
> The nights you watched and wired and dug and piled sandbags on
>   parapets?
> Do you remember the rats; and the stench
> Of corpses rotting in front of the front-line trench –
> And dawn coming, dirty-white and chill with a hopeless rain?
> Do you ever stop and ask, 'Is it all going to happen again?'

Under the Treaty of Versailles, signed on 28 June 1919, victors and vanquished alike promised to respect and to maintain the graves of 'military foreigners' on their soil. Those graves soon became places of pilgrimage for families and friends. The dignity of the headstones in the cemeteries of all the combatants brought serenity to the troubled landscape. 'Life is not worth living if we brood too much,' wrote one bereaved father, Sir Henry Dickens (Charles Dickens's son); 'we have to make an effort not to forget it, but to bear it in resignation and in proud remembrance.' Dickens, whose son Cedric has no known grave, wrote this letter five days after the Treaty of Versailles promise was made.

★

Ninety years after the Battle of the Somme, the rural landscape has been restored. The woods that had been reduced to shattered stumps of trees and churned-up soil are woods once more. The villages that had been reduced to rubble, not even their church spires standing, are villages again. Each was awarded the Croix de Guerre for the tenacity of its inhabitants. Each has its own war memorial to the villagers who fell fighting with the French armies on all the war fronts, including Salonika, Gallipoli, Italy and the Western Front.

The trenches that scarred the Somme landscape and were the focal point of the struggle in 1916 have been filled in, with the exception of a few that have been kept, no longer as deep or as fierce as they used to be, as memorials and souvenirs. Only one of the craters, Lochnagar, made by the massive underground explosions of 1 July 1916 remains as a testimony to that destructive, and yet not decisive, moment of the battle.

The most significant change in the landscape of the Somme is the proliferation of First World War cemeteries. These are visible from every road and every vista: the well-ordered expanses of tombstones of those who were killed. In the French National Cemetery at Rancourt there are 8,566 burials, more than half of them in four large ossuaries. This is the largest French cemetery on the Somme, created by bringing many graves from the surrounding battlefields.

There is also a German military cemetery at Rancourt: 11,422 German soldiers are interred there, of whom 7,494 lie in a mass grave. In the German military cemetery at Fricourt lie the remains of 17,000 German soldiers. The remains of soldiers in fields and isolated graves were brought to Fricourt from seventy-nine communes in the surrounding region. In 1929, eleven years after the Armistice, the German War Graves Agency began work at Fricourt on landscaping and permanent architectural features. Work stopped while still incomplete in September 1939, on the outbreak of the Second World War. It was not until more than half a century later, following a Franco-German Agreement of 19 July 1966, that the German War Graves Agency returned to Fricourt to finish building and landscaping the First World War cemetery. Two soldiers are often buried in a double grave under each cross. Many crosses have three and even four names inscribed on them. The remains of 11,970 soldiers interred at Fricourt lie in four large communal graves. Of these burials, the names of 6,477 remain unknown. The names of those who are known to be buried in the communal graves are inscribed on metal tablets at the back of the cemetery.

The Commonwealth War Graves Commission – earlier the Imperial War Graves Commission – maintains more than sixty war cemeteries on the Somme battlefield itself, and a further hundred and twenty in the rear areas and in the areas fought over in March and August 1918. On a visit to France and Flanders in 1922, when the first cemeteries were dedicated, King George V declared, 'We can truly say that the whole circuit of the earth is girdled with the graves of our dead.' The King added that in the course of his pilgrimage, as it was called, 'I have many times asked myself whether there can be more potent advocates of peace upon earth through the years to come, than this massed multitude of silent witnesses to the desolation of war.'

The Commonwealth War Graves Commission cemeteries include those that were made at the casualty clearing stations for men too seriously wounded to survive the journey by hospital train to the hospitals near the coast. There are also the cemeteries of those who died while in hospital: the Military Cemetery at Etaples is one of the largest on the Western Front – many of the dead of the Somme lie there among the 11,431 burials, of whom 658 are German. On the Somme itself, each Commonwealth War Graves Commission cemetery has an identical, solemn Cross of Sacrifice, designed by a leading architect, Sir Reginald Blomfield, trim lawns, neat bushes, carefully attended flower beds, and row after row of gravestones.

Memorials have been established on the Somme battlefield in every decade from the 1920s until today. In October 1922 a New Zealand Memorial to the Missing was unveiled in Caterpillar Valley Cemetery. New Zealand troops had fought on the Somme for twenty-three consecutive days.

On 7 June 1925, laden with honours, including the prestigious British Order of Merit, Field Marshal Earl Haig returned to the Somme for the opening of the Newfoundland War Memorial Park south-west of Beaumont-Hamel. Eighty-four acres of the former battlefield had been purchased and the park created from funds subscribed 'by the Government and Women of Newfoundland'. It is dominated by the statue of a caribou calling out in anguish at Newfoundland's losses. Below the statue are three bronze plaques, on which are inscribed the names of the 591 members of the Royal Newfoundland Regiment who were killed in action and have no known grave. The regiment was the only one in the First World War to be given the designation Royal – in recognition of its wartime contribution to the Allied cause.

One aim of the Newfoundland War Memorial Park was to preserve the trench system where the Newfoundlanders had fought and died on 1 July 1916. At the entrance to the park is a plaque that states, of the battle on July 1, 'strategic and tactical miscalculations led to a terrible slaughter.'

Within the Newfoundland Park are three Commonwealth War Graves cemeteries. One of them, Hunter's Cemetery, has forty-one graves. All but one of the men had been killed on 13 November 1916. The cemetery is built in what had been a large shellhole. There is also a statue of a kilted Scottish Highlander, erected in memory of the 51st (Highland) Division, which had fought on that same narrow battle-ground on 13 November 1916. A few yards from the Highlander, a Celtic memorial cross commemorates the 51st Division's losses at High Wood in July 1916. Just outside the park is the Hawthorn Ridge Cemetery No. 1, which contains 152 British and 1 Newfoundland burial. The Newfoundlander is Private Joseph Evans, killed in action at the age of twenty-two on the first day of the battle.

Field Marshal Earl Haig died on 29 January 1928, before he could lead a pilgrimage of 10,000 veterans and civilians to Flanders and the Somme. In his place, Lady Haig led the sombre journey. The Prince of Wales joined it when they reached Béthune. On August 6, in a succession of trains arriving at ten-to-fifteen-minute intervals, the pilgrims alighted at Beaucourt Station, scene of fierce fighting in November 1916. For twenty-four hours they toured the battlefield, on foot, by car and by charabanc. 'Among the sadness', write Major and Mrs Holt in their *Battlefield Guide to the Somme*, 'was the unfailing humour of the Tommy. "I wonder if my blinkin' leg is still up there?" mused a one-legged veteran, looking up at Beaumont-Hamel. "Well, I dunno; somebody's bin muckin' abaht 'ere since I was 'ere larst", commented another.'

Returning to the River Ancre long after battle had raged there, Edmund Blunden wrote:

> The struggling Ancre had no part
>   In these new hours of mine,
> And yet its stream ran through my heart;
>   I heard it grieve and pine,
> As if its rainy, tortured blood
>   Had swirled into my own,
> When by its battered bank I stood
>   And shared its wounded moan.

On 31 July 1932 the Prince of Wales unveiled the Thiepval Memorial to the Missing, the largest British war memorial in the world. On its massive pillars are inscribed the names of 73,335 British and South African soldiers who were killed on the Somme and have no known grave. The Menin Gate at Ypres has the names of 54,338 British and Commonwealth soldiers who were killed in the Ypres Salient between 4 August 1914 and 15 August 1917 and have no known grave. Because there was no room on the panels for the names of a further 34,888 who were killed between 16 August 1917 and 11 November 1918, they are inscribed on the memorial wall at the back of the Tyne Cot Cemetery five miles to the north-east; many of them had earlier fought on the Somme.

A fourth memorial to the missing, at Arras, has the names of 34,739 British and Commonwealth soldiers killed in the central sector of the British Expeditionary Force area of operations who likewise have no known grave. Such was the destructive power of artillery, the intensity of the fighting, and the time it often took before the bodies could be reached that 197,300 British and Commonwealth troops killed on the Western Front between 1914 and 1918, including those whose remains were found, could not be identified.

In the winter of 1932–3 a small joint cemetery was created next to the Thiepval Memorial, to represent the dead of both France and the British Commonwealth. Of the 300 Commonwealth burials there, 239 are unidentified. The remains had been found between December 1931 and March 1932, some as far north as Loos and as far south as Le Quesnel, but most from the Somme battlefields of July to November 1916. Of the 300 French dead, 253 are unidentified.

The Somme was chosen as the site of another memorial for the whole Western Front, and at Easter 1939, five months before the outbreak of the Second World War, Lieutenant Colonel Graham Seton Hutchison, who had served with the Machine Gun Corps in the attack on High Wood on 15 July 1916, unveiled a memorial plaque in the town hall in Albert to the 60,000 dead and wounded members of the Machine Gun Corps.

Over the years, more and more memorials have been established. The Tank Corps Memorial at Pozières, an obelisk with four miniature tanks, recalls the first appearance of tanks in battle, on 15 September 1916. The fence around the memorial is made from tank gun barrels and driving chains. The site was chosen because it was the final tank assembly point on the night of September 14.

The South African memorial in Delville Wood, with its sculpture of a struggling Castor and Pollux, is a powerful reminder of the battle for the wood, as is the wood itself, which, with its now ninety-year growth of trees and foliage, and its one surviving wartime tree, a hornbeam, is maintained as a memorial. Also in Delville Wood is a small memorial to Corporal Joseph Davies and Private Albert Hill, both of the 10th (Service) Battalion, Royal Welch Fusiliers, who won the Victoria Cross 'close to this spot' on 20 July 1916.

Facing Mametz Wood is a magnificent red dragon, sculpted in iron, grasping a strand of barbed wire in its claw, commemorating the Welshmen who fought and were killed in the battle for the wood. At the edge of High Wood is a memorial to the Black Watch and Cameron Highlanders who fought and died there. Nearby is a memorial to the 9th (Glasgow) Battalion, Highland Light Infantry, and a short walk away, the memorial cross to the 47th Division, unveiled at a ceremony on 13 September 1925.

During the Second World War, the Somme was quickly overrun by the German Army on its sweep to the English Channel at Abbeville. The gardener at Serre Road Cemetery No. 2, Ben Leach, who had taken part in the capture of Montauban on 1 July 1916 with the Manchester Pals, stayed on after the German occupation and, working with the French Resistance, helped twenty-seven Allied airmen who had been shot down over the Somme escape to the Spanish border. He hid many of them in the cemetery tool shed.

With the German occupation in 1940, General Rawlinson's former headquarters at Querrieu became a German headquarters. Among the Germans who used it were General Erwin Rommel, then command-ing the 7th Panzer Division, General Heinz Guderian, the Panzer chief, and Field Marshal Goering, head of the German Air Force.

The German conquest of the Somme battlefields in 1940 was rapid, although there was heavy fighting in and around Amiens when the Germans broke through the former Somme front line and took the city on 18 May 1940, when all the houses west of the cathedral were destroyed by the German bombardment. Amiens was retaken on 31 August 1944 by the British Second Army, whose tanks and armoured vehicles moved swiftly eastward across the once battle-scarred land-scape, passing the many First World War cemeteries as they advanced. Once more Amiens became a British hospital centre: No. 25 and No. 121 General Hospitals were set up there in October 1944, remaining until April 1945. Saint-Pierre Cemetery contains 676 Commonwealth burials of the First World War and 82 from the Second World War.

Several strange echoes of the Battle of the Somme have been heard in recent decades. In 1992, episode eight of the Young Indiana Jones Chronicles, the film story of a fictional adventurer, was set on the Somme, where the seventeen-year-old American-born Indiana Jones, enlisting in the Belgian Army as 'Corporal Defense', was in charge of a section. In the words of the film promotion, 'Almost succumbing to despair, as his life becomes an endless round of artillery barrages, nerve gas attacks and decaying corpses, Indy fears that death will be his only way out.' He is then captured by the Germans and confined to a prisoner-of-war camp, from which he escapes.

In 1995 a British Army football, flat and misshapen by age, was found on a rubbish dump near Mailly-Maillet, a village where troops had been billeted just behind the front line. The ball was taken to Dominique and Melanie Zanardi, owners of the Le Tommy Café at Pozières, who restored it to something like its original condition. The laces are missing, but the holes are visible. The ball still contains the remnants of a bladder, with the name Gamage's Defiance. Gamage's department store in London was famous for its sporting goods.

Monuments continued to be unveiled eighty years and more after the battle. In Authuille village church, a few minutes' walk from the military cemetery, is a monument, unveiled in 1996, on the eightieth anniversary of the battle, dedicated 'to the eternal memory' of the officers, non-commissioned officers and men of three of the battalions of Kitchener's Army: the 15th (Glasgow Tramways), 16th (Boy's Brigade) and 17th (Glasgow Commercials) Battalions of the Highland Light Infantry, who had fought and died near the village on 1 July 1916.

On 10 September 1997 a plaque was unveiled by the roadside facing Mouquet Farm, informing the passer-by, 'Many of the men who fought and were lost in 1916 remain beneath this land forever; unknown, but never forgotten by their homeland Australia.' Three times as many Australians fought on the Western Front as at Gallipoli. Of the 60,000 Australians killed in action in the First World War, 46,000 were killed on the Western Front.

At Longueval crossroads, once the site of a ferocious British artillery bombardment before its capture by the 9th (Scottish) Division on 19 July 1916, and now a bustling crossroads once more, is the statue of a piper, white and imposing on his cairn, playing his black bagpipes. On the wall behind him are incised the cap badges of all those regiments that lost pipers in the fighting. The statue was unveiled and blessed on 20 July 2002, at a ceremony in which the poem 'The Piper' by Ron Venus was read. It is a moving experience to stand at that crossroads today – in sight, as so often in villages on the Somme, of the French war memorial to their dead of 1914–18 – and to read the poem aloud:

> 'Take my pipes,' the Piper said,
> 'And lay me down to sleep.
> The sights I've seen have broke my heart
> And caused my soul to weep.'
>
> 'Take my pipes,' the Piper said,
> 'And wrap me in my plaid.
> The sights I've seen have made me cold
> And all I feel is sad.'
>
> 'Take my pipes,' the Piper said,
> 'And my hearty tartan kilt.
> My friends have gone and left my side,
> Dragged down by mud and silt.'

'Take my pipes,' the Piper said,
'And play them far away.
Their sound's too sweet to carry far
Upon this dreadful day.'

'But stay . . . ! Don't take my treasured pipes,
I'll need them by my side
When I take up my Scottish lads
To the land on the other side.'

There are five Commonwealth War Graves Commission cemeteries within a mile of the Pipers' Memorial.

On Armistice Day 2004 a cairn was erected in Contalmaison to the memory of the football players and club members of Heart of Midlothian Football Club who had fallen in action. A plaque depicts two men, a soldier and a footballer. 'Sometimes I go past the cairn and there have been scarves or souvenirs from football clubs left there,' the Mayor of Contalmaison, Bernard Sénéchal, reflected a year later. 'This has given our village new life.'

The visitor to the Somme in the opening years of the twenty-first century can explore the villages, woods, rivers and rivulets, hills and valleys that were at the centre of the fighting between July and November 1916. The trenches, dugouts and redoubts have long gone, except in a few specially preserved or reconstructed sites, but the war cemeteries remain.

Every headstone in each cemetery, each name on the long lists of those whose bodies were never found, hides a human being, a man, a story, a cry of pain and a grieving family. Each visitor reacts differently, alone with his or her thoughts, or with friends who can share emotions of that ninety-year-old charnel house.

One such visitor, fifty years after the First World War, was the Scottish-born songwriter Eric Bogle. So moved was he by the war cemeteries that, picking a name at random to represent all the fallen, he wrote the song 'No-Man's Land':

Well, how do you do, Private William McBride.
Do you mind if I sit here down by your graveside?
I'll rest for a while in the warm summer sun
I've been walking all day, and I'm nearly done.

And I see by your gravestone, you were only nineteen
When you joined the glorious fallen in 1916.
And I hope you died quick, and I hope you died clean.
Or, Willie McBride, was it slow and obscene?

(*Refrain, after each verse*)
Did they beat the drum slowly; did they play the pipes lowly;
Did the rifles fire o'er you as they lowered you down?
Did the bugles sound The Last Post in chorus;
Did the pipes play The Flowers of the Forest?

And did you leave a wife or a sweetheart behind;
In some loyal heart is your memory enshrined?
And, though you died back in 1916,
To that loyal heart are you always nineteen?

Or are you a stranger without even a name,
Forever enshrined behind a glass frame,
In an old photograph, torn and tattered and stained,
And fading to yellow in a bound leather frame?

The sun's shining down on these green fields of France.
The warm wind blows gently, and the red poppies dance.
The trenches have vanished, long under the plough.
No gas and no barbed wire, no guns firing now.

But here in this graveyard it's still No Man's Land.
The countless white crosses in mute witness stand
To man's blind indifference to his fellow man,
And a whole generation who were butchered and damned.

And I can't help but wonder now, Willie McBride,
Do all those who lie here know why they died?
Did you really believe them when they told you 'The Cause'?
Did you really believe this war would end wars?

Well, the suffering, the sorrow, the glory, the shame,
The killing, the dying, it was all done in vain.
For Willie McBride, it all happened again,
And again, and again, and again, and again.

Unknown to Eric Bogle when he wrote this song, a Private William
McBride is buried in Authuille Military Cemetery. Serving in the Royal
Inniskilling Fusiliers, he had been killed in April 1916, near Thiepval,

two and a half months before the Battle of the Somme. I visited his grave while writing this book, and read aloud Eric Bogle's lament at his graveside.

Once it was parents who came to see the graves of their sons, widows the graves of their husbands, and children the graves of their fathers. Now it is grandchildren, nieces, nephews, great-nieces and great-nephews of the soldiers who fought on the Somme who make that pilgrimage. British schoolchildren also visit the Somme in increasing numbers, the First World War having entered their school curriculum.

Starting in 1977, Major and Mrs Holt (Tonie and Valmai Holt) have conducted battlefield tours on the Somme, as well as on many other battlefields, including Gallipoli. Their largest single groups on the Somme were for the seventieth anniversary in 1986 and the seventy-fifth in 1991, each about 350 strong. The Holts have also developed tours that specialize in studying specific interests such as poetry or padres. Reflecting on their work, which has been a major incentive for visitors to the Somme, they write, 'Though visiting the beautiful Commonwealth War Graves Commission cemeteries is not the be all and end all of a battlefield tour, we determined right at the beginning of our ventures that if we ever found ourselves walking along a line of headstones without feeling the sorrow radiating from the personal messages we would stop immediately. So far that has not happened. We feel proud to be able to cry.'

In the ten years before the ninetieth anniversary of 1 July 1916, the number of visitors to the Somme battlefields more than doubled. The Somme Tourist Authority estimated the total number for 2004 at 200,000. That year the Newfoundland War Memorial Park register recorded 44,000 British visitors, 22,100 French and 4,500 others. As many as 500 coaches of schoolchildren visit Lochnagar Crater each year – 25,000 schoolchildren in all. Every July 1 and November 11 – Armistice Day – wreaths, poppies, crosses and messages are laid at the crater, as at all the Somme cemeteries and memorials, by veterans groups, civic dignitaries and private visitors.

Five days before Armistice Day 2004, a ceremony took place at the New Zealand Memorial at Longueval, when the remains of an unidentified New Zealand soldier were entrusted to the New Zealand government. The remains had been exhumed by staff of the

Commonwealth War Graves Commission from Caterpillar Valley Cemetery – Plot 14, Row A, Grave 27 – and were later laid to rest within the Tomb of the Unknown Warrior at the National War Memorial in Wellington, New Zealand. An inscription at the site of the grave records this disinterment and special reburial.

Hardly a day passes on the Somme when a wreath is not laid at one or other of the cemeteries and memorials that define the battlefield. On Armistice Day 2005 a wreath laid at Lochnagar Crater served as a reminder of the future lost generations of Britons, Frenchmen and Germans – men and women of many nationalities who were never born as a result of the battle. The wreath was in memory of Second Lieutenant Ernest Apps, 2nd Battalion, Wiltshire Regiment, who died in 1985 at the age of ninety. The note with the wreath read, 'Had he not survived the Battle of the Somme, we – all 25 of his descendants – would not have existed.'

The battlefield of the Somme remains, ninety years after the battle, a sombre, powerful and constant memorial, and salutation, to the vast armies of men who fought there: those who were killed, those who were wounded, and those who survived with only the mental scars of the savage conflict. The agony of war took its toll on the Somme in full measure. The heroism and horror of war were seen there without disguise, unembellished and unadorned.

Maps

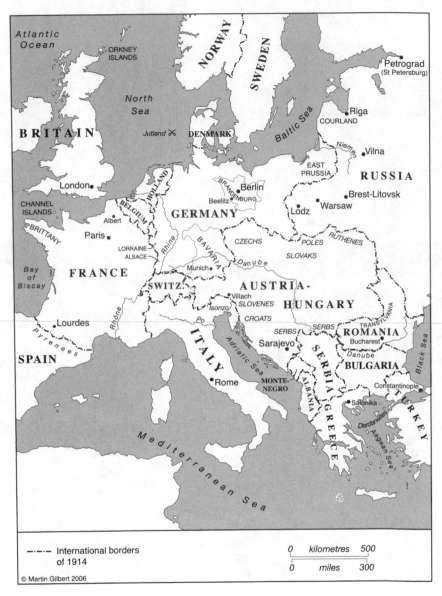

1. Europe on the eve of war, June 1914

2. The Western Front line of trenches from the North Sea to the Swiss border

3. The British Expeditionary Force sector of the front under Haig's command

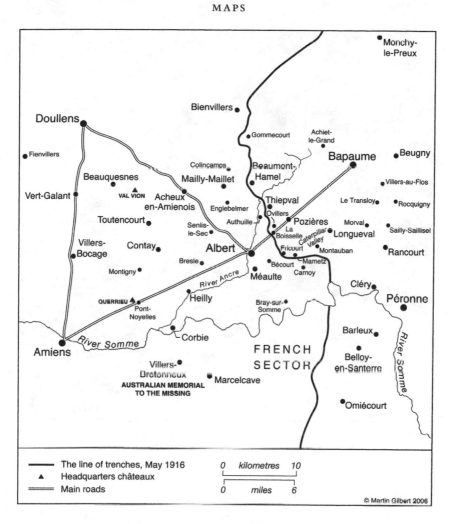

4. The Somme region before the battle

5. One battalion's journey: Newfoundland–Britain–
Gallipoli–the Somme

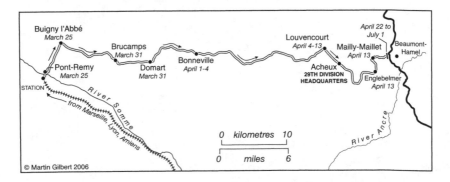

6. One battalion's journey: Pont-Remy to the front line

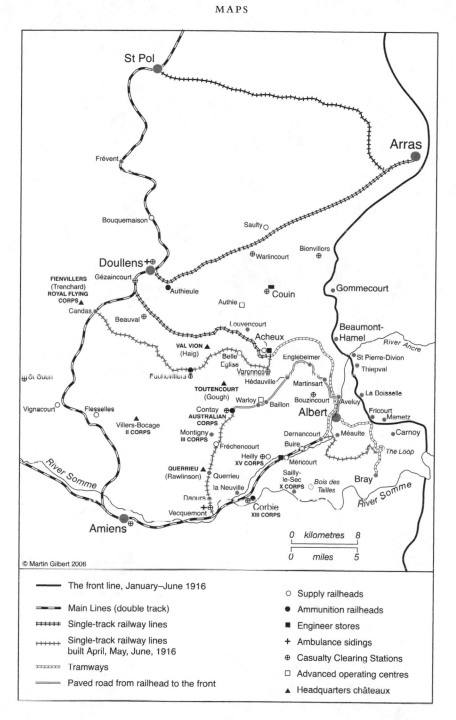

7. Preparing for battle, April–June 1916

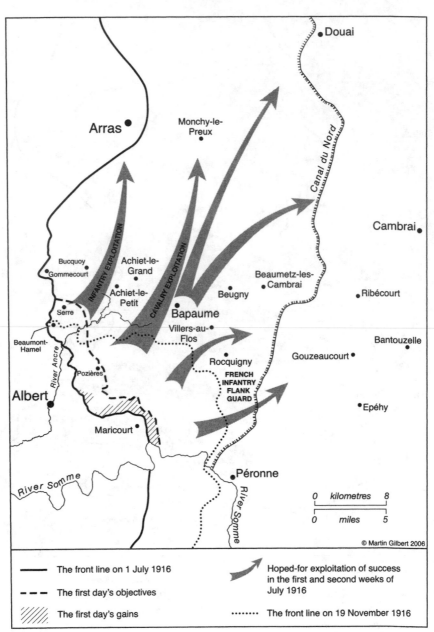

Douai

Arras

Monchy-le-
Preux

Canal du Nord

Cambrai

Bucquoy
Gommecourt
Achiet-le-
Grand

INFANTRY EXPLOITATION

Achiet-le-
Petit

Beaumetz-les-
Cambrai

Ribécourt

Serre

CAVALRY EXPLOITATION

Beugny

Beaumont-
Hamel

River Ancre

Bapaume

Villers-au-
Flos

Bantouzelle

Poziéres

Rocquigny

Gouzeaucourt

Albert

FRENCH
INFANTRY
FLANK
GUARD

Epéhy

Maricourt

River Somme

Péronne

River Somme

| 0 | kilometres | 8 |
| 0 | miles | 5 |

© Martin Gilbert 2006

—— The front line on 1 July 1916	Hoped-for exploitation of success in the first and second weeks of July 1916
– – – The first day's objectives	
///// The first day's gains	•••••• The front line on 19 November 1916

8. The Somme, 1 July 1916: first-day objectives and the plan for a breakthrough

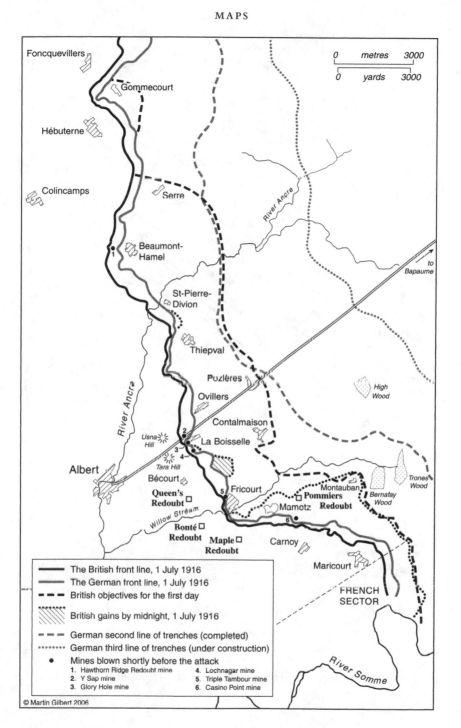

9. The first day of battle, 1 July 1916

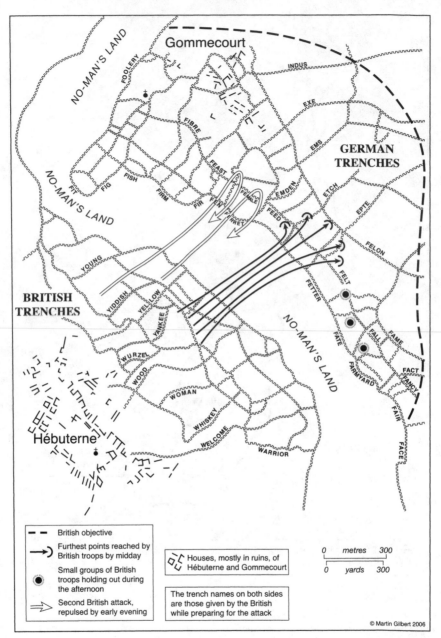

10. Gommecourt: the attack on the German trench lines, 1 July 1916

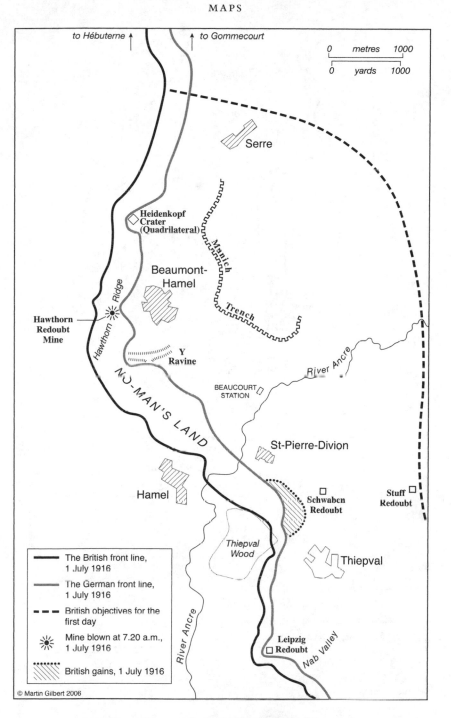

to Hébuterne

to Gommecourt

| 0 | metres | 1000 |
| 0 | yards | 1000 |

Serre

Heidenkopf Crater (Quadrilateral)

Munich

Beaumont-Hamel

Trench

Hawthorn Redoubt Mine

Hawthorn Ridge

Y Ravine

River Ancre

BEAUCOURT STATION

NO-MAN'S LAND

St-Pierre-Divion

Hamel

Schwaben Redoubt

Stuff Redoubt

Thiepval Wood

Thiepval

——— The British front line, 1 July 1916

——— The German front line, 1 July 1916

– – – British objectives for the first day

☀ Mine blown at 7.20 a.m., 1 July 1916

⋯⋯ British gains, 1 July 1916

River Ancre

Leipzig Redoubt

Nab Valley

© Martin Gilbert 2006

11. From Serre to Leipzig Redoubt: 1 July 1916

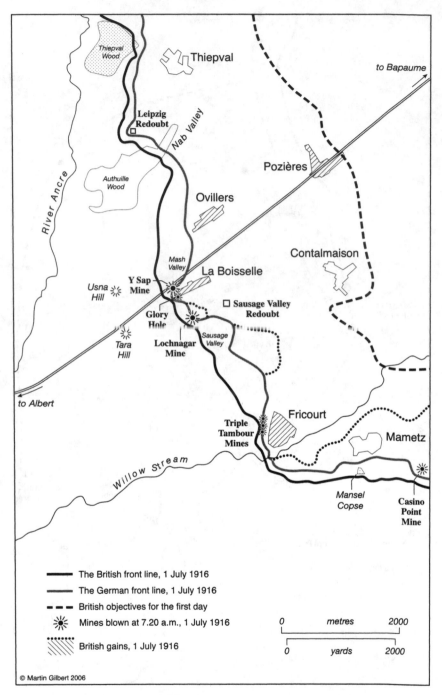

Thiepval
Wood

Thiepval

to Bapaume

Leipzig
Redoubt

Nab Valley

Pozières

River Ancre

Authuille
Wood

Ovillers

Contalmaison

Mash
Valley

La Boisselle

Usna
Hill

Y Sap
Mine

Sausage Valley
Redoubt

Glory
Hole

Sausage
Valley

Lochnagar
Mine

Tara
Hill

to Albert

Fricourt

Triple
Tambour
Mines

Mametz

Willow Stream

Mansel
Copse

Casino
Point
Mine

—— The British front line, 1 July 1916

—— The German front line, 1 July 1916

- - - British objectives for the first day

☀ Mines blown at 7.20 a.m., 1 July 1916

▨ British gains, 1 July 1916

| 0 | metres | 2000 |
| 0 | yards | 2000 |

© Martin Gilbert 2006

12. From Leipzig Redoubt to Mametz: 1 July 1916

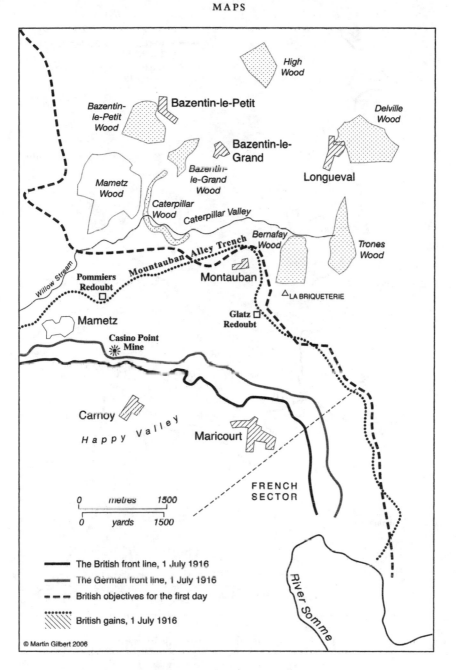

High
Wood

Bazentin-
le-Petit
Wood

Bazentin-le-Petit

Delville
Wood

Bazentin-le-
Grand

Bazentin-
le-Grand
Wood

Mametz
Wood

Longueval

Caterpillar
Wood

Caterpillar Valley

Bernafay
Wood

Trones
Wood

Mountauban Alley Trench

Willow Stream

Pommiers
Redoubt

Montauban

LA BRIQUETERIE

Mametz

Glatz
Redoubt

Casino Point
Mine

Carnoy

Happy Valley

Maricourt

FRENCH
SECTOR

0   metres   1500

0   yards   1500

——— The British front line, 1 July 1916

——— The German front line, 1 July 1916

– – – British objectives for the first day

///// British gains, 1 July 1916

River Somme

© Martin Gilbert 2006

13. The eastern sector of the British line, 1 July 1916

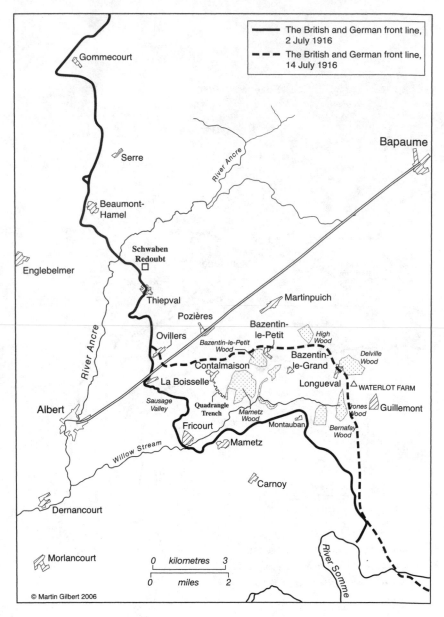

14. The fighting from 2 to 31 July 1916

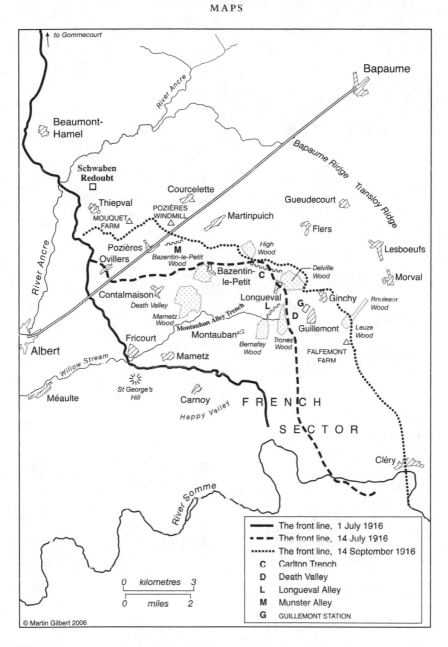

to Gommecourt

Bapaume

River Ancre

Beaumont-
Hamel

Bapaume Ridge

Transloy Ridge

Schwaben
Redoubt

Courcelette

Gueudecourt

Thiepval

POZIÈRES
WINDMILL

Martinpuich

MOUQUET
FARM

Flers

Pozières

M

High
Wood

Lesboeufs

Ovillers

Bazentin-le-Petit
Wood

Bazentin-
le-Petit

C

Delville
Wood

Morval

River Ancre

Contalmaison

Death Valley

Longueval

L

Ginchy

G

Rouleaux
Wood

Mametz
Wood

Montauban Alley Trench

Montauban

D

Guillemont

Leuze
Wood

Fricourt

Bernafay
Wood

Trones
Wood

FALFEMONT
FARM

Albert

Willow Stream

Mametz

Méaulte

St George's
Hill

Carnoy

F R E N C H

Happy Valley

S E C T O R

Cléry

River Somme

———	The front line, 1 July 1916
– – –	The front line, 14 July 1916
········	The front line, 14 September 1916
C	Carlton Trench
D	Death Valley
L	Longueval Alley
M	Munster Alley
G	GUILLEMONT STATION

0   kilometres   3
0   miles   2

© Martin Gilbert 2006

15. The fighting in August 1916

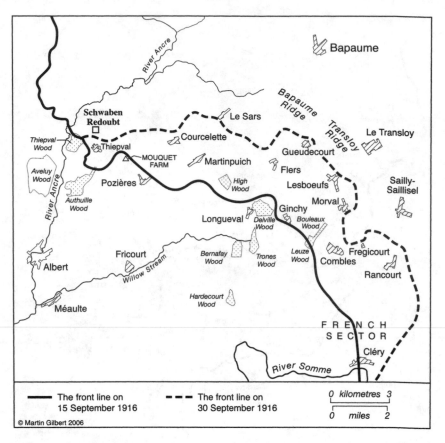

16. The fighting in September 1916

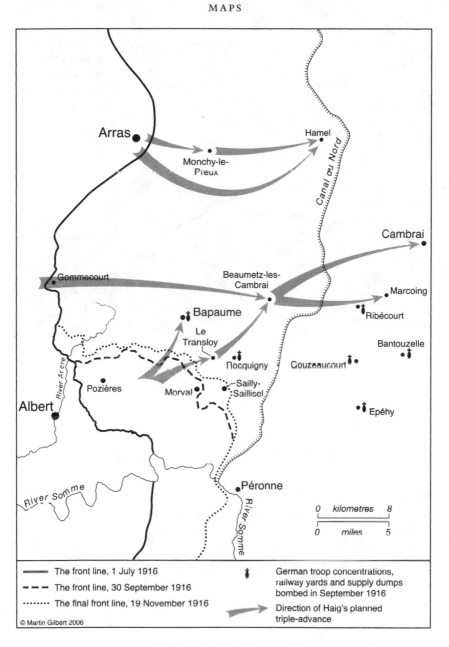

The following labels appear on the map:

Arras

Hamel

Monchy-le-Preux

Canal du Nord

Cambrai

Gommecourt

Beaumetz-les-Cambrai

Marcoing

Bapaume

Ribécourt

Le Transloy

Bantouzelle

Rocquigny

Gouzeaucourt

River Ancre

Pozières

Sailly-Saillisel

Morval

Epéhy

Albert

River Somme

Péronne

River Somme

| 0 | kilometres | 8 |
| 0 | miles | 5 |

——— The front line, 1 July 1916

– – – The front line, 30 September 1916

.... The final front line, 19 November 1916

German troop concentrations, railway yards and supply dumps bombed in September 1916

Direction of Haig's planned triple-advance

© Martin Gilbert 2006

17. The October Plan, 1916

287

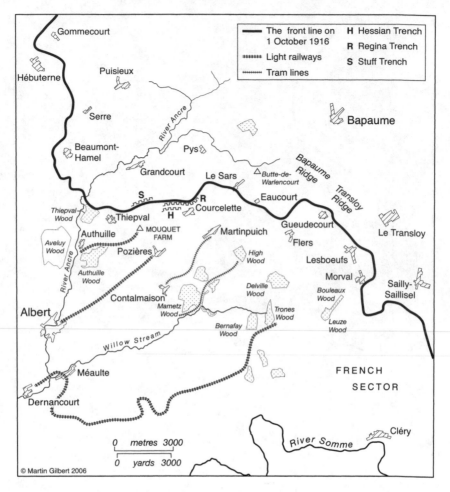

18. The fighting in October, and from 1 to 11 November 1916

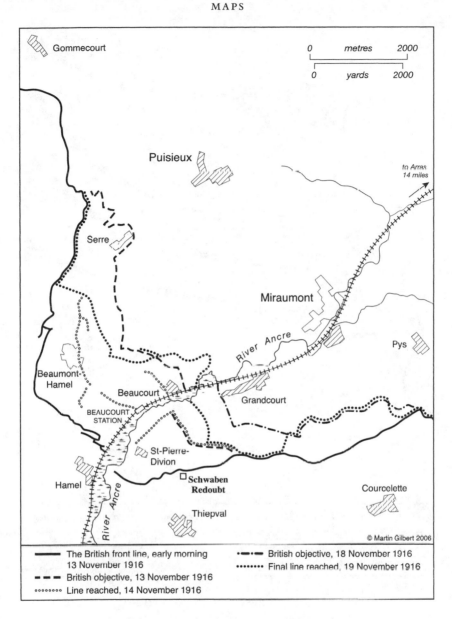

Gommecourt

0   *metres*   2000

0   *yards*   2000

Puisieux

to Arras
14 miles

Serre

Miraumont

Pys

Beaumont-
Hamel

Beaucourt

River Ancre

BEAUCOURT
STATION

Grandcourt

St-Pierre-
Divion

Hamel

River Ancre

☐ Schwaben
   Redoubt

Courcelette

Thiepval

© Martin Gilbert 2006

—— The British front line, early morning 13 November 1916	·—·— British objective, 18 November 1916
– – – British objective, 13 November 1916	········ Final line reached, 19 November 1916
°°°°°°° Line reached, 14 November 1916	

19. The fighting on the Ancre, 12–18 November 1916

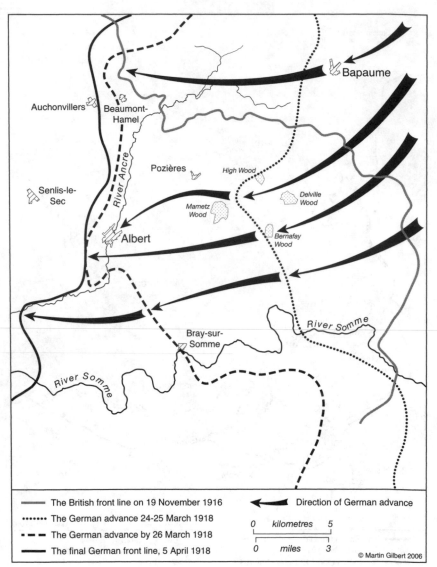

20. The Somme battlefield, March 1918

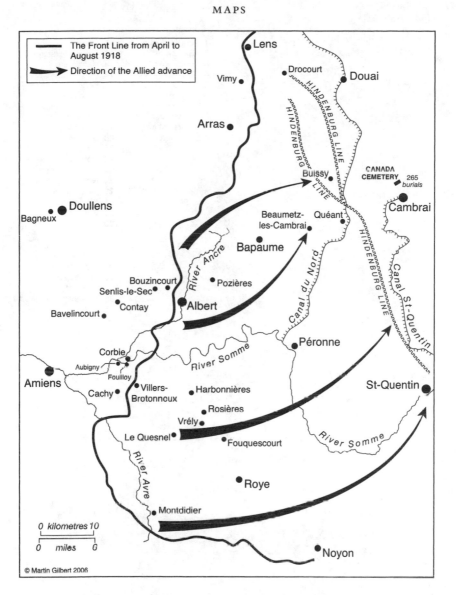

The Front Line from April to August 1918

Direction of the Allied advance

Lens

Drocourt
Douai

Vimy

HINDENBURG LINE
HINDENBURG

Arras

Buissy
CANADA
CEMETERY   265
           burials

Doullens
Bagneux

Beaumetz-
les-Cambrai   Quéant

Cambrai

LINE

Bapaume

River Ancre

Canal du Nord

HINDENBURG LINE

Bouzincourt
Senlis-le-Sec   Pozières
Contay
Bavelincourt   Albert

Péronne

Canal St-Quentin

Corbie

River Somme

Aubigny
Fouilloy

Amiens

Cachy   Villers-
        Brotonneux   Harbonnières

St-Quentin

Rosières
Vrély
Le Quesnel   Fouquescourt

River Somme

Roye

River Avre

Montdidier

0 kilometres 10

0   miles   0

© Martin Gilbert 2006

Noyon

21. The Somme battlefield, August 1918

291

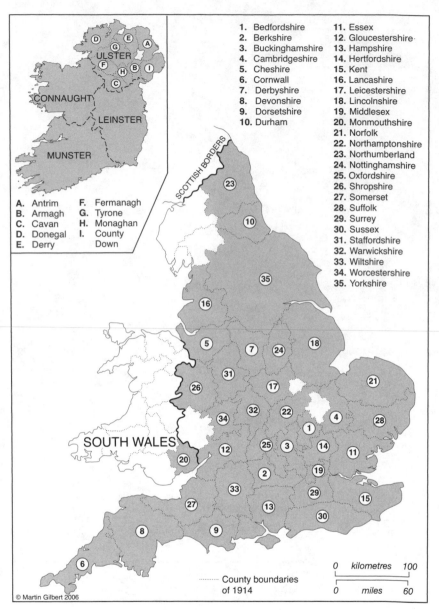

1. Bedfordshire
2. Berkshire
3. Buckinghamshire
4. Cambridgeshire
5. Cheshire
6. Cornwall
7. Derbyshire
8. Devonshire
9. Dorsetshire
10. Durham
11. Essex
12. Gloucestershire
13. Hampshire
14. Hertfordshire
15. Kent
16. Lancashire
17. Leicestershire
18. Lincolnshire
19. Middlesex
20. Monmouthshire
21. Norfolk
22. Northamptonshire
23. Northumberland
24. Nottinghamshire
25. Oxfordshire
26. Shropshire
27. Somerset
28. Suffolk
29. Surrey
30. Sussex
31. Staffordshire
32. Warwickshire
33. Wiltshire
34. Worcestershire
35. Yorkshire

A. Antrim
B. Armagh
C. Cavan
D. Donegal
E. Derry
F. Fermanagh
G. Tyrone
H. Monaghan
I. County Down

ULSTER
CONNAUGHT
LEINSTER
MUNSTER

SCOTTISH BORDERS

SOUTH WALES

County boundaries
of 1914

0 kilometres 100
0 miles 60

© Martin Gilbert 2006

22. British counties whose regiments fought on the Somme

23. Places in Britain mentioned in the text.

24. Home towns and villages of some of the dead in a single
Commonwealth War Graves Commission cemetery:
Fricourt New Military Cemetery

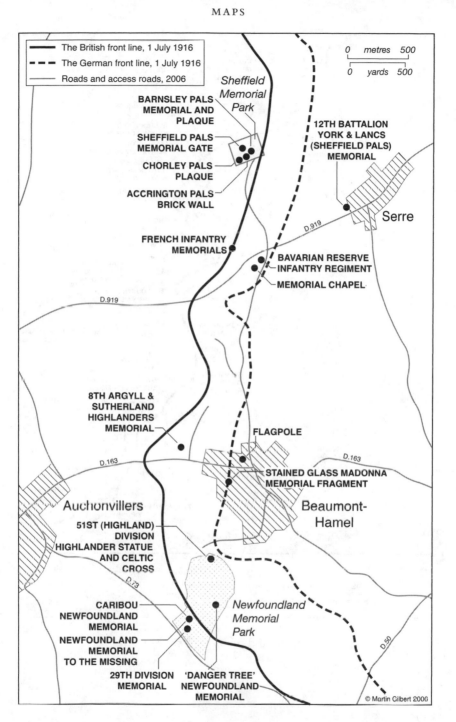

The British front line, 1 July 1916
- - - The German front line, 1 July 1916
Roads and access roads, 2006

0   metres   500
0   yards   500

Sheffield Memorial Park

BARNSLEY PALS MEMORIAL AND PLAQUE

SHEFFIELD PALS MEMORIAL GATE

CHORLEY PALS PLAQUE

ACCRINGTON PALS BRICK WALL

12TH BATTALION YORK & LANCS (SHEFFIELD PALS) MEMORIAL

Serre

D.919

FRENCH INFANTRY MEMORIALS

BAVARIAN RESERVE INFANTRY REGIMENT

MEMORIAL CHAPEL

D.919

8TH ARGYLL & SUTHERLAND HIGHLANDERS MEMORIAL

FLAGPOLE

D.163

STAINED GLASS MADONNA MEMORIAL FRAGMENT

D.163

Auchonvillers

Beaumont-Hamel

51ST (HIGHLAND) DIVISION HIGHLANDER STATUE AND CELTIC CROSS

D.73

CARIBOU NEWFOUNDLAND MEMORIAL

NEWFOUNDLAND MEMORIAL TO THE MISSING

Newfoundland Memorial Park

29TH DIVISION MEMORIAL

'DANGER TREE' NEWFOUNDLAND MEMORIAL

D.50

© Martin Gilbert 2006

25. Monuments and memorials, Serre to Beaumont-Hamel

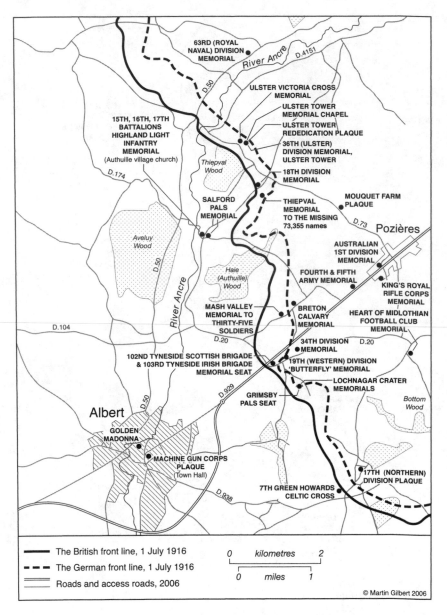

63RD (ROYAL NAVAL) DIVISION MEMORIAL

River Ancre

D.4151

D.50

ULSTER VICTORIA CROSS MEMORIAL

15TH, 16TH, 17TH BATTALIONS HIGHLAND LIGHT INFANTRY MEMORIAL (Authuille village church)

ULSTER TOWER MEMORIAL CHAPEL

ULSTER TOWER REDEDICATION PLAQUE

36TH (ULSTER) DIVISION MEMORIAL, ULSTER TOWER

D.174

Thiepval Wood

18TH DIVISION MEMORIAL

SALFORD PALS MEMORIAL

THIEPVAL MEMORIAL TO THE MISSING 73,355 names

MOUQUET FARM PLAQUE

D.73

Pozières

Aveluy Wood

D.50

AUSTRALIAN 1ST DIVISION MEMORIAL

River Ancre

Haie (Authuille) Wood

FOURTH & FIFTH ARMY MEMORIAL

KING'S ROYAL RIFLE CORPS MEMORIAL

HEART OF MIDLOTHIAN FOOTBALL CLUB MEMORIAL

D.104

MASH VALLEY MEMORIAL TO THIRTY-FIVE SOLDIERS

BRETON CALVARY MEMORIAL

D.20

34TH DIVISION MEMORIAL

D.20

102ND TYNESIDE SCOTTISH BRIGADE & 103RD TYNESIDE IRISH BRIGADE MEMORIAL SEAT

19TH (WESTERN) DIVISION 'BUTTERFLY' MEMORIAL

D.929

GRIMSBY PALS SEAT

LOCHNAGAR CRATER MEMORIALS

Bottom Wood

Albert

D.50

GOLDEN MADONNA

MACHINE GUN CORPS PLAQUE (Town Hall)

17TH (NORTHERN) DIVISION PLAQUE

D.938

7TH GREEN HOWARDS CELTIC CROSS

—— The British front line, 1 July 1916

- - - The German front line, 1 July 1916

══ Roads and access roads, 2006

0   kilometres   2

0   miles   1

© Martin Gilbert 2006

26. Monuments and memorials west of Pozières

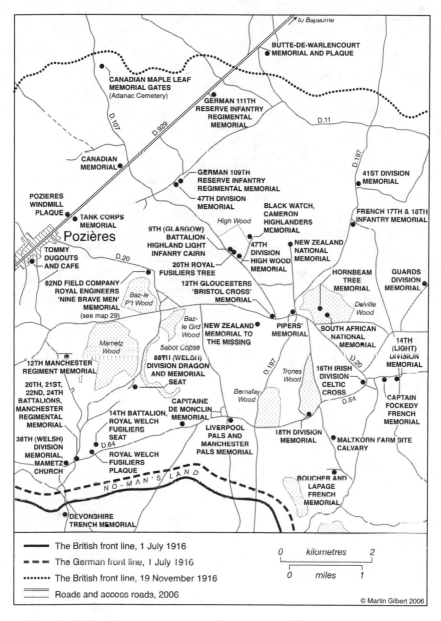

27. Monuments and memorials east of Pozières

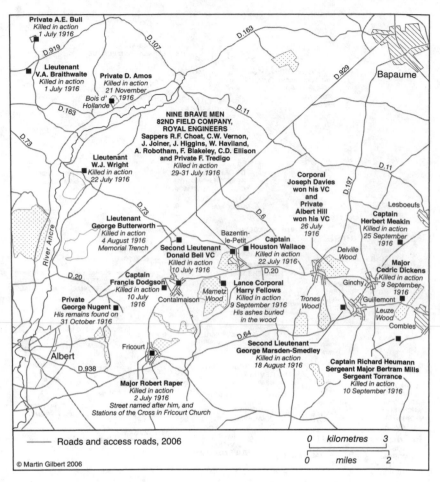

Private A.E. Bull
Killed in action
1 July 1916

D.919

D.107

D.163

D.929

Bapaume

Lieutenant
V.A. Braithwaite
Killed in action
1 July 1916

Private D. Amos
Killed in action
21 November
1916

Bois d'
Hollande

D.163

D.11

D.73

NINE BRAVE MEN
82ND FIELD COMPANY,
ROYAL ENGINEERS
Sappers R.F. Choat, C.W. Vernon,
J. Joiner, J. Higgins, W. Haviland,
A. Robotham, F. Blakeley, C.D. Ellison
and Private F. Tredigo
Killed in action
29-31 July 1916

Lieutenant
W.J. Wright
Killed in action
22 July 1916

Corporal
Joseph Davies
won his VC
and
Private
Albert Hill
won his VC
26 July
1916

D.11

D.197

Lesboeufs

Captain
Herbert Meakin
Killed in action
25 September
1916

Lieutenant
George Butterworth
Killed in action
4 August 1916
Memorial Trench

D.73

Bazentin-
le-Petit

D.6

Captain
Houston Wallace
Killed in action
22 July 1916

Delville
Wood

Major
Cedric Dickens
Killed in action
9 September
1916

River Ancre

Second Lieutenant
Donald Bell VC
Killed in action
10 July 1916

D.20

Ginchy

Guillemont

Leuze
Wood

Combles

Captain
Francis Dodgson
Killed in action
10 July
1916

Contalmaison

Mametz
Wood

Lance Corporal
Harry Fellows
Killed in action
9 September 1916
His ashes buried
in the wood

Trones
Wood

D.20

Private
George Nugent
His remains found on
31 October 1916

D.64

Fricourt

Second Lieutenant
George Marsden-Smedley
Killed in action
18 August 1916

Albert

D.938

Captain Richard Heumann
Sergeant Major Bertram Mills
Sergeant Torrance
Killed in action
10 September 1916

Major Robert Raper
Killed in action
2 July 1916
Street named after him, and
Stations of the Cross in Fricourt Church

——— Roads and access roads, 2006

0   kilometres   3

0   miles   2

© Martin Gilbert 2006

28. Private memorials on the Somme

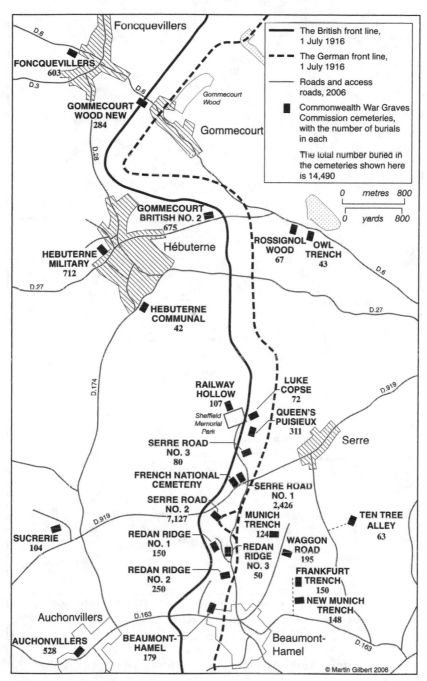

The British front line,
1 July 1916

The German front line,
1 July 1916

Roads and access
roads, 2006

Commonwealth War Graves
Commission cemeteries,
with the number of burials
in each

The total number buried in
the cemeteries shown here
is 14,490

0   metres   800
0   yards   800

Foncquevillers

FONCQUEVILLERS
603

GOMMECOURT
WOOD NEW
284

Gommecourt
Wood

Gommecourt

GOMMECOURT
BRITISH NO. 2
675

Hébuterne

ROSSIGNOL   OWL
WOOD   TRENCH
67   43

HEBUTERNE
MILITARY
712

HEBUTERNE
COMMUNAL
42

RAILWAY
HOLLOW
107

LUKE
COPSE
72

Sheffield
Memorial
Park

QUEEN'S
PUISIEUX
311

SERRE ROAD
NO. 3
80

Serre

FRENCH NATIONAL
CEMETERY

SERRE ROAD
NO. 1
2,426

SERRE ROAD
NO. 2
7,127

TEN TREE
ALLEY
63

MUNICH
TRENCH
124

SUCRERIE
104

WAGGON
ROAD
195

REDAN RIDGE
NO. 1
150

REDAN
RIDGE
NO. 3
50

FRANKFURT
TRENCH
150

REDAN RIDGE
NO. 2
250

NEW MUNICH
TRENCH
148

Auchonvillers

AUCHONVILLERS
528

BEAUMONT-
HAMEL
179

Beaumont-
Hamel

© Martin Gilbert 2006

29. Commonwealth War Graves Commission cemeteries from
Foncquevillers to Beaumont-Hamel

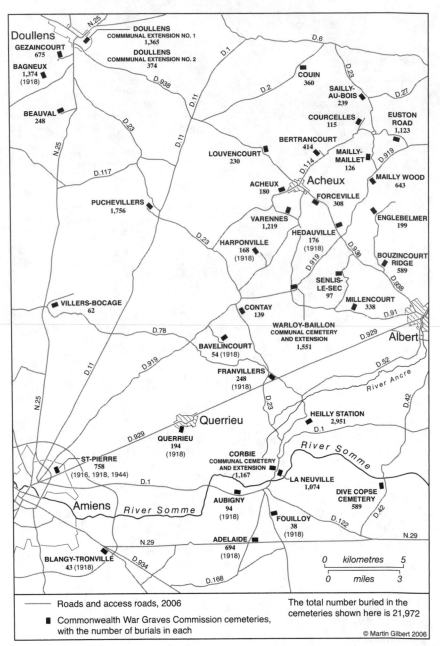

Doullens
GEZAINCOURT
675
BAGNEUX
1,374
(1918)
BEAUVAL
248
PUCHEVILLERS
1,756
VILLERS-BOCAGE
62
N.25
D.25
N.25
D.117
D.938
D.23
D.11
D.11
D.11
DOULLENS
COMMMUNAL EXTENSION NO. 1
1,365
DOULLENS
COMMMUNAL EXTENSION NO. 2
374
D.1
D.2
COUIN
360
SAILLY-
AU-BOIS
239
COURCELLES
115
BERTRANCOURT
414
LOUVENCOURT
230
MAILLY-
MAILLET
126
ACHEUX
180
Acheux
FORCEVILLE
308
VARENNES
1,219
HARPONVILLE
168
(1918)
HEDAUVILLE
176
(1918)
SENLIS-
LE-SEC
97
CONTAY
139
WARLOY-BAILLON
COMMUNAL CEMETERY
AND EXTENSION
1,551
MILLENCOURT
338
Albert
BAVELINCOURT
54 (1918)
FRANVILLERS
248
(1918)
HEILLY STATION
2,951
QUERRIEU
194
(1918)
Querrieu
CORBIE
COMMUNAL CEMETERY
AND EXTENSION
1,167
LA NEUVILLE
1,074
DIVE COPSE
CEMETERY
589
ST-PIERRE
758
(1916, 1918, 1944)
AUBIGNY
94
(1918)
FOUILLOY
38
(1918)
Amiens
River Somme
ADELAIDE
694
(1918)
BLANGY-TRONVILLE
43 (1918)
D.6
D.23
D.27
EUSTON
ROAD
1,123
D.919
MAILLY WOOD
643
ENGLEBELMER
199
D.114
D.938
D.919
BOUZINCOURT
RIDGE
589
D.888
D.91
D.929
D.52
River Ancre
D.42
River Somme
D.1
D.23
D.929
D.1
D.122
D.42
N.29
N.29
D.934
D.168
D.78
D.919
D.11

0   kilometres   5

0   miles   3

Roads and access roads, 2006

■ Commonwealth War Graves Commission cemeteries,
with the number of burials in each

The total number buried in the
cemeteries shown here is 21,972

© Martin Gilbert 2006

30. Commonwealth War Graves Commission cemeteries behind
the lines

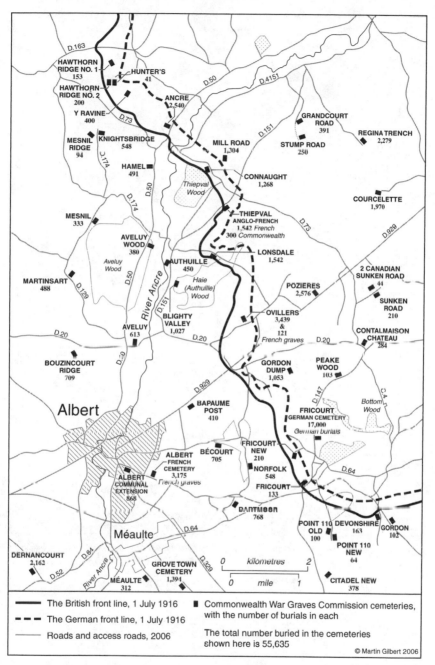

The British front line, 1 July 1916
The German front line, 1 July 1916
Roads and access roads, 2006

Commonwealth War Graves Commission cemeteries, with the number of burials in each

The total number buried in the cemeteries shown here is 55,635

© Martin Gilbert 2006

31. Commonwealth War Graves Commission cemeteries from Hawthorn Ridge to Méaulte

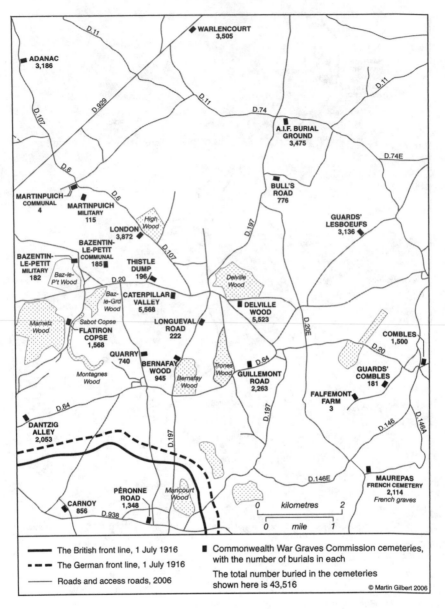

The British front line, 1 July 1916

- - - The German front line, 1 July 1916

Roads and access roads, 2006

■ Commonwealth War Graves Commission cemeteries, with the number of burials in each

The total number buried in the cemeteries shown here is 43,516

© Martin Gilbert 2006

32. Commonwealth War Graves Commission cemeteries from Warlencourt to Carnoy

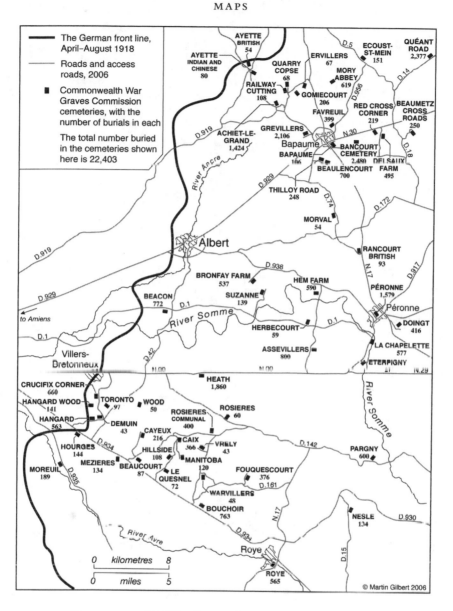

The German front line, April–August 1918

Roads and access roads, 2006

Commonwealth War Graves Commission cemeteries, with the number of burials in each

The total number buried in the cemeteries shown here is 22,403

AYETTE BRITISH 54

AYETTE INDIAN AND CHINESE 80

QUARRY COPSE 68

RAILWAY CUTTING 108

GOMIECOURT 206

ERVILLERS 67

MORY ABBEY 619

FAVREUIL 399

GREVILLERS 2,106

ACHIET-LE-GRAND 1,424

River Ancre

Bapaume

BAPAUME 106

BANCOURT CEMETERY 2,480

DELSAUX FARM 495

D.5

ECOUST-ST-MEIN 151

QUÉANT ROAD 2,377

RED CROSS CORNER 219

BEAUMETZ CROSS ROADS 250

BEAULENCOURT 700

THILLOY ROAD 248

MORVAL 54

Albert

RANCOURT BRITISH 93

BRONFAY FARM 537

HEM FARM 590

PÉRONNE 1,579

BEACON 772

SUZANNE 139

Péronne

DOINGT 416

to Amiens

River Somme

HERBECOURT 59

ASSEVILLERS 800

LA CHAPELETTE 577

ETERPIGNY 27

Villers-Dretonneux

HEATH 1,860

River Somme

CRUCIFIX CORNER 660

HANGARD WOOD 141

HANGARD 563

TORONTO 97

WOOD 50

ROSIERES COMMUNAL 400

ROSIERES 60

DEMUIN 43

CAYEUX 216

CAIX 366

VRELY 43

PARGNY 600

HOURGES 144

HILLSIDE 108

MANITOBA 120

MEZIERES 134

BEAUCOURT 87

LE QUESNEL 72

FOUQUESCOURT 376

MOREUIL 189

WARVILLERS 48

BOUCHOIR 763

NESLE 134

River Avre

Roye

ROYE 565

© Martin Gilbert 2006

0 kilometres 8

0 miles 5

33. Commonwealth War Graves Commission cemeteries in the Somme area established as a result of the fighting in 1917–18

Appendix

Approximate size of army formations

Once battle began, most battalions – the basic formation in any attack – were under strength.

Army (under a general)	200,000 men
Corps (lieutenant general)	50,000 men
Division (major general)	12,000 men
Brigade (brigadier general)	4,000 men
Regiment (colonel)	2,000 men
Battalion (lieutenant colonel or major)	1,000 men
Company (captain)	250 men
Platoon (second lieutenant)	60 men
Section (lance corporal)	15 men

Bibliography of Works Consulted

Books specifically about the Battle of the Somme

Barry Cuttell, *One Day on the Somme, 1st July 1916*. Peterborough: GMA Enterprises, 1997

—— *148 Days on the Somme, 2nd July to 26th November 1916*. Peterborough: GMA Enterprises, 2000

Martin Marix Evans, *The Battles of the Somme*. London: Weidenfeld & Nicolson, 1996

A. H. Farrar-Hockley, *The Somme*. London: B. T. Batsford, 1964

John Giles, *The Somme Then and Now*. London: Battle of Britain International, 1986

Peter Hart, *The Somme*. London: Weidenfeld & Nicolson, 2005

Tonie and Valmai Holt, *Major and Mrs Holt's Battlefield Guide to the Somme*. Barnsley: Leo Cooper, 4th edition, 2003

Illustrated Michelin Guides to the Battle-Fields (1914–1918), *The Somme, Volume 1: The First Battle of the Somme (1916–1917) Albert–Bapaume– Péronne*. Clermont-Ferrand: Michelin Tyre Company, 1925

Peter H. Liddle, *The 1916 Battle of the Somme: A Reappraisal*. London: Leo Cooper, 1992

Chris McCarthy, *The Somme: The Day-by-Day Account*. London: Cassell, 1993

Lyn Macdonald, *Somme*. London: Michael Joseph, 1983

Martin and Mary Middlebrook, *The Somme Battlefields: A Comprehensive Guide from Crécy to the Two World Wars*. London: Viking, 1991

Mike O'Connor, *Airfields and Airmen: Somme*. Barnsley: Leo Cooper, 2002

Anne Powell (editor), *The Fierce Light: The Battle of the Somme, July–November 1916, Poetry and Prose*. Aberporth: Palladour Books, 1996

Robin Prior and Trevor Wilson, *The Somme*. New Haven and London: Yale University Press, 2005

Paul Reed, *Walking the Somme*. Barnsley: Leo Cooper, 1997

Gary Sheffield, *The Somme*. London: Cassell, 2003

Jack Sheldon, *The German Army on the Somme, 1914–1916*. Barnsley: Pen and

Sword Military, 2005

Books about phases and aspects of the Battle of Somme

Nigel Cave, *Beaumont Hamel: Newfoundland Park*. Barnsley: Leo Cooper, 1994
—— *Delville Wood*. Barnsley: Leo Cooper, 1999
—— *Gommecourt*. Barnsley: Leo Cooper, 1998
Peter Charlton, *Pozières: Australians on the Somme, 1916*. London: Leo Cooper/ Secker & Warburg, 1986
Gerald Gliddon, *VCs of the First World War: The Somme*. Norwich: Gliddon Books, 1991
Jack Horsfall and Nigel Cave, *Serre*. Barnsley: Leo Cooper, 1996
Graham Keech, *Pozières*. Barnsley: Leo Cooper, 1998
Graham Maddocks, *Liverpool Pals*. London: Leo Cooper, 1991
Martin Middlebrook, *The First Day on the Somme*. London: Purnell Book Services, 1971. Reprinted by Leo Cooper, Barnsley, 2003
Terry Norman, *The Hell They Called High Wood: The Somme, 1916*. Barnsley: Leo Cooper, 2003 (reprint)
Paul Reed, *Courcelette*. Barnsley: Leo Cooper, 1998
Michael Renshaw, *Beaucourt*. Barnsley: Leo Cooper, 2003
Lieutenant Colonel W. A. Shooter, OBE, *Ulster's Part in the Battle of the Somme, July to November 1916*. Belfast: The Somme Association, 1996
Michael Stedman, *Guillemont*. Barnsley: Leo Cooper, 1998
—— *La Boisselle, Ovillers, Contalmaison*. Barnsley: Leo Cooper, 1997

Document volumes and reference works

Max Arthur, *Forgotten Voices of the Great War: A History of World War I in the Words of the Men and Women Who Were There*. London: The Lyons Press, 2002
—— *Symbol of Courage: A History of the Victoria Cross*. London: Sidgwick & Jackson, 2004
Keith Bartlett (editor), *Somme*. London: Public Record Office, The National Archives, no date (portfolio of documents)
J. H. Borlaston, *Sir Douglas Haig's Despatches (December 1915–April 1919)*. London: J. M. Dent, 1919
Cemeteries and Memorials in Belgium and Northern France. Maidenhead: Commonwealth War Graves Commission and Michelin, 2004
Brigadier General Sir James E. Edmonds, *Military Operations France and Belgium, 1916, Sir Douglas Haig's Command of the 1st July: Battle of the Somme.*

London: Macmillan, 1932. Reprinted by the Imperial War Museum, London, and Battery Press, Nashville, 1993

A. D. Ellis, *The Story of the Fifth Australian Division*. London: Hodder & Stoughton, no date (*c.*1920). Reprinted by Naval and Military Press, Uckfield, 2002

Histories of Two Hundred and Fifty-One Divisions of the German Army which Participated in the War (1914–1918). Washington DC: War Department (Document No. 905), 1920. Reprinted by the London Stamp Exchange, London, 1989

History of the Corps of Royal Engineers: Volume Five, The Home Front, France, Flanders and Italy in the First World War. Chatham: The Institution of Royal Engineers, 1952

Sidney C. Hurst, *The Silent Cities: An Illustrated Guide to the War Cemeteries and Memorials to the 'Missing' in France and Flanders, 1914–1918*. London: Methuen, 1929

Captain Wilfrid Miles, *Military Operations France and Belgium, 1916, 2nd July 1916 to the End of the Battles of the Somme*. London: Macmillan, 1938. Reprinted by the Imperial War Museum, London, and Battery Press, Nashville, 1992

Gary Sheffield and John Bourne (editors), *Douglas Haig: War Diaries and Letters*. London: Weidenfeld & Nicolson, 2005

Memoirs and diaries containing recollections of the Battle of the Somme

Edmund Blunden, *Undertones of War*. London: Four Square, The New English Library, 1928

Joy B. Cave (editor), *I Survived, Didn't I? The Great War Reminiscences of Private 'Ginger' Byrne*. London: Leo Cooper, 1993

Oliver Lyttelton, Viscount Chandos, *The Memoirs of Lord Chandos*. London: The Bodley Head, 1962

Viscountess D'Abernon, *Red Cross and Berlin Embassy, 1915–1926: Extracts from the Diaries of Viscountess D'Abernon*. London: John Murray, 1946

General Sir Hubert Gough, *Soldiering On*. London: Arthur Barker, 1954

Robert Graves, *Goodbye to All That*. London: Cassell, 1929

John Jackson, *Private 12768: Memoirs of a Tommy*. Stroud, Gloucestershire: Tempus Publishing, 2004

Cecil Lewis, *Sagittarius Rising*. London: Peter Davies, 1936

Chris Littler (editor), *The Diary of Thomas Frederick Littler, July–December 1916*. http://www.firstworldwar.com/diaries/littlerdiary2.htm. Copyright Michael Duffy, 2000–2005

Harold Macmillan, *Winds of Change, 1914–1939*. London: Macmillan, 1966

Paul Maze, *A Frenchman in Khaki*. London: William Heinemann, 1934

Lord Moran, *The Anatomy of Courage*. London: Constable, 1945

Siegfried Sassoon, *Memoirs of an Infantry Officer*. London: Faber and Faber, 1930

R. B. Talbot Kelly, *A Subaltern's Odyssey: A Memoir of the Great War, 1915–1917*. London: William Kimber, 1980

R. H. Tawney, *The Attack and Other Papers*. London: George Allen & Unwin, 1953. Reprinted by Spokesman, Nottingham, 1981

Henry Williamson, *The Golden Virgin*. Edinburgh: Macdonald & Co., 1957

Biographies

Ann Clayton, *Chavasse – Double VC*. London: Leo Cooper, 1992

Bill Newton Dunn, *Big Wing: The Biography of Air Chief Marshal Sir Trafford Leigh-Mallory, KCB, DSO and Bar*. Shrewsbury: Airlife Publishing, 1992

Peter C. Ford, *Captain B. H. Radford: Otherwise known as Basil Hallam*. http://www.crossandcockade.com

Paul Freyberg, *Bernard Freyberg, VC*. London: Hodder & Stoughton, 1991

Martin Gilbert, *Plough My Own Furrow: The Story of Lord Allen of Hurtwood as Told through his Writings and Correspondence*. London: Longmans, 1965

—— *Winston S. Churchill*, vol. iii, Document Volumes, August 1914–December 1916. London: William Heinmann, 1972

Alistair Horne, *Macmillan, 1894–1956, Volume 1 of the Official Biography*. London: Macmillan, 1988

Lawrence James. *Imperial Warrior: The Life and Times of Field Marshal Viscount Allenby, 1861–1936*. London: Weidenfeld & Nicolson, 1993

Ian Kershaw, *Hitler, 1889–1916: Hubris*. London: Allen Lane, 1998

Richard Lovell, *Churchill's Doctor: A Biography of Lord Moran*. London: Royal Society of Medicine Services Limited, 1992

Major General Sir Frederick Maurice, *The Life of General Lord Rawlinson of Trent, from His Journals and Letters*. London: Cassell, 1928

John W. Wheeler-Bennett, *Hindenburg: The Wooden Titan*. London: Macmillan, 1936

General works

Jack Alexander, *McCrae's Battalion: The Story of the 16th Royal Scots*. Edinburgh: Mainstream Publishing, 2004

Max Arthur, *Last Post: The Final Word From Our First World War Soldiers*. London: Weidenfeld & Nicolson, 2005

Robert B. Asprey, *The German High Command at War: Hindenburg and*

Ludendorff and the First World War. New York: Little, Brown, 1991

C. T. Atkinson, *The Queen's Own Royal West Kent Regiment, 1914–1919*. London: Simpkin, Marshall, Hamilton, Kent, 1924

Maurice Baring, *Flying Corps Headquarters, 1914–1918*. Edinburgh: William Blackwood, 1968

D. S. Barnes, *This Righteous War*. Huddersfield: Richard Netherwood, 1990

Alexander Barrie, *War Underground*. London: Frederick Muller, 1962

C. E. W. Bean, *Official History of Australia in the War of 1914 to 1918*. Sydney: Angus & Robertson, 6 volumes, 1929

Vera Brittain, *Testament of Youth: An Autobiographical Study of the Years 1900–1925*. London: Victor Gollancz, 1933

Malcolm Brown, *The First World War: A Great Conflict Recalled in Previously Unpublished Letters, Diaries and Memoirs*. London: Sidgwick & Jackson, 1991

John Buchan, *The History of the South African Forces in France*. Edinburgh: Thomas Nelson & Sons, 1920

Winston S. Churchill, *The World Crisis, 1916–1918*, Part One. London: Thornton Butterworth, 1927

—— *Marlborough: His Life and Times*, vol. ii. London: George G. Harrap, 1934

Rev. E. C. Crosse, *The Defeat of Austria as Seen by the 7th Division*. London: H. W. S. Deane, 1919 (includes material about the Battle of the Somme)

Daniel G. Dancocks, *Gallant Canadians: The Story of the Tenth Canadian Infantry Battalion, 1914–1919*. Markham, Ontario: The Calgary Highlanders Regimental Funds Foundation, 1990

George A. B. Dewar and Lieutenant Colonel J. H. Boraston, *Sir Douglas Haig's Command, December 19, 1915, to November 11, 1918*. London: Constable, 2 volumes, 1922

Charles Edmonds, *A Subaltern's War*. London: Peter Davies, 1929

John Ellis, *Eye-Deep in Hell*. London: Croom Helm, 1976

Sir Frank Fox, *The Royal Inniskilling Fusiliers in the World War*. London: Constable, 1928

John Garth, *Tolkien and the Great War: The Threshold of Middle-earth*. Boston: Houghton Mifflin, 2003

W. Grant Grieve, *Tunnellers: A History of the Tunnelling Companies, Royal Engineers, in the World War*. London: H. Jenkins, 1936. Reprinted by Barbarossa Books, Bainbridge Island, Washington State, 1999

Michael Hammerson (editor), *No Easy Hopes or Lies: The World War 1 Letters of Lt. Arthur Preston White*. London: London Stamp Exchange, 1991

Donald Hankey, *A Student in Arms*. London: Andrew Melrose, 1918

Amanda Harlech (editor), *Letters and Diary of Alan Seeger*. Paris: Edition

7L/Steidl, 2001 (first printed in 1917)

—— *Poems by Alan Seeger*. Paris: Edition 7L/Steidl, 2001 (first printed in 1916)

Trevor Henshaw, *The Sky Their Battlefield: Air Fighting and the Complete List of Allied Air Casualties from Enemy Action in the First War*. London: Grub Street, 1995

Captain F. C. Hitchcock, MC, *'Stand To': A Diary of the Trenches*. London: Hurst & Blackett, 1937. Reprinted by Gliddon Books, Norwich, 1998

Mike Hodgson, *Remembered: The Men on the Mareham-le-Fen War Memorial*. Boston, Lincolnshire: Lancfile Publishing, 2004

Douglas Jerrold, *The Royal Naval Division*, London: Hutchinson, 1923

H. A. Jones, *The War in the Air: Being the Story of the Part Played in the Great War by the Royal Air Force*. London: Hamish Hamilton, 2 volumes, 1928

Nigel H. Jones, *The War Walk: A Journey Along the Western Front*. London: Robert Hale, 1983

John Keegan, *The Face of Battle: A Study of Agincourt, Waterloo and the Somme*. London: Jonathan Cape, 1976

Rudyard Kipling, *The Irish Guards in the Great War: Edited and Compiled from Their Diaries and Papers*. London: Macmillan, 2 volumes, 1923

Bernard Lewis, *Swansea Pals: A History of the 14th (Service) Battalion, The Welsh Regiment in the Great War*. Barnsley: Pen and Sword, 2004

Peter H. Liddle, *The Soldier's War, 1914–1918*. London: Blandford Press, 1988

David Macfarlane, *The Danger Tree: Memory, War, and the Search for a Family's Past*. Toronto: Macfarlane, Walter & Ross, 1991

Graham Maddocks, *Liverpool Pals: 17th, 18th, 19th, and 20th Battalions The King's (Liverpool Regiment)*. London: Leo Cooper, 1991

John Masefield, *The Old Front Line*. London: Heinemann, 1917

Frank Mitchell, *Tank Warfare: The Story of the Tanks in the Great War*. London: Nelson, 1933. Reprinted by Spa Books and Tom Donovan, Stevenage, 1987

J. B. Montagu, *History of the 9th (Service) Battalion, The York and Lancaster Regiment, 1914–1919*. London: privately printed, 1934

Colonel G. W. L. Nicholson, *The Fighting Newfoundlander: A History of The Royal Newfoundland Regiment*. Ottawa: Government of Newfoundland, 1964

Neal W. O'Connor, *Aviation Awards of Imperial Germany in World War I and the Men who Earned Them*. Princeton, New Jersey: Foundation for Aviation World War 1, volume 2, 1990

Lieutenant Colonel the Right Hon. Sir Frederick Ponsonby, *The Grenadier Guards in the Great War of 1914–1918*. London: Macmillan, 3 volumes, 1920

Anne Powell, *A Deep Cry: First World War Soldier-Poets Killed in France and*

Flanders. Stroud, Gloucestershire: Sutton Publishing, 1998

Robin Prior and Trevor Wilson, *Command on the Western Front: The Military Career of Sir Henry Rawlinson, 1914–1918.* Oxford: Blackwell Publishers, 1992

Julian Putkowski and Julian Sykes, *Shot at Dawn.* Barnsley: Wharncliffe Publishing, 1989

David Raw, *Bradford Pals: A Comprehensive History of the 16th–18th & 20th (Service) Battalions of the Prince of Wales Own West Yorkshire Regiment, 1914–1918.* Barnsley: Pen and Sword, 2005

Donald Richter, *Chemical Soldiers: British Gas Warfare in World War I.* Lawrence, Kansas: University Press of Kansas, 1992

Lieutenant Colonel H. R. Sandilands, *The 23rd Division, 1914–1919.* Edinburgh: William Blackwood, 1925

Siegfried Sassoon, *The War Poems.* London: Faber and Faber, 1983

Leonard Sellers, *The Hood Battalion, Royal Naval Division: Antwerp, Gallipoli, France, 1914–1918.* London: Leo Cooper, 1995

Alasdair Sutherland, *Never More: The Story of Tongue, Melness and Skerray War Memorials.* Tongue, Sutherland: Woodend Publishing, 2000

Robert Thompson, *Ballymoney Heroes, 1914–1918.* Coleraine: Robert Thompson, 1999

—— *Bushmills Heroes, 1914–1918.* Coleraine: Robert Thompson, 1995

—— *Portrush Heroes, 1914–1918.* Coleraine: Robert Thompson, 2001

Tonbridge School and the Great War of 1914 to 1919. London: The Whitefriars Press, 1923

Barrie Thorpe, *Private Memorials of the Great War on the Western Front.* Reading, Berkshire: The Western Front Association, 1999

Richard Van Emden, *Boy Soldiers of the Great War: Their Own Stories for the First Time.* London: Hodder Headline, 2005

Ray Westlake, *Kitchener's Army.* Staplehurst, Kent: Spellmount, 1989

Captain A. V. Wheeler-Holohan and Captain G. M. C. Wyatt (editors), *The Rangers: Historical Records from 1959 to the Conclusion of the Great War.* London: Harrison & Son, 1921

Everard Wyrall, *History of the Somerset Light Infantry, 1914–1919.* London: Methuen, 1927

Journals

Gun Fire, ed. A. J. Peacock, York Educational Settlement, York

The Poppy and the Owl, Journal of the Friends of the Liddle Collection, Leeds University Library

Articles

Winston S. Churchill, 'Douglas Haig' (obituary). *Nash's Magazine*, November 1928

Owen Slot, 'France preparing to pay respects to the fallen heroes from Hearts'. *The Times*, 10 November 2005

Film and DVD

The Battle of the Somme. William F. Drury (producer), Geoffrey Malins and Charles Urban (directors). British Topical Committee for War Films. First shown on 10 August 1916

The Somme. London: Channel Four. First transmission, 22 November 2005

The Trenches of Hell. The Young Indiana Jones Chronicles, Episode Eight, Lucasfilm Ltd. First transmission, 28 September 1992

Website

http://www.cwgc.com (Commonwealth War Graves Commission). Contains a listing of all British and Empire soldiers, sailors and airmen killed in action, with their units, ages when known, date of death, and cemetery or memorial to the missing. Also contains indispensable information about all Commonwealth War Graves cemeteries, including those on the Somme.

Index

compiled by the author